The Transparent State

This book examines the transformation of transparency as a metaphor in West German political thought to an analogy for democratic architecture, questioning the prevailing assumption in German architectural circles that transparency in governmental buildings can be equated with openness, accessibility, and greater democracy.

The Transparent State: Architecture and Politics in Postwar Germany traces the development of transparency in German political and architectural culture, tying this lineage to the relationship between culture and national identity, a connection that began before unification of the German state in the eighteenth century and continues today. The Weimar Republic and Third Reich periods are examined although the book focuses on the postwar period, looking at the use of transparency in the three projects for a national parliament: the 1949 Bundestag project by Hans Schwippert, the 1992 Bundestag building by Günter Behnisch, and the 1999 Reichstag renovation by Foster and Partners.

Transparency is an important issue in contemporary architectural practice; this book will appeal to both the practicing architect and the architectural historian.

Deborah Ascher Barnstone is an architect, academic, and designer. Her work includes a special issue of the *Journal of Architecture Education* dedicated to transparency in twentieth-century architecture (with Anthony Vidler), and she has chaired sessions addressing transparency and approaches to architectural modernism at two annual meetings of the Association of Art Historians. Her design practice has explored both spatial and material transparency; transparency in politics and architecture was the subject of her dissertation. She has taught architectural design in Germany as well as in the United States where, with a Ph.D. in German architectural history, she is currently Associate Professor at Washington University.

The Transparent State

Architecture and politics in

postwar Germany

Deborah Ascher Barnstone

Routledge
Taylor & Francis Group

LONDON AND NEW YORK

First published 2005 by Routledge
2 Park Square, Milton Park, Abingdon, Oxon OX14 4RN

Simultaneously published in the USA and Canada
by Routledge
270 Madison Ave, New York, NY 10016

Routledge is an imprint of the Taylor & Francis Group

© 2005 Deborah Ascher Barnstone

Typeset in Univers by
Florence Production Ltd, Stoodleigh, Devon
Printed and bound in Great Britain by
TJ International, Padstow, Cornwall

British Library Cataloguing in Publication Data
A catalogue record for this book is available from the British Library

Library of Congress Cataloging in Publication Data
A catalog record for this book has been requested

ISBN 0–415–70019–1

To my father who inspired me to pursue the study of history with his excellent example and to my mother who always believed I could do it

Contents

Illustration credits

Akademie der Künste, Sammlung Baukunst, Berlin 2.1, 2.2, 2.5, 2.15

Akademie der Künste, Sammlung Baukunst, Berlin, photographer: Foto Orgel-Köhne 2.14

Bauhaus Archiv, Berlin 2.4, 2.6, 2.9, 2.10, 2.11

Bauhaus Archiv, Berlin, photographer: Günter Lepkowski 2.7

Bauhaus Archiv, Berlin, photographer: Markus Hawlik 2.8

Behnisch & Partner 6.2, 6.3, 6.4, 6.5, 6.6, 6.9

Behnisch & Partner, photographer: Christian Kandzia 6.1, 6.7, 6.8, 6.10, 6.11, 6.12, 6.13, 6.14, 6.15, 6.16, 6.17, 6.18, 6.19, 6.20, 6.21

Bundesbildstelle Berlin 3.2, 3.3, 5.12, 7.2, 7.24

Bundesbildstelle Berlin, photographer: Berndt Kühler 7.1, 7.4

Bundesbildstelle Berlin, photographer: Julia Fassbender 7.19, 7.25

Bundesbildstelle Bonn 1.1, 1.2, 1.3, 2.12, 5.11

Bundesbildstelle Bonn, photographer: Georg Bauer 3.1

Bundesbildstelle Bonn, photographer: Julia Fassbender 2.13

Foster and Partners 7.6, 7.7, 7.8, 7.9, 7.10, 7.11, 7.12, 7.13, 7.14

Foster and Partners, Depot Conradi 7.16, 7.17, 7.21, 7.22, 7.23

Foster and Partners, photographer: Nigel Young 7.5, 7.15, 7.18, 7.20

Foster and Partners, photographer: Tom Miller 7.3

Photographer: Axel Föhl 2.3, 4.1, 4.2

Schwippert Archiv, Architecture Museum, Technical University (TU), Munich 5.2, 5.3, 5.4, 5.5, 5.6, 5.17

Schwippert Archiv, Germanisches Nationalmuseum, Nuremberg 5.1, 5.7, 5.8, 5.9, 5.10, 5.13, 5.14, 5.15, 5.16

Preface

The first summer I spent in West Germany was the summer of 1989, coincidentally the summer that Günter Behnisch's radical design for a transparent glass national parliament was approved for construction by the Bundestag. I distinctly remember listening to emotional discussions among architect friends about the Behnisch design; they never questioned the transparent aspect of the project but heatedly debated its other design merits. I recall looking at articles in the West German popular and architecture press, and being astonished at the importance accorded transparency. To my foreign sensibility, transparent state architecture did not seem to have any relationship to the architectural expression of democracy, yet it was this very notion that I encountered again and again. "Transparency equals democracy" was the dictum West Germans assumed Benisch had embodied in his proposal for a see-through glass structure. While not universally accepted, the aphorism formed the center of discussions about Behnisch's design. Here, in the summer of 1989, my fascination with transparency began.

By November of 1989, the Berlin Wall was breached. As souvenir hunters carried off bits of the Wall, the imminent unification of East and West loomed. These events might have affected notions about national identity, the appropriate architectural representation of the state, and, consequently, the importance of transparency. But the Behnisch project continued unchanged in spite of the November events and, later, in spite of the vote to relocate much of the German government apparatus, including the parliament, to Berlin.

When parliament turned its attention to questions of how to renovate the Reichstag, the members called for transparency once again. This time, because of the limitations dictated by a renovation project, the requested transparency was constrained; the brief asked for a transparent plenary chamber, but not a transparent building. Many of the new structures for the government built near the Reichstag resorted to transparent glass-enclosed architecture also. Stefan Braunfels and Axel Schultes are two architects who elected to use transparency in their Berlin projects although stylistically the buildings are very different.

The obsession with transparency was not restricted to state architecture. By the 1980s, the visionary ideas of the interwar period seemed to be everywhere and transparency used for every architectural type conceivable. The ascendancy of transparency dates to the end of the Second World War. Today transparent glass is the esthetic choice for every building type: banks, shopping malls, private homes, office complexes, gas stations, train stations, airports, factories, and museums. Furthermore, the use of transparent glass seems to transcend ideological lines since architects of every stripe use it. Examples from the 1940s and 1950s include the Schneider-Esleben Garage in Düsseldorf (1949); Eiermann's Chancellery of the German Embassy in Washington, DC (1950, 1962–64); Pfingstberg Church by Carlfried Mutschler in Mann (1958); and the Wilhelm Lehmbruck Museum by Manfred Lehmbruck in Duisberg (1956, 1959–64). Recent examples include Helmut Jahn's BMW building at Potsdamer Platz in Berlin; the new train station at Frankfurt Airport and Von Gerkan and Marg's Lehrter Bahnhof in Berlin (not yet complete); Norman Foster's office buildings in Düsseldorf; Pablo Molestina's Kimmerle House in Metzingen; the new Volkswagen factory in Leipzig; Günter Behnisch's Akademie der Künste in Berlin (not yet complete); the Smart Car showrooms around the country; the Center for Eastern European Studies and Research in Bonn; and the CDU headquarters in Berlin. With the exception of storefronts, where the use of transparent display windows on the street was designed to attract customers and therefore had an explicitly functional rationale, the explosion in glass construction has not been functional but esthetic, except for state buildings where it has been explicitly ideological. Dreams of glass buildings date to the 1920s but the technology that enables them has largely developed since 1945 with a surge in new technology in the 1980s. Although certain journalists recognize the irony in the insistence on transparent glass construction for the national parliament when this is the preferred esthetic for commercial projects, the ideology has persisted. The postwar parliaments relied on the embodiment of transparency as an analogy in formal, spatial, and stylistic ways while eschewing the style, symbols, and references used for democratic parliaments elsewhere and Germany's own long tradition of building town halls and state parliaments. These facts begged the question: is transparency simply a fashion in German postwar architectural circles or is it part of a deeper ideology connected to Germany's unique history?

Ideologies supporting transparent architecture are difficult to summarize or categorize because of the range of architectural transparency and because of the numerous interpretations of the term "transparency" itself. In optics, transparency refers to a matterial that transmits light so that we can see through it. In architecture, this usually translates into the use of see-through glass as the primary building material, but other materials are also transparent such as crystal, finely woven and diaphanous fabrics, and lattice screens. The modern fascination with making interior and exterior space continuous is yet another manifestation of transparency. In philosophy, transparency refers to the ability of the light of the mind to pass through a concept so that its true nature, or hidden essence, is perceptible. The Platonic ideal describing a higher order visible through material form underscored classical architecture practice. The anthroposophist, Rudolf Steiner, adopted a similar notion of transparency to his architectural program for buildings like the Gotheanum, whose materials were opaque but whose meaning was transparent to the initiated. In political thinking transparency is linked to open and accessible government, while in sociology it connotes a pluralistic society. Modern discourse is rife with other myths concerning transparency: the transparency of the soul to nature, the self to others, and the self to society.[1]

Today, transparency is a catchword for corporations, government, academia, and for institutions of every size and description, for the internet and the ways in which it connects the world. It is almost impossible to open a newspaper or magazine without seeing some reference to transparency usually framed as a positive characteristic, as a goal we should unquestionably aspire to. In this sense, transparency is familiar and for that reason alone, if for no other, it demands closer scrutiny. We meet transparency in one guise or another daily – at work, in the news, in our built environment. But do we understand its complexity, its many dimensions?

Visionary architects at the beginning of the century like Bruno Taut and other members of the German Crystal Chain group posited futuristic utopian societies whose progressive cultural values were echoed in the transparent glass architecture. Writers like Arthur Korn simply saw the transparent potential inherent in glass construction as the most modern of building techniques, the sign of technological prowess.[2] For Korn, buildings constructed using material and spatial transparency were revolutionary; building transparently therefore had a moral and ethical imperative attached to it. Colin Rowe and Robert Slutzky wrote their explication of "transparency" in 1955 in part to counter what they viewed as the one-dimensional understanding of the term in architectural circles, namely the obsessive use of transparent materials for their "progressive" constructive aspect and the neglect of perceptual and intellectual transparency.[3] Rowe and Slutzky proposed two types of transparency in architecture in their essay, "Transparency: Literal and Phenomenal." "Literal transparency" described the material quality of being see-through while "phenomenal transparency" described the perceptual quality that allows the mind to discern the underlying governing concept or spatial concept.[4] Rowe and Slutzky's analysis only touched the surface of the subject, however. Furthermore, they wrote from their perspective in the US where transparency in architectural circles did not seem to extend beyond formal, spatial, and material concerns. In Germany after the war, transparency went increasingly deeper into realms that were only tangentially related to architectural expression.

This is the study of the intersection between the dimensions transparency assumes in German politics and parliamentary architecture after the Second World War. It probes the relationship between political notions of transparency and architectural ones, trying to fathom how and why the two were linked together and whether this link has any real merit. Art historical methods did not seem adequate to explain the interconnection between political ideology and architectural expression nor did historical method offer the modes with which to read the architecture. In Chapter 1 I explain how I approached the methodological challenge of working across two very different disciplines. As Carl Schorske once explained,

> The [textual analyst] aims at the greatest possible illumination of a cultural product, relativizing all principles of analysis to its particular content. The historian seeks rather to locate and interpret the artifact temporarily in a field where two lines intersect. One line is vertical, or diachronic, by which he establishes the relation of a text or a system of thought to previous expressions in the same branch of cultural activity (painting, politics, etc.). The other is horizontal, or synchronic; by it he assesses the relation of the content of the intellectual object to what is appearing in other branches or aspects of a culture at the same time.[5]

To borrow Schorske's metaphor, I have attempted to weave together the connections between architecture and politics. The artifacts I analyze are the three federal parliament buildings designed and constructed since 1945: Hans Schwippert's 1949 Bundeshaus in Bonn, Günter Behnisch's 1992 Bundeshaus in Bonn, and Norman Foster's 1999 Reichstag renovation in Berlin. Because the national parliament is one intersection between architecture and politics, those buildings make ideal cases with which to study transparency ideology as an architectural phenomenon. Key to interpreting the individual works of architecture is the method for formal, spatial, and stylistic analysis discussed at length in Chapter 1, while the reading of political transparency is a straightforward interpretation of the factual record. The sources used were a combination of primary and secondary ones. The chapters analyzing transparency in the political realm primarily rely on secondary sources since they are not an attempt to discover new material about West Germany but, rather, an attempt to frame well-known material about the postwar period in a new light. The chapters analyzing the architectural projects, by contrast, rely mostly on primary sources including archival materials such as personal letters, manifestoes, interviews with important protagonists, contemporary newspaper and magazine articles, competition briefs, minutes from competition juries, presentation drawings, construction documents, and conceptual sketches. The conceptual sketches are key because they convey the design intention, often showing formal and spatial concepts in an idealized way that was not realized In the built object, while the buildings show the extent to which each architect was able to achieve his goals.

I am reminded of the great historian of Germany, Gordon Craig, who admonished his readers about how difficult it is to make any assessments or generalizations about the Germans.[6] I am not attempting to do more than pose and speculate about one German Question. German history has been rife with questions. In his book *Society and Democracy in Germany*, Ralf Dahrendorf re-phrases the "German Question" as a series of questions about German democracy, social, and political concerns; the "special" history that encompasses National Socialism and Auschwitz, the contradiction between political failure and cultural success, and even national identity. This book tries to ascertain why transparency ideology has been so persistent in postwar Germany despite all the evidence to suggest that it is flawed, even incorrect, then explores the potential ties to recent German history, memory, postwar politics, and notions of national identity. This is my German Question.

Acknowledgments

As with any project of this length and complexity I am indebted to many colleagues, friends, and professional acquaintances for their help who are, unfortunately, too numerous to list. But a few must be singled out because of their extraordinary contribution to my efforts. My sincerest heartfelt thanks to Professors Franziska Bollerey, Andrei Markovits, and Gerhard Fehl for their careful readings, copious corrections, and insightful criticism of the work. Without their input, the book would be infinitely less refined and less thorough. Professor Bollerey's warm enthusiasm and support gave me confidence when I sorely lacked it. I owe thanks to Dr Irmtraud Frfr von Andrian-Weburg and her archivists at the Germanisches Nationalmuseum in Nuremberg, Dr Gerhard Kabierske and Heidi Fischer at the Südwestdeutsches Archiv für Architektur und Ingenieurbau in Karlsruhe, and Dr Annemarie Jäeggi at the Bauhaus Archiv in Berlin, for helping me find my way through archival material that was often not cataloged and tedious to wade through. Extra special thanks too to Elmar Leucht at the Bundesarchiv in Bonn for helping me find newspaper articles key to my research that I had trouble finding elsewhere and for giving me unrestricted access to the microfilm reading room where I uncovered priceless source material.

From the start, people have given generously of time and resources to the project. A German Academic Exchange Service grant allowed me to complete my research in 2003. The Bundesbildstelle donated 25 photographs, the Germanisches Nationalmuseum gave another 12. Michael Obert, Dietmar Kansy, Peter Conradi, Mark Braun, Heinrich Wefing, David Nelson, and Detlef Lenz gave of their time in key interviews. Two invaluable wells of source material came from personal generosity: Michael Cullen shared his copious private collection, the product of years of work on German architecture; and former MP Peter Conradi made his depot of records of Building Commission meetings available to me. To Carola Franke-Höltzermann at Behnisch & Partner, as well as to Christian Kandzia and Günter Behnisch, goes my deepest gratitude for the time they spent helping me and for their gift of photographs for the book (all of which Mr Kandzia took himself). At Foster and Partners, I owe equal thanks to Elizabeth Walker for digging through their archives to satisfy my odd requests, to David Nelson for his time, and to Lord Foster for the gift of firm images for publication.

Acknowledgments

I must thank Pablo Molestina and Renate Kimmerle for a kind of support without which I would not have been able to conduct my research. Pablo and Renate gave me a bed when I needed one – again and again over five long years of research visits. They put me up in times of need and put up with me graciously even when I was under stress.

My father, Abraham Ascher, has offered the kind of advice only a father can give along with a wealth of professional expertise that made tackling my first solo book project so much easier. I am sure he looks forward to some months without my frantic calls asking for help! My husband, Robert, and my beloved children Alexander and Maya, have put up with countless weeks without Mommy – without their tolerance, love, and support this book would not have been written. Lastly, this book owes whatever merits it has to the generous support of all these people, and many others. For any shortcomings it might have, I can only blame myself.

Pullman, March 15, 2004

Chapter 1

Transparency
ideology

From which origins the parliamentary building should be formed is
primarily a political and secondarily an architectonic question.

Adolf Arndt[1]

Abstraction, transparency, simultaneity, and symbolization are
means of expression which appear both at the dawn of art and
today.

Sigfried Giedion[2]

"He who builds transparently, builds democratically," is a truism of parliamentary architecture in the Federal Republic of Germany adopted to further
several postwar myths: the occasion of a Zero Hour; the existence of a democratic architecture and its opposite, a totalitarian one; the likening of an open
society with a transparent one; and the equating of a democratically elected
parliament with an accessible one.[3] The saying suggests that democracy is
transparent and for this reason, a see-through federal parliament building
exemplifies this transparency both in its workings and in its architecture.[4] "He
who builds a democracy makes a transparent society, government, and
economy" would be an accurate inversion of the trope to delineate certain
goals of postwar West German political renewal. Indeed, the move towards
transparency lies at the heart of the Federal Republic: open public access to
the political process especially to the elected representatives, active public
participation in the political system, an open market economic system, a free
press, and guaranteed civil liberties such as freedom to express one's opinion,
freedom of conscience, and freedom to dissent. But a drive towards transparency is not the same as transparency achieved. Rather, it is the expression

of a desire, a goal, an ideal, but not the real state of things. The drive towards transparency, then, was a weapon against the past, intentionally incorporated into the West German constitution, the Basic Law, to militate against a potential relapse into totalitarianism, state-sponsored racism, and a closed society. Translated into architecture, this interest has evolved since the late 1940s into a dominant ideology for state buildings, especially the national parliaments, although neither the meaning intended by its proponents, nor the possible interpretations, have remained static over time.[5]

The three federal parliament buildings constructed since the Second World War, Hans Schwippert's 1949 Bonn Bundeshaus, Günter Behnisch's 1992 Bonn Bundeshaus, and Norman Foster's 1999 renovation of the Berlin Reichstag, all exploit transparency as the principal architectural analogy (Figures 1.1, 1.2, and 1.3). They do so because the ideological thinking supporting transparency posits the new architecture as the antithesis of historic state buildings like the Reichstag, the embodiment of democratic values, and the symbol of the open society. Although Germany today is certainly an open society and a successful democracy, it is neither a transparent society nor a transparent democracy. In fact, a truly transparent society and democracy does not exist. Nor are the parliament and its workings transparent. The ideology supporting transparency has persisted in spite of these facts. Based on collective memory and consensus about what events should never be repeated, transparent government is supposed to act as a preventative measure, a guarantee. It offers the false hope that things and events that are visible are controllable. Transparency in architecture responds to a collective desire to forget on the part of West Germans feeling guilty about National Socialist excesses, and the desire to begin anew by creating a *Stunde Null* (Zero Hour); transparency is the basis for a new German myth.

The list of those advocating transparency – political, societal and architectural – as the foundation for the new order in West Germany is lengthy. It includes parliamentarians like Adolf Arndt, Carlo Schmid, and Theodor Heuss, and architects like Hans Schwippert, Paul Baumgarten, Sep Ruf, and Günter Behnisch. By 1970, even the parliamentary Building Committee believed it must mandate transparent architecture for the new *Bundehaus* and government complex in Bonn, a mandate repeated again and again thereafter including for the competition for the Reichstag renovation in the 1990s.[6] If "he who builds transparently, builds democratically," is taken as a hypothetical assertion applied to West German parliamentary architecture after the Second World War, the statement can be tested with a series of questions. Do those who build opaquely, build undemocratically? Is it possible to build transparently for a totalitarian or authoritarian regime? The answers to both questions seem obvious because so many constructed examples exist that refute each one. Opaque buildings are not necessarily undemocratic, and yes, it is possible to construct transparently for a totalitarian or authoritarian regime. Among the numerous examples of opaque, massive, monumental, democratic parliaments the American Capitol in Washington, DC, and the French Assemble Nationale in Paris stand out, while transparent buildings used to further undemocratic ideologies include Giusseppe Terragni's masterpiece, the Casa del Fascio in Como built to support Italian Fascism, and the Palace of the Republic in East Berlin designed to promote the East German brand of Communism. If the hypothesis is so easy to disprove, why has it not only continued to be accepted in the Federal Republic but also gained wider and wider currency over the past 55 years?

Although easily proved false, "he who builds transparently, builds democratically," does have buried in it some important facts about postwar German parliamentary architecture. The expression sets up a relationship between the political realm and meaning in state architecture, as well as between the concept of transparency in politics and in state buildings. It is here that the real interest lies since after the Second World War West German architects intentionally attempted to invent modern iconographic systems based on new formal, spatial, and stylistic models for the design of a national parliament. Transparency offered a convenient ideal to parliamentarians eager to distance West Germany from the Third Reich, Weimar Republic, and East Germany, and to architects equally determined to distance their work from the ideological and symbolic programs of the other regimes. In the case of each parliamentary project, the architect drew on the contemporary understanding of West German political identity as a source for architectural

1.1
The Bonn Bundeshaus as designed by Hans Schwippert, seen from the Rhine River in 1949.
Schwippert Archiv, Germanisches Nationalmuseum, Nuremberg.

invention. And, in both the political and the architectural realms, transparency served as the agent that defined the parameters for action. Furthermore, the numerous parallels between notions of transparency in political identity and state architecture evolved over time, as West Germany progressed from a hopeful new state to a mature democracy. What the linkage between transparency and democracy does not address is the extent to which it establishes a false metaphor and false analogy for both the state and state architecture since neither is truly transparent. Myths by definition are rarely based on fact, but derive their strength from their emotional appeal to collective desires. In the case of West Germany after 1945, there was an overwhelming desire to be open and to be anything but what had come before. Transparency offers the hope that West Germans have achieved this collective goal of national reinvention.

1.2
The Bonn Bundeshaus as designed by Günter Behnisch, seen from the Parliament Plaza in 1992.
Bundesbildstelle Berlin.

I

Adolf Arndt, the distinguished German lawyer, member of the first Bundestag in 1949, *Geschäftsfuhrer* for the SPD from 1949 to 1963, and foremost legal

1.3
The renovated Reichstag as designed by Foster and Partners, seen from the West side.
Bundesbildstelle Berlin.

expert in the SPD, repeatedly addressed the issue of building for democracy. In 1960 he delivered his most famous speech at the opening of the Berlin Building Week, *Bauen für die Demokratie* (Building for Democracy), a speech that has been republished repeatedly in West Germany since: in the architecture press (*Bauwelt* ran the speech in January 1961), in collections of essays about the new West German state, and in special single editions. In that and other speeches and essays, Arndt asked for a state architecture that at once demonstrated the spirit of the West German community and the spirit of the time – no mean feat in a country whose civil service was still dominated by former Nazis. Furthermore, it is significant that the speech was first delivered in Berlin with East Germany as backdrop and the memory of National Socialist excesses clearly motivating some of Arndt's argument.[7] In Arndt's view, West Germany's new democratic society was based on transparency. By this Arndt meant that West German society had open public access to its elected officials and to parliamentary proceedings, pluralism and individualism, freedom of expression and conscience, and popular participation in government. Because of his interpretation of West German democracy, Arndt called for transparency in state architecture as well.[8] "Shouldn't there be a connection between the public principles of democracy and inner and outer transparency and accessibility in our public buildings?"[9] Arndt was convinced that West German democracy needed some sort of unique architectural expression. Speaking in the city Hitler and Speer once planned to redesign, where certain architectural remnants of their megalomania like the Reichsbank and the Aviation Ministry still stood, and where reminders of the Prussian monarchy and the Wilhelmine empire like Schloss Charlottenburg and the Reichstag also survived, the lack of a style for the new West Germany must have been all the more apparent. Interestingly, Arndt's demand came 11 years after the architect Hans Schwippert identified transparent architecture as the most appropriate representation of West German democratic government, but long before the notion gained common currency among West German architects and parliamentarians.[10] In his defense of the design for the Bundeshaus, Schwippert recognized the originality in his proposition. He claimed to have built the "first modern parliament"; to have anchored West German parliamentary architecture firmly in the present, the up-to-date, and the innovative.[11] By transparent architecture, both Schwippert and Arndt meant see-through glass structures whose visual accessibility could be understood as an analogy for the openness, accessibility, and egalitarianism to which the new Federal Republic aspired and whose architecture would promote greater public participation in government as well as help West Germans identify with democracy.

While Schwippert's and Arndt's arguments were part of a larger postwar debate on the appropriate architectural style for post-Nazi Germany, a dispute that divided into two camps – those who favored the return to historic styles or regional traditions as a means of reconstructing confidence and historic continuity versus those who advocated the adoption of a contemporary style that would represent a clear break with the National Socialist past and link with the world-famous architecture of the Weimar Republic – transparency did not become a popular ideology until the 1980s. This is not to say that there were not dozens of state parliaments and town halls constructed from Achern (1964) to Ahlen (1977), from Dorsten (1957) to Bocholt (1978), whose primary material was glass rendering the envelope see-through in the proper light conditions. But the discourse supporting these physically transparent state buildings rarely equated transparency with democracy or the open society.[12] Only a handful of federal projects engaged in this discourse before the 1980s when the second parliament building, the Behnisch Bundeshaus, was being designed. The date of the first competition for the new Bundeshaus and government quarter in 1970 marks the beginning of transparency's true ascendance in German architectural discourse.[13] In that brief, the commissioning agent of parliament called for a transparent building whose design made parliament accessible to the public.[14] The 1993 brief for the Reichstag renovation reveals the logic underlying calls for transparent building in the political realm. It refers to Article 42, Paragraph 1 of the German Basic Law that mandates open (*offen*) public access to the workings of government.[15] The mandate to make the workings of government physically accessible was part of a larger Bill of Rights modeled on the American one that guaranteed an open society – free speech, freedom of conscience, free press, tolerance, and pluralism – qualities that Arndt and others associated with transparency in government and society. By the 1990s, many German parliamentarians clearly wished to believe that state architecture should symbolically reflect the political transparency called for in the constitution. Why did transparency become so important for the national parliament, but nowhere else? Most likely because it is the one building type closely connected with national political identity – the most visible public expression of the new Germany both nationally and internationally. In the years after the war, the FRG was extremely sensitive to how it was perceived abroad, particularly in the former occupying countries, Great Britain, France, and the United States. Local and state government buildings have a limited, mostly regional, audience whereas the national parliament has a presence both inside and outside the country.

II

The national parliament building is an important and potent political symbol of a democratic country like West Germany because it is the seat of government, the home of the constitution, and the place where law is debated and enacted. Yet there is no single form or style for parliament buildings or state buildings either in West Germany, or abroad. Indeed, there is no single form, spatial configuration, or style for democratic state architecture as differentiated from architecture associated with totalitarian, authoritarian, or any other governmental system. In Germany, there was no national parliament building before the late nineteenth century when the Reichstag was designed and constructed, although there was a succession of state parliaments and town halls dating back to the late Middle Ages and after 1663 the national assembly, the Reichstag, held its meetings in the newer section of the Regensburg Town Hall built in 1660.[16] The *Rathaus*, or town hall, did not follow a uniform stylistic formula, rather the buildings were designed to fit prevailing architectural fashion, nationalistic ideologies of style, and local tastes, so that the *Rathaus* in Tangermünde (first half of the fifteenth century) was decidedly Gothic, rendered in brick adorned with bar tracery, rose windows, arched openings covered with tracery, astragals, and pinnacles while that in Frankfurt am Main (1624) was in a typical seventeenth century Rhineland style with stucco façades, steeply gabled roof supported by richly carved wooden members and gingerbread ornamentation in contrast to the town hall in Marburg that tried to express nineteenth-century bourgeois pride through its neo-gothic appearance.[17] The lack of a uniform style did not mean that there were not elements common to most of the *Rathäuser* like the clock tower, that was initially placed at the center of an axial composition, then later at the corner of the building where the tower had a prominent civic presence.[18] In his study of postwar *Rathäuser*, Martin Damus points to several fundamental societal changes that account for the lack of a uniform design approach as well as for the profoundly different way twentieth-century *Rathäuser* are designed compared with their antecedents.[19] Damus's observations are particularly interesting because they seem to apply to the *Landtage*, State Parliaments, and to the national parliament as well. Before the twentieth century, the town hall was conceived as a place for the town council to meet and the council room, the *Ratsaal*, was not only the most important space in the building but also the generating space around which the rest was placed. The building was meant to represent the unique aspects of the town for which it was designed, namely the local industry and the prominent families and their businesses. The wealthy and influential members of the *Rat* therefore largely determined the style in which the building would be constructed. With the advent of participatory democracy came a new concept of government in which the common citizen was elevated to an equal level with the rich merchant and aristocrat; at the same time, the bureaucracy that serves the people replaced the town council as the most important governmental entity. The modern town hall therefore typically devotes only 2 percent of the total square footage to the town council chamber and the remaining 98 percent serves the bureaucracy as opposed to the medieval *Rathaus* whose meeting room was the most important chamber in the building and scaled accordingly.[20] The modern building is constructed to serve the people while the traditional town hall was designed to represent them – not their political identity, but their cultural one.[21] The same is true at the national level, the modern parliament is not an analogy for West German cultural identity, but for West German political identity – the way the country understands itself as a democracy.

It is true that there was no stylistic uniformity among the various town halls and state parliament buildings but there were only a limited number of plan configurations for the plenary chamber. The most usual form was based on the antique theater. A half circle, at the center of the form stood the speaker's podium with the seats for the president and the government behind and the seats for the representatives in front of the podium. At times the half circle was squared to make a multi-sided centrally focused shape whose ordering system was essentially the same as the half circle. Other plenary chambers took the rectangle as their organizing form. The best-known example is the English Parliament in London. In the case of a rectangular plan, whether square or otherwise, the speaker's podium was located at one side of the square so that, in fact, there was little difference between this plan type and the others. The greatest difference was the manner in which the representatives were arranged. In London, the representatives sit on either side facing one another while at the Berlin Herrenhaus the representatives sat side-by-side facing the president rather than each other.

With no national historic precedents to draw on, the architect of the Reichstag, Paul Wallot, relied heavily on foreign precedents for the plan layout, especially the placement of the plenary chamber and the inclusion of a dome, all elements common to many of the design proposals from the 1872 Competition.[22] Wallot's resulting design was highly eclectic, mixing elements from many different styles in a manner that garnered a great deal of criticism in its day.[23] Wallot was equally dependent on applied symbol for his project for the Reichstag adorning façades and interiors with a complex, meaning-laden, sculptural program that combined internationally recognized symbols with ones particular to Germany. Symbol assigns meaning by association, application, or convention. According to Hegel, symbol is defined as "an external existent given or immediately present to contemplation, which yet is to be understood not simply as it confronts us immediately on its own account, but in a wider and more universal sense."[24] The female figure of Athena holding scales is a symbol for "justice" and the laurel and oak wreaths are symbols for "victory." On a larger scale, buildings with societal and cultural significance themselves can become symbols. It was because they recognized the symbolic power embedded in state architecture that the French revolutionaries inscribed *Liberté*, *Egalité*, and *Fraternité* on the old monarchical structures. Yet they did not feel the need to raze the old structures nor to invent new formal and spatial solutions for state buildings – the same neo-classical architecture served monarchic and republican rule equally well! The French example shows how neo-classical models served notions of power and authority regardless of the political system from which they emanated. Stated otherwise, the French example shows how historically unimportant architectural style is to the political system state buildings serve. Similar to the *Rathäuser* designed to show the cultural identity of the town as well as its power and wealth, typical state architecture was designed to show the power and authority of the state rather than the type of political system. In this sense, the West German quest for a special style for democratic state buildings is unusual if not unique.

III

In order to understand the elements constituting the new style West German architects developed, certain key concepts need to be explained, followed by an explication of the method used to read the new architecture. Transparency is so important to this study that a full chapter is devoted to understanding its meaning in West German architecture while a second two chapters analyze its meaning in the West German postwar political arena. Other key terms that require definition are: metaphor, analogy, and "representative," especially the phrase, "representative architecture," for which a short discussion follows. Metaphor and analogy need to be distinguished from one another because they are so often conflated. The two terms also need to be discussed in relationship to actual transparency, referred to as "literal" transparency in architectural discourse, since this too figures in the architecture.

Without some definition of metaphor, it would be impossible to understand how transparency operates in the West German consciousness. Ironically, by definition, metaphors are fluid linguistic devices that are almost impossible to pin down. Nevertheless, a brief working definition ensues, for without some basis for understanding what constitutes a metaphor it would be impossible to discuss transparency. Metaphors are words and concepts used to describe, qualify, or stand in for another concept. Metaphors are fundamental to language and the ways in which human beings understand, or qualify their understanding of, the world. According to the linguist George Lakoff and philosopher Mark Johnson, metaphor forms the basis for all linguistic structure and for language itself.[25] Furthermore, Lakoff and Johnson maintain that, "the most fundamental values in a culture will be coherent with the metaphorical structure of the most fundamental concepts in the culture."[26] Further, they demonstrate the ways in which metaphoric concepts form the basis for the entire human conceptual system.

> The concepts that govern our thought are not just matters of the intellect. They also govern our everyday functioning, down to the most mundane details. Our concepts structure what we perceive, how we get around in the world, and how we relate to other people. Our conceptual system thus plays a central role in defining our everyday realities. If we are right in suggesting that our conceptual system is largely metaphorical, then the way we think, what we experience and what we do every day is very much a matter of metaphor.[27]

Perhaps even more importantly, Lakoff and Johnson assert that metaphor lies at the heart of any human thought process and conceptual system. If their assertion is true, then an analysis of the different metaphors used in any particular language should reveal some, if not all, of the fundamental values of the culture to which that language belongs. Equally, analysis of the metaphors used by one person should reveal the fundamental cultural values held by that person. Fundamental values include how the society is structured in terms of social, political, and economic order; what sort of achievements are esteemed; and what kind of cultural production is supported. If the analysis of metaphor can help uncover some of these, then it offers a powerful analytical tool for linguistic study as well as for cultural, historical, and political study.

Lakoff and Johnson identify three basic types of metaphor: structural, orientational or spatialization, and ontological. A structural metaphor conceptually frames one idea in terms of another. For example, "I gave you that idea" suggests that ideas are things that can be exchanged.[28] An orientational metaphor is one in which a whole series of concepts is systematically structured in relationship to one another. Orientational metaphors usually indicate spatial orientation: up/down, in/out, front/back, and so on. For instance, "Happy is up; sad is down" is an orientational metaphor in English with expressions that include: "I'm feeling up. That boosted my spirits . . . I'm feeling down. I'm depressed."[29] Ontological metaphors are ones in which abstract ideas or experiences are understood as objects with distinct qualities. "Once we can identify our experiences as entities or substances, we can refer to them, categorize them, group them, and quantify them – and, by this means, reason about them."[30] The metaphor transparency usually operates as an ontological metaphor since it assumes the position of subject, or entity, in concepts such as "a democratic Parliament building must somewhat symbolize openness," and "transparency equals democracy," "transparent buildings for open government," "the material naturally has its particular semantic . . . the cube is out of glass – that is associated with openness, transparency, checkability, and honesty."[31] Lakoff and Johnson offer a number of ways the ontological metaphor can manifest itself including: referring, quantifying, identifying aspects, identifying causes, setting goals, and motivating actions.[32] It is also possible that any single metaphor is used in several different ways, which is, in fact, the case with transparency in West German political and architectural discourse.

A cursory look at the various manifestations of the transparency metaphor in German political and architectural discourse suggests several readings. The metaphor "transparency equals democracy," for instance, is one in which the metaphor is certainly referring. It can also be understood as quantifying. That is, the phrase suggests that the use of transparency in parliamentary architecture is a desired and valued characteristic in a democracy and in the institutional representation of that democracy. At the same time, the metaphor identifies these qualities as ones that are associated with democracy versus some other forms of government. The implication is that where there is transparency, there is democracy but not totalitarianism, despotism, monarchical rule, or communism. Further, despite the certainty implied in the word "equals," the metaphor may reflect a desire for openness, accessibility, and honesty since it may be the manifestation of the belief that when one condition exists, i.e. transparent architecture or transparent political discourse, that the condition democracy must also exist or may come into existence. It is easy to disprove both statements. Tatlin's famous proposal for a *Monument to the Third International* is one of many examples of a transparent government building designed for, and symbolizing, Stalin's regime rather than a democratic one. Similarly, many of the National Socialist aphorisms could be described as transparent since their meaning was completely clear and their intent was a transparent social connection between people, state, and Führer. The phrase, "*Ein Volk, Ein Reich, Ein Führer*" accurately represents the synthesis of the German nation the National Socialists hoped to achieve. The expression does not, however, demonstrate the utter lack of transparency such a synthesis would create, the unitary, opaque society the phrase symbolizes. Thus transparency can be misleading, it does not necessarily guarantee the kind of openness and clarity implied in the word. If this is true in linguistic terms, it can also be true in architectural ones. That is, although transparency in government architecture may express the desire for open democracy, it may not prove or guarantee that open democracy actually exists.

Jan Esche is one of many German authors whose writing intimates the value of democratic government measured in terms of transparency: the dialog between people and elected representatives, between representatives and chancellor, the role of the press, the relationship between Germany and her foreign allies, and so on can all be assessed relative to the degree of transparency.[33] In other words, the degree to which these many layers of political and societal relationships are open, honest, clear, and checkable is equal to their value.

Transparency acts as a metaphor in political and architectural discourse, but not in the architecture itself because metaphors relate to ideas and language but not to things. The relational patterns formed by objects to other objects, and by ideas to objects are called "analogies."[34] Thus, the formal, spatial, and stylistic use of transparency in postwar West German architecture is analogical. Although some metaphors can be considered analogies, because they share relational information, the two are different. As the authors of *The Analogical Mind* are careful to point out, "metaphors can be based on common object attributes" while analogies cannot. They are founded on structural relationships – the "process of establishing a structural alignment between two represented situations and then projecting inferences . . . An alignment consists of an explicit set of correspondences between the representational elements of the two situations."[35] The use of transparent formal and spatial systems, as well as see-through materials, in West German state architecture is therefore analogical because it suggests the relationship between the physical structure of democratic government and society, and the material and spatial structure of the buildings. The structure of democratic government in this case means a political system open to public observation and participation, and differences in race, conscience, and political beliefs.

The way in which metaphor and analogy are used reveals a great deal about attitudes towards the state, the official architecture, and to history. By analyzing texts describing the goals for the architecture, defending it or criticizing it, it is possible to construct a set of norms, desires, goals, and fundamental values for state architecture present in postwar Germany. After identifying these values, norms, desires, and goals from texts describing the architecture, it is possible to work backwards in order to deduce more general underlying cultural attitudes that informed the architectural belief systems. This is particularly true since state architecture is the embodiment of someone's image of the country, and of political identity, in built terms.

Besides its position relative to a particular cultural product, transparency must also be situated relative to its position in time, or history. As is true of all words and ideas, the notion of transparency differs depending on the historic moment, the cultural context, and the language in which it is used. Thus, it is impossible to equate a nineteenth- with a twentieth-century notion of transparency, or the English language notion of "transparency" with the French notion *transparence*, or the German *Transparenz*.[36] The philosopher of cognitive science, Hilary Putnam, points to the difficulties in translating words from one language to another since their contexts, and therefore their meanings, will be different. Furthermore, Putnam asserts that all "reference is a social phenomenon." Putnam goes on to declare that, "meaning is interactional. The environment itself plays a role in determining what a speaker's words, or a community's words, refer to."[37] In other words, in order to understand fully the meaning of a word, it has to be examined in the social and historical context in which it is used. In the case of transparency, it continued to be used as a metaphor for democracy in the Federal Republic from 1949 onwards. Although as Putnam no doubt would predict, its sense did change in subtle ways related to changes in the German political context, mostly by acquiring additional shades of meaning rather than losing existing ones or altering them.

That language changes over historic time is a statement of fact without a statement of cause. But in order to fully understand the underlying cultural values revealed through metaphor and analogy, the expressed desires and hidden fears revealed in linguistic choices, it is necessary to discover the historic events that caused the change in meaning or usage. As Maurice Halbwachs explained, it is necessary to uncover the collective memory or memories that define the social identity of a group.[38] The key here is that transparency began as a metaphor for a desired condition but became an analogy for democracy in Germany as it was embodied in architectural projects over the last 50 years.

One primary reason that transparency ideology developed after the establishment of West Germany was the persistent need for a means with which to represent the state architecturally. The terms *Repräsentativ* or *Repräsentation* and *Selbstdarstellung* are used throughout the German literature discussing and analyzing government architecture. The word *Selbstdarstellung* is formed by combining *Selbst* (self) and *Darstellung* (to show or to portray), literally to mean, "to show oneself." When "self-portrayal" is used in the architectural sense, the author intends the reader to understand the presentation of the most important qualities of the self – character, content, physical attributes, and belief systems – through all available means: architectural drawings, sketches, buildings, construction details, writings, and any other ways by which architecture can be portrayed. Both the German and English words are based on the Latin roots, *repraesentare*, which means "to show," from and *re-*, "again," and *praesentare*, "to present." In English, representative is derived from "represent" which is formed by joining "re-" with "present," literally to mean "to show again." The implication is that whatever is portrayed is not new and likely has been seen and understood before. The word's additional meanings include, "typical, having good prestige value, creating a good impression, and creating the correct impression." The term is used to convey the positive worth of a piece of architecture as the means for showing the state.

Representation is a central issue in art history too large to discuss at length here. One question key to the analysis of artworks is what does the work "re-present," that is, present again. The approach assumes that any work of art, or architecture, is "evidential in nature."[39] The art historian Donald Preziosi explains the traditional approach to interpreting art as follows:

> Art objects of all kinds came to have the status of historical documents in the dual sense that (1) each was presumed to provide significant, often unique, and, on occasion, profoundly revealing evidence for the character of an age, nation, person or people; and that (2) their appearance was the resultant product of a historical milieu, however narrowly or broadly framed.[40]

The technique used to create the artwork is all-important to this particular art historical method. In the case of West German state architecture, it can be said to "re-present" notions about the nature of West German democracy in the form of a building. Further, the changes in formal, spatial, and stylistic approach signaled by the first Bundeshaus project parallel an altered collective mentality in West Germany – one in which transparency seems to be the ideal analogy for democracy in architecture.

Lastly, the first German romance with transparency arose in conjunction with the great innovative movement of twentieth-century German architecture, Neues Bauen, and retained a connection to Neues Bauen after

1945. The term Neues Bauen (New Buildings) was coined after the turn of the twentieth century to refer to architecture whose esthetic seemed to present a novel approach to design, one that responded to the social conditions of industrial society, mass production techniques, and new materials whose buildings were simple, often asymmetrically formulated, unadorned volumes with flat roofs and large glass surfaces. The architects associated with the Neues Bauen believed they had uncovered the formal, material, and spatial means to represent the Zeitgeist, the spirit of their times, and they thought their approach to design was trans-national and trans-cultural in nature. Alternatively called Neues Bauen, International Style, Neue Sachlichkeit (New Objectivity), Rationalismus (Rationalism), *Funktionalismus* (Functionalism), and *Kronstruktivismus* (Constructivism), as Detlef Mertins rightly points out, so many names proliferated because none seemed to fully capture the richness and variety of work produced. The approach was generally thought of to be without style; at least in the period before the Second World War because it was a reaction against the style-oriented architectural production of the nineteenth century and tended to stress the functional and rational motivations for design over the stylistic.[41] Like so many new movements, as Manfredo Tafuri asserts, Neues Bauen claimed to be anti-historical in nature.[42] It was only with Philip Johnson and Henry Russell Hitchcock's International Style Exhibition and book in 1932, and Alfred Barr's preface to the book *The International Style*, that the word "style" was more widely applied to Neues Bauen work although the term was in circulation already in the 1920s.[43] Critics and writers Walter Curt Behrendt and Adolf Behne are two people who used Neues Bauen in book titles during the 1920s. Behne published *Neues Wohnen – Neues Bauen* in 1927, the same year that Behrendt presented *Der Sieg des Neuen Baustils* (The Victory of the New Building Style). Furthermore, the Weissenhofsiedlung (1927) sponsored by the Deutsche Werkbund, and organized by Mies van der Rohe, offered the public the unique opportunity to tour constructed examples of the new architecture. For this study, the German term Neues Bauen is the most appropriate, rather than any of the others, for two reasons: because it is a broad term compared with Functionalism, for example, but not so broad as International Style, and because it was used in West Germany after 1945 when debates over how to rebuild revived many of the prewar arguments. There is a key difference between the prewar and postwar Neues Bauen architecture that should be noted. Whereas buildings designed before the war were based on the ideological underpinnings of Neues Bauen, those designed after the war tended to appropriate the stylistic elements of the movement without much of the ideology. This occurred because of the changed political, economic, and social conditions brought on by the war that further justify the addition of the word "style" after Neues Bauen to describe the production dating after 1945.

IV

In his essay, "How Buildings Mean," Nelson Goodman argues that in order to understand what a building means, we have to identify how that building conveys meaning.[44] Goodman outlines four distinct ways of meaning: denotation, exemplification, metaphorical expression, and mediated reference. Denotation describes the ways a building may convey meaning in a straightforward, easily legible manner. A typical way denotation operates is through written literature explaining the architect's intentions for the building; Hans Schwippert's manifesto on the importance of glass construction is a good example of denotation. Exemplification explains the use of architectonic devices, the formal, spatial, and material means with which a building is organized and constructed, in order to convey an idea. Using see-through glass and open floor plans to connote transparency are forms of exemplification. Goodman uses the phrase "metaphorical expression" to describe the embodiment of metaphor in architecture. In this case, Goodman's terminology is not specific enough; architecture actually conveys meaning analogously, not metaphorically (see above). Analogous expression in the cases presented here includes the utilization of transparent architecture to indicate honest, open, and accessible parliament. Much of this study is devoted to exploring the means with which architects created analogous architectonic systems to express notions of German political identity. The fourth category, mediated reference, applies to culturally created meaning. An example present in Germany was the belief that the Reichstag represented failed democracy. This idea arose because the failed Weimar parliament had met in the Reichstag building. Goodman's four categories are helpful tools but limited. They are not specific enough about the method with which each category should be approached and, as Lawrence Vale points out, they do not comprise an analytic model.[45] Nor do they offer a means with which to examine *why* particular meanings apply. Much of this text therefore relies on traditional historical research methodology within the four areas Goodman identifies.

The descriptive categories developed by architectural historians to analyze classical architecture are inadequate to the analytical task at hand since they apply to design systems that were very different from those adopted in the twentieth century. Paradoxically in their book, *Classical Architecture*, Alexander Tzonis and Liane Lefaivre use an analysis of classical architecture to suggest a way to devise a formal system that could be applied to architecture in any style at any period in history. The system they propose developed by reading surviving texts from the periods "in which classical architecture was shaped in order to find out how classical architecture was seen, how it was talked about, and what the categories are through which classical buildings were originally conceived and perceived."[46] For classical architecture, especially during the Greek and Roman periods, very little documentary evidence remains but for German architecture from 1920 onwards, there is an abundance of evidence that includes manifestoes written by the architects, correspondence between architects, newspaper and journal reviews of buildings, and critical essays by contemporary architectural historians. More importantly, while differences exist in the terminology used, there is an astonishing consistency in the language suggesting that even from the very beginning, some consensus existed, or very quickly developed, about what constituted the new design system.

The West German architects who were interested in transparency before and immediately after the Second World War were members of the avant-garde and sympathizers, if not members, of the Neues Bauen. Hans Schwippert lived in Berlin in the 1920s and 1930s where he befriended Bruno Taut and Mies van der Rohe, joined the avant-garde group called the Zehner Ring (Ring of Ten), and began to experiment with formal elements of the Neues Bauen architecture.[47] After the war, Schwippert joined the ranks of West German architects advocating the Neues Bauen style as the most appropriate for the postwar period (see Chapter 5 for a lengthier discussion of this subject). By the time Günter Behnisch began work on his project, the debate had greatly altered but one thing had not: the importance of contemporary design on the West German scene and its lineage from Neues Bauen. Even unification has not much altered the terms of the debate. Most importantly, the new ways of designing and seeing form and space that developed in the 1920s continue to inform architectural discourse even today.[48] Therefore the criteria for formulating an evaluative system for the postwar parliamentary projects should cull from the writings about the Neues Bauen, those proselytizing for it, defending it, and explaining it.

It is possible to reduce the fundamental categories for discussion into four distinct areas: formal, spatial, stylistic, and holistic. Since the sides to the stylistic debate that dealt with state architecture in West Germany were largely delineated during the years immediately after the war, the stylistic determinants pertain more directly to the first parliamentary project than to the second or third.[49] "Style" usually describes attributes in a work of art or architecture that are common to a group of works, thereby tying them together, although it can also refer to a sense of elegance, panache, and originality. Therefore, Lazlo Moholy-Nagy, Raoul Hausmann, Hans Arp, and Ivan Puni could declare in 1921 "Reject styles! We demand a world without styles in order to arrive at *style!* Style is never plagiarism!"[50] The stylistic analysis will be left at a minimum, however, for the simple reason that all three parliamentary projects are somewhat different stylistically although they share formal and spatial qualities.

In architectural discourse the word "form" generally has one of two meanings: the property of things as they are known to the senses, often understood as their shape, and the property of things as they are known to the mind, their meaning. As Adrian Forty makes clear, the confusion often attached to the use of the word "form" in English is less apt to occur in German where there are two separate words for these different concepts, *Gestalt*, for the former and *Form* for the latter.[51] For the purposes of this study, both senses apply. The *Form* of each building will be examined in relationship to notions of political and societal transparency; the *Gestalt* will be broken into a series of sub-categories. Formal considerations, in the sense of *Gestalt* include identifying the use of: (a) line, (b) plane (or surface), (c) volume, (d) structure, and (e) materials within some simple regulating geometric order. Qualifying characteristics of form mentioned over and over again in contemporary texts include: simplicity, clarity, proportion, rationality, and openness. Giedion, after Van Doesburg, identifies line, surface, volume, space, and time as the "elementary forms of architecture."[52] In his essay explicating elementary construction, "Towards a Plastic Architecture" (1924), Van Doesburg refers to many of the same elements as Giedion adding light, color, and material to the catalog.

In "Towards a New Architecture," Le Corbusier points to line (contour), surface, and mass as three critical elements in contemporary architecture, although in his view, line is largely used to regulate the ordering system, which he believes is based in geometry and the plan. Le Corbusier was extremely concerned with order and systematic method to design, as Adolf Behne emphasizes. Behne also was quick to remind his readers that Le Corbusier's system was individual. It was similar to, but at the same time quite different from the systems other contemporary architects were using. Van Doesburg advocated a geometric system based on rectangular units. Erich Mendelsohn wrote that:

> Architecture establishes the conditions of its animated masses from its own laws: the dynamic condition, movement of space (seen in outline as its linear element), the rhythmic condition, the relationship of masses (seen in elevation as its surface projection), and the structural condition or balance of movement (seen in plan and section as their structural elements).[53]

In his writing on architecture, Schwippert distinguishes between "form" and "content," sometimes using the German word *Form* and sometimes *Gestalt* to refer to the shape of things, and always the word *Inhalt* (content) for ideas.[54] He readily acknowledges the difficulty of discussing and defining "form," then suggests that form is only the intermediary for something else, something human. "I use the word 'form' henceforth in the sense of 'forming,' 'formal events,' and 'gestures.'"[55] Schwippert's view is close to that of the German writer and historian Friedrich Schiller, whom Schwippert quoted extensively in his own speeches and writing. When trying to pinpoint the underlying qualities of "good form," Schwippert repeatedly points to "Cleanness, clarity, situation, rational dimensions, realized from perfect light and proportion, and fashioned from rational purposes" as characteristics of good form as well as "transparency (*Durchsichtigkeit*), lightness, openness."[56] Finally, Schwippert refers to the need for order in form making, to the architect's task lying in finding a way to give form to the unseen. "Form," he wrote in notes to himself in 1943, "is not a photographic copy of 'reality' but beyond (and inside) making archetypes and timeless examples visible."[57] When describing successful design he said, "formal work has material, form and conceptual structures. It relates to the material, spiritual and intellectual realms. . . ."[58] For Schwippert, form and idea are not the same thing, although one will certainly embody the other.

Behnisch uses similar terms to describe form-making in general and specifically at the Bundeshaus. He makes clear the absolute connection between ideas and form in architecture. "The architectural idea and the imaginative conception of reality are at the centre of our planning. . . ."[59] And when describing the process of building for a democracy he wrote, "We architects make material, visible, and credible in the experiential world, that which already exists in the realm of ideas."[60] The forms Behnisch makes visible are open, not closed, in every sense possible. "One fundamental characteristic of Modern Architecture is its openness towards the circumstances, demands etc. of its time."[61] Behnisch goes on to describe the "open, democratic" aspect the building was to have and how it is composed of "elements," "surfaces and lines." Elsewhere, Behnisch describes the plenary chamber as "the open room." Openness to the landscape, to the sky, and between individual spaces, is an aspect of most Behnisch designs. For Behnisch, "the essence of the 'building' lay not in its protective outer shell, that which, in former times, represented a house; not primarily the roof or the wall, either. Instead, it is the localities that are prominent, both within and outside the walls – in one place a tree, in another a staircase floating in space, the location for plenary meetings and the Rhine riverbed. . . ."[62] When discussing the various schemes developed for the Reichstag renovation, Norman Foster uses language similar to Behnisch and Schwippert. He discusses the need for "open" architecture, for "lightness," for renewed connections between exterior and interior, and vertically between the floors.[63] For the first competition, he felt, "that the building had, metaphorically at least, to be 'blown apart' in a very novel way."[64] In other words, the closed neo-classical form of the old building had to be made open; the old ideas and symbols had to be replaced. Underlying all of these projects, then, is the common notion that form is the expression of an idea, and that form uses clear, straightforward geometry to order simple, basic (archetypal) elements.

Spatial analysis forms the second part of the readings of architectural projects in this book but, like form, space is a slippery term. Furthermore, it is extremely difficult to discuss one without the other since the two are so interdependent in twentieth-century architecture. As a concept in the architectural vocabulary, "space" is relatively new – it only entered common usage in the 1890s.[65] Furthermore, it was the German architect and theorist Gottfried Semper who, in *Der Stil*, first referred to space, by explaining the primary purpose of architecture as the enclosing of space.[66] By the 1920s, however, the use of "space" had proliferated. Adrian Forty identifies three senses in which the word was most often used as "space as enclosure, space as continuum, and space as extension of the body."[67] "Space Conception" is Sigfried Giedion's term from *Space, Time and Architecture*, coined to explain new notions of space in art and architecture.[68]

> The essence of space as it is conceived today is its many-sidedness, the infinite potentiality for relations within it. Exhaustive description of an area from one point of reference is, accordingly, impossible; its character changes with the point from which it is viewed. In order to grasp the true nature of space the observer must project himself through it.[69]

Giedion's definition is far from unique – similar ones exist in writings by Gropius, Taut, Van Doesburg, Le Corbusier, Arthur Korn, Adolf Behne, and many others – but Giedion's text is one of the most clearly written. Indeed, Giedion goes on to talk about the moving point of reference in spatial concepts of modern physics, which he relates to compositional strategies evident in Cubism, Neo-Plasticism, Elementarism, and Futurism. Mies van der Rohe called architecture, "the will of the age conceived in spatial terms."[70] For him, space was the fundamental quality that distinguished "modern" architecture from classical architecture.[71] In his seminal book *Der Moderne Zweckbau* (*The Modern Functional Building*) (1926), Adolf Behne refers to a similar group of criteria. Instead of "space conception" Behne discusses "shaped space" but the idea is essentially the same as Giedion's.[72]

Writing the same year that Giedion first delivered his lectures on Space, Time, and Architecture at Harvard University, Lazlo Moholy-Nagy addressed the complex and elusive meaning of "space" in his essay "Modern Art and Architecture" (1936) in a direct and comprehensive manner. In the essay, he explains the essence of what he calls the "new art" by writing "it is an attempt to get into accord with the new conception of space."[73]

Moholy-Nagy grapples with the many different nuances "space" can have. He lists 44 different types of space in order to illustrate how difficult it is to pinpoint one, comprehensive definition for the term. In the end, Moholy-Nagy prefers the definition that comes from physics, "Space is the relation between the position of bodies. Therefore: spatial creation is the creation of relationships of position of bodies (volumes)."[74] The understanding of space comes primarily through visual observation of dynamic forces operating in the architecture such as movement, relationships between masses and light, vertical, horizontal, and diagonal elements, and interpenetrations.[75]

Like other contemporaries, Schwippert writes about "space" and "spatiality," referring again and again to the "spatial will." By "spatial will" Schwippert seems to mean the drive towards an architectural space that is dictated by program, site, functional requirements, and the idea behind the design informed by a sensitivity to contemporary society and its needs. He acknowledges that new materials, such as glass and steel, and new building techniques are especially suited to the contemporary will to space.[76] Reading further, Schwippert's concept of space is close to that of Giedion and Moholy-Nagy in that transparency, relations between objects, and movement inform it. "We do not need to speak of the interior spatial possibilities . . . transparency, distance, openness, we win all of this with the material [steel]."[77] He calls for "spatiality . . . as a light, moving, lightweight and open spatial sequence. . . ."[78]

Behnisch too refers constantly to "space" and "space-making" in explications of his design work. The most striking aspect of his approach to spatiality is how central openness is, not only to the space itself, but to the process of enclosing it. Behnisch advocates using an open process, soft pencil or charcoal drawings that are imprecise and therefore indefinite so as to leave the design as "open" as possible "and therefore allowing more subtle forces to emerge."[79] Behnisch even suggests that his open method of working is anti-totalitarian and democratic. When describing space itself at the Bundeshaus, Behnisch writes of "flowing spaces" that are only loosely circumscribed by open spatial barriers such as handrails. The spatial experience Behnisch, and others writing about the Bundeshaus, convey is one of multiple vantage points: the landscape is visible in every direction from the building interiors while the interior spaces are visible from everywhere inside and outside, because internal partitions are either transparent glass, screens, or handrails. The total effect is akin to Giedion's impression of the Bauhaus building where simultaneous views overlap spaces that are, in fact, distinct. Foster is explicitly concerned with the spatial development of the Reichstag interiors. He criticizes the Paul Baumgarten renovation from the 1960s because it "was at odds with the original form of the building. His planning was horizontally constrained, with little vertical connection or emphasis."[80] Foster continues, "Spatially, Wallot's Reichstag was highly compartmentalized . . . We have gouged through the building from top to bottom, opening it up . . . ."[81] Not only did the Foster team create vertical connections where they did not exist in any of the earlier schemes, they restored vertical spaces, two interior court-yards, that had been eliminated during the 1960s renovation. Similar logic was applied to the new dome, "the spatial grandeur of Wallot's building was crushed by the uniform horizontality of Baumgarten's new floor levels; the new chamber and cupola cuts through these levels to provide a powerful vertical emphasis."[82] Foster uses words like "layers" and "interlocking" to describe the new spatial condition his design will create and, indeed, the internal transparency coupled with the opening of floors in both plan and section creates spatial connections and vistas through the structure that are similar to those Behnisch and Schwippert constructed at the Bundeshaus in their respective projects.

Space then is the relation between things understood from multiple perspectives, often by moving through the space, versus form, the thing in itself. Form encloses space. The elements that are ordered to make form therefore enclose and define space so that although it is possible to describe form without describing the space it encloses, the inverse would be im-possible. Space touches on quality, emotional content, the intangible aspects of architecture that can be excluded from purely formal analysis which, as Tzonis and Lefaivre point out, are purely descriptive, not qualitative.[83]

Finally, the notion of a holistic architecture dates to well before the Neues Bauen period but was very much a part of the discourse. Often referred to as "organic," the quality is one Berlage extolled in his 1907 lectures in Zürich in which the parts relate so intimately to one another and to the whole that nothing seems additive or superfluous. Walter Behrendt wrote that the

> inner tensions of the spatial organism are brought into a pure and harmonious relationship . . . The whole building will again become a unified organism, whose individual parts entail each other and are held in tension. This way of designing no longer permits chance ornament, superfluous ornament, or applied decoration. One and the same driving force produces forms and proportions altogether integrated, a characteristic that Jacob Burckhardt has described as the most distinctive sign of all original and organic styles.[84]

Behrendt's assessment is echoed by many of his contemporaries who want the new architecture to return to the origins of design, to the most basic, fun-damental principles. Behne explains the benefits of the new design by writing that, "a building achieves a much broader and better inner unity; it becomes more organic by abandoning the old conventions and formalisms of represen-tation, which inhibit the materialization of necessary form."[85] Architects did not agree on the precise means with which to achieve a holistic design: various proportional systems were proposed by Berlage and Le Corbusier, for instance. Berlage famously developed a system using triangles to regulate plans, sections, and façades while Le Corbusier created the modular based on the human body. Others propose strict adherence to a functional rationale for the building in order to create a cohesive design. In *Neues Wohnen – Neues Bauen* from 1927, Behne even suggests that there is no single method for generating the new architecture.[86] At first Behne asserts that the new approach is too new to have developed its own methodology but he then goes on to write that the "way to a totality is through simplicity only."[87] Ludwig Hilberseimer agrees with Behne and perhaps states the case in the most straightforward and emphatic manner of all. In his very brief introduction to the buildings presented in *Internationale Neue Baukunst* (*International New Building Art*) Hilberseimer points to the functional characteristic, material uses, industrial and social concerns common to all the projects that together "affirm the correct balance of the individual elements. The juxtaposition forms the unity of the building works."[88] Hilberseimer goes on to compare the new architecture to the old, condemning the lack of concern for the building as organism in the "façade architecture" of the nineteenth century. He concludes by writing that it is the mutual dependency of the individual parts, that read as a unified whole, that gives the buildings their worth and their meaning. But it is Walter Gropius who, perhaps, puts the case most succinctly and beautifully in his 1925 book, *Die Neue Architektur und Das Bauhaus* (*The New Architecture and the Bauhaus*) when he affirms that architecture is more than constructive technique, "the other, the aesthetic satisfaction of the human soul, is just as important as the material. Both find their counterpart in that unity which is life itself."[89] Art and life: architecture and life, should be one and the same.

V

Three distinct moments in West German history – in 1949, 1989, and 1999 – lie at the core of this study, moments that are significant to German political and architectural history. West Germany officially came into existence on September 7, 1949; East and West Germany began the process of unification when the Wall was first breached on November 9, 1989; and 1999 marked the installation of the unified parliament in Berlin. These dates also correspond with the completion of a new parliament building, or the approval of a new design for one. It is only in the case of the Behnisch project, in fact, whose construction straddled unification and a sea change in both the German political landscape and notions of political identity, for which the design completion date has been selected rather than the construction completion date. For the three projects used as cases here, conceptual meaning is intimately tied to contemporary notions of political identity whether they reflect the truth or not. Furthermore, if political identity is taken as a constituent part of national identity, then these projects also represent notions of national identity especially at the time they were designed and built. The intention here is to read accepted notions of political identity in a novel way in order to trace the ways the ideology of transparency has shifted and changed its meaning over time. A brief history of transparency in West German architectural and art historical realms is also presented because the projects draw as much on architectural and art historical models as they do on ones from the political realm. Whereas the political meaning of transparency served to help justify transparency in state architecture to members of the political class, the architectural and art historical meanings made transparency appealing to architects and others involved in the arts in West Germany. Indeed, the confluence of meanings of transparency from different disciplines in state architecture offers one explanation for the appeal the metaphor and the analogy have held. Next, the study analyzes the parliamentary projects both as works of architecture and as embodiments of the transparency analogy and other contemporary notions of political identity.

It is important to add that for the purposes of this discussion, notions of German "political identity" are never presented as widely held popular ideas, but rather as part of the belief system of either one individual, or a small group. Thus, the comparison is of German political identity as interpreted by three architects: Hans Schwippert, Günter Behnisch, and Norman Foster, with the complicity of their design teams and the politicians responsible for commissioning the works. While there may be parallel beliefs held by many others in the German population, this book does not in any way attempt to prove that that is, or is not, so. On the other hand, since few individuals hold beliefs completely unique to themselves, it is possible to infer that other contemporaries of each architect would have agreed with the analogical reading each architect made of Germany at the time. Indeed, the contemporary press supports this view in each case.

Each of the three projects is a combined reaction to the historic image of German state architecture under the Kaisers, and for the brief period during the Third Reich, and the contemporary political situation in Germany. The understanding of transparency, or *Durchsichtigkeit*, in 1949 is profoundly influenced by the aftermath of the Second World War, the political situation in Germany at the time both as a nascent democracy and as an emerging member of the West European community of nations. The use of the Germanic word *Durchsichtigkeit*, as opposed to the Latinate *Transparenz*, may be a holdover from the Third Reich and the National Socialist tendency to promote Germanic words over "foreign" ones. The political situation in 1949, at the time Schwippert completed the Bundeshaus, was tenuous at best. Germany had just been defeated and divided into four zones, each governed by an occupying force that was Russian, British, American, or French. While the British, Americans, and French had agreed to unite their zones to create the German Federal Republic, the Russians absorbed East Germany into the ring of communist satellites in Eastern Europe. On June 20, 1948 the three Western zones reformed the currency by abolishing the old Reichsmark and replacing it with the Deutsch Mark at a conversion rate of 10:1. According to the distinguished historian Peter Pulzer, it was the currency reform more than any other measure that "set the seal on the division of Germany" for it tied the Western zones to the American dollar while the Eastern currency was tied to the Soviet rouble.[90] In 1949 the German Federal Republic was born to fend off Russian intervention in the Western sectors. Out of a patently unsuccessful democracy, a new parliamentary democracy emerged whose future was unknown.

By the 1980s, the internal and external political landscape had changed dramatically and architectural language changed with it. Texts describing the Bundestag project by Günter Behnisch use the word *Transparenz* instead of *Durchsichtigkeit*, although Hans Schwippert only referred to transparency as *Durchsichtigkeit*. That is, sometime between 1948 and 1970, the discourse abandons the German-language word in favor of the Latinate one that is the root for the word transparency in many languages, among them English, French, and Italian. This shift, albeit subtle, reflects similar attitudinal shifts perceptible in the contemporary political landscape that sought to internationalize West Germany, to make the country transparent to its neighbors. By the time the decision to rebuild the Reichstag was taken on June 20, 1991, Germany was united as one nation. The Soviet empire was crumbling and a new political order emerging. Germany, it had long been clear, was more than a small part of the West European community, it had developed into one of the driving forces behind the European Union. By the time of the completion of the Reichstag in 1999, a decade after unification, optimism had soured in the face of reality. Unification forced a different kind of transparency on West Germany, the kind of transparency that occurs when you look at your reflection in the mirror, and for the first time, see yourself as others do.

The ideology of transparency, then, is the basis for two parallel and interrelated studies – one, of one myth of the dominant political identity in the FRG in 1949, 1989, and 1999, and the other, of the translation of that myth into architectural form, space, and material. Transparency as ideology is compared with transparency in reality both in the built object and in the political realm. Finally, I ask the question "why transparency in West German parliamentary architecture?" Transparent state architecture is not unique to the Federal

Republic of Germany after the war, but it is far more common here than anywhere else, and the arguments for and against it are more public, more heated, and have lasted for almost 60 years. Furthermore, West Germany is the only country in which transparent architecture is so strongly equated with expressions of democratic government and where the national parliament has been rendered transparent in some way on three distinct occasions. What historic circumstances account for this?

To say that the architects of each parliamentary project acted in concert with the contemporary political situation is to say that, in each case, the architect's choice of analogical reference and symbol for his building can be read in the context of the contemporary political scene. Sometimes the analogies directly reflect aspects of the political realm, other times they are an interpretation, still other times they represent a desired condition, for politics or state, rather than a real one, yet other times they convey an ideal. In every case, the project confronts historic German state architecture in one way or another – by rejecting and countering historic models and by creating either a direct or indirect dialog with history. If the political aspirations of the FRG can be described as the movement towards an open, egalitarian, and transparent society, then these can be compared with the closed, elitist, and opaque aspect of National Socialist Germany, and even of Wilhelmine Germany. On the other hand, if transparency is a goal for postwar West Germany, the question must be asked how much transparency really exists in 1949, 1989, and 1999? Furthermore, how transparent are the state buildings designed to serve this ideology materially, formally, and spatially? If transparency in every realm is a myth, why has it persisted – what ends does it serve? One thing is certain – it is impossible to generalize about stylistic attributes of architecture in any era. But since 1945 a group of German architects has pitted a vision of official German architecture under the Kaisers and Hitler as monumental, solid, massive, stone, opaque, and neo-classical; against a vision of the new architecture as posited by Schwippert, Behnisch, and Foster as diminutive, steel and glass, fragile, and contemporary, but more than anything transparent.

Chapter 2

Transparency in German architecture before and after the War

Reconstruction? Technically, economically, impossible, say I; what say I? Spiritually impossible! Already the word 're' does not appeal to me. It sounds like 'repeat' and 'restore'!

Otto Bartning in 1946[1]

The photographs showing the sea of rubble that constituted Berlin in 1945 are legendary but the extent to which the country and its infrastructure were destroyed and needed to be rebuilt is not widely known. When Germany surrendered on May 7, 1945 the country was in ruins of a magnitude that is difficult to grasp. About 7 million Germans were dead (3,760,000 military personnel and 3,810,000 civilians), and as many as 20 million others became homeless refugees when they fled the advancing Russian army or were expelled from Eastern Europe.[2] Another 2 million wounded resided in Germany after 1945. Allied bombs assaulted 199 cities all told, 41 of which were major urban centers.[3] The extent of the devastation varied from 50–60 percent in the large cities to as much as 100 percent in the smaller and mid-sized cities.[4] The bombs alone were not responsible for the damage because fires often broke out and wreaked as much, if not more, havoc than the bombs. The Allied campaign focused mainly on industrial areas in the Ruhrgebiet located along the Rhine River stretching from Frankfurt in the South to Duisburg in the North, and dense city centers, the location of much historic architecture. The infrastructure that needed to be replaced and rebuilt in 1945 included bridges and roads; railways; airports; factories; electric generators; and communications networks, but fully and partly destroyed building stock represented the largest portion of infrastructure that required attention. It is hard to collect precise statistics documenting the extent of the destruction in Germany in 1945 – cities seem to have recorded the degree of devastation differently, records may have been lost in the intervening decades, and in many places no records were kept until some years after the war. But some figures do exist. Only 1,000 of 13,000 km of rail in the British Zone functioned; none of the numerous waterways were open. All 22 rail bridges over the Rhine were gone, as well as most of the other bridges in Germany.[5] While industrial facilities were Allied targets these escaped relatively unscathed with a mere 20 percent reduced to rubble. In the case of mining and steel installations only 10 percent were demolished.[6] Housing stock suffered the most; in the American Zone overall approximately 81 percent of housing was destroyed or damaged.[7]

According to Douglas Botting, postwar calculations of the scope of Germany's devastation yielded the following facts: "it would take 16 years to clear the rubble out of Berlin, using ten trains a day, each train pulling fifty wagons."[8] Further, it was also calculated that the devastated areas of Germany were covered in 400 million cubic metres of rubble. If that figure is correct it is equivalent to a country the size of Great Britain completely covered in rubble to a height of several meters. Eyewitnesses agreed that Germany was in a terrible state and that the country faced a long, painstaking reconstruction effort. The questions architects would face were numerous. What was the appropriate way to rebuild? Should historic city centers be reconstructed as they had been before the war, or in a reasonable facsimile of their former state? Or, did the wartime devastation present an opportunity to construct anew, to make German cities the most modern and technologically advanced in the world? Was style an appropriate issue to consider when so many millions of Germans were homeless? Should not architects be concerned with efficient, economical, and rapid building techniques?

I

In the same way that West Germany had to reinvent itself as a political entity after the war, West German architects had to search for new ways to delimit architecture. In broader cultural terms, the necessity of starting anew had its parallel in the "*Nullpunkt*" or "*Stunde Null*" (zero point or zero hour), first declared by members of the literary society, the Group of 47.[9] In the attempt to define the new German culture, artists repudiated historic German myth and culture, and delineated fresh images and metaphors for their national identity. It is important to understand that the *Nullpunkt* in literature represented the desire to invent a new German language as the basis for postwar culture. The Nazis were famous for their manipulations of language in such euphemisms as "The Final Solution" and in their intense propaganda efforts. At the same time, they appropriated and distorted much of the great German cultural achievements of the past making it difficult to harness national pride to many of them after 1945, at least in the immediate postwar years. The National Socialists used Wagner's music for their rallies, Hegel's and Nietzsche's philosophy to justify some of their ideas, and Goethe's writings as emblems of the Great Germany past. Any attempt to redefine German culture therefore had to begin with language, the foundation for metaphor and expression, and then emanate from there.

In architectural terms, the *Stunde Null* had to establish a new set of metaphors, analogies, and stylistic prerogatives for all buildings, especially for those representing the state, since things connected with the state had been the most sullied by the experience of the Third Reich. The response to the *Stunde Null* declaration varied, as did its acceptance as a concept. But the notion of Germany as a *Tümmerfeld* (expanse of ruins), architectural, urban, societal, and political, was widely held. In an article titled, "*Auf dem Tümmerfeld der Bauformen*," ("From the expanse of ruins of building forms"), Walther Schmidt argues that a positive end can result from the postwar architectural ruin and chaos.[10] For Schmidt the danger of the situation in 1947 was to romanticize the past, then rebuild Germany according to a faulty memory, or an intentionally altered one, in a pseudo-historic manner without giving room for the full range of architectural and urban solutions possible. Schmidt's article is one of many that appeared soon after the end of the war, when the debate began as to how to rebuild, in which style (if any), and for which reasons. As Schmidt himself points out, the architectural debate centered on old prewar themes reframed in reference to experiences during the Third Reich and its aftermath: historicism versus reinstated functionalism, reconstructing the historic fabric versus building completely new cities, the popular appeal of traditional "*Heimat*" housing versus the efficiency of new construction materials and methods; organic, open versus classical city planning; manufactured products versus local handicrafts; prefabricated versus site-built work. Transparency does not figure overtly in the debate for many years although Neues Bauen buildings exploited transparent construction; transparency enters the discussion around 1961 but becomes commonplace and ideological only in the early 1970s (see Chapter 1).

II

When West German architects and politicians call for transparency in state buildings they do not necessarily understand the term in one and the same way. Transparency has a series of connotations that are related, but different, and come from several disparate sources: from art and architectural history, from common usage, from philosophy, political theory, and literature, although the art and architectural understandings are the most important for this discussion. Transparency in architecture after 1920 can be divided into two general categories: esthetically and ideologically motivated. The former describes projects whose use of transparent glass was inspired by its appearance; while ideological transparency describes buildings whose see-through aspect reflects some larger concern that sometimes relates to notions about hygiene, social conditions, or politics. The motivations behind West German calls for transparency are equally varied. In some cases the speaker desires literal transparency, as in a see-through plenary chamber in order to facilitate public surveillance of parliament and, thereby, visual control. In other cases transparency is a metaphor for the desired condition, as in political discourse where it is equated with openness, accessibility, and pluralism, articulated goals for the West German state. In still other cases transparency is used as an analogy. The transparent plenary chamber is an analogy for transparent parliament – that is, the see-through seat of parliament is meant to suggest that the parliament itself is open and visible. Equally important, Germany's unique history has endowed transparency with special meaning that is different from its meaning anywhere else in the Western world – from France, England, and the United States. Thus transparency has to be understood as a layered and complex term whose usage is at times literal, at times metaphorical, and at times analogical.

According to Duden's etymology of the German language, "*Transparenz*" entered the language at the beginning of the eighteenth century. Formed from the Latin roots *trans* for "through" and *parere* for "appear," the word describes a material condition in which light is transmitted through a substance so that views can also penetrate that substance. For this reason, glass is the building material most often associated with the physical quality of "transparency" but other materials are also transparent, such as lattice screens, diaphanous fabrics, punched metals, and Plexiglas. Spatial transparency can be said to occur when the boundaries between distinct spaces in plan or section are visually penetrable or do not exist. Phenomenal transparency, as Colin Rowe and Robert Slutzky pointed out, occurs when the visual clues permit the viewer to "see" with his or her mind's eye obscured and concealed spaces.[11] Moreover, open architectural form is also transparent in that it allows penetration, whether visual or otherwise, across membranes,

spatial dividers, and disparate functions. Sigfried Giedion based his assessment of architectural transparency on strategies developed in Cubist painting.[12] According to Giedeon, architectural transparency occurred when it was
possible to see multiple aspects of a building or multiple spaces simultaneously. Giedeon defined open forms as ones whose interior and exterior were
transparent to one another. Further, he saw this transparency between inside
and outside as dissolving the boundaries between the subject and object
by creating a condition in which the two were interacting so consistently that
they could fuse.[13] Because transparent materials transmit light, radiate it
outwards and allow it to shine inwards, light is intimately tied to any discourse on transparency. Because seeing through is the principal way in which
transparency is recognized, vision and sight are also closely linked with
transparency. The idea of seeing through is, in fact, the dominant notion that
permeates many of the different uses of "transparent." Seeing through is connected to physical properties described as "transparent" as well as a whole
slew of metaphors associated with the term including candor, being easily
understood and detected, openness, and even honesty and truthfulness.
In each of these cases, being transparent is equated with the lack of conceal-
ment, artifice, masks, and hidden motives. In the last 20 years or so, transparency has become a mantra for corporate honesty, institutional candor as
well as governmental openness the world over, not just in West Germany.
When people ask for transparent institutions they mean ones in which it is
possible to see the true motivations, goals, operational structures, and achievements of an organization without veils, masks, and manipulations of the truth.

The huge glass windows typical of traditional Dutch bourgeois
housing are an example both of the kind of transparency now popular everywhere, and the paradoxes inherent in such a condition. Beginning in the fifteenth and sixteenth centuries the Dutch began to construct larger and larger
transparent glass windows on domestic façades facing the public street. The
practice was in keeping with Calvinist doctrine demanding open relations
between members of society since only virtuous people, ones with nothing to
hide from public view, could live in such an exposed condition. The demand for
larger glass surfaces also paralleled middle class desires to display their
wealth.[14] The contrast with the typical punched openings of German middle
class housing is palpable. But the passers-by were not supposed to actually
look into the interiors – they were only supposed to be able to! Transparency
thus implies control through surveillance – things that can be seen can be controlled while opacity implies the opposite – things that remain hidden or
obscured cannot be controlled.

The notion of a transparent society, most recently referred to as
the "open society" in the writings of Jürgen Habermas and Ralf Dahrendorf in
Germany, and as "open institutions" by Charles de Gaulle and André Malraux

in France, is the open, egalitarian, politically democratic society first en-
visioned by liberal thinking philosophers but expanded upon in the twentieth
century, especially in the postwar period. Transparency as a political goal for
democratic society has its origins in the writing of Jean Jacques Rousseau
who imagined the French post-revolutionary society as one in which there
were no secrets between individual citizens and between citizen and the
state.[15] The true revolutionary would strip off social pretense in the interests
of the good of the community. Polis and state would blend into one as
self-interest dissolved in the face of perfect transparency. Rousseau's ideas
were disseminated in Germany soon after they were published in France. But
German political philosophy developed its own notions of transparency first
articulated in debates over how to construct the social contract between
citizens and the state. Eighteenth and nineteenth century thinkers like
Immanuel Kant, Johann Gottlieb Fichte, and Georg Wilhelm Friedrich Hegel
did not refer to transparency per se but were already concerned with philosophical questions that today are considered part and parcel of transparent
government, namely the proper means of citizen representation and participation in government, the amount of access the public should have to
government, who should hold the franchise, and how to balance the rights of
the individual with the best interests of society as a whole.[16] Given his background in political philosophy, it is not surprising that Adolf Arndt would coin
the term *"Durchsichtigkeit"* to describe the ideal conditions for a modern
democracy, especially since Arndt saw the problem of state architecture as
first a political, and secondly an architectural challenge.[17] He begins his famous
speech "Democracy as Building Client" by asking the question whether architecture for a democracy should have a special, a different appearance from
architecture designed for a non-democratic state.[18] Arndt sees state architecture as a didactic tool through which citizens can learn their roles as political
beings, responsible to one another and to society.[19] Thus, "Should not there
be a connection between the public principles of democracy and an outer and
inner transparency and accessibility of her public buildings?"[20] Arndt extended
the liberal notions of the social contract to include state architecture. For him,
state architecture should be as much a means to guarantee the rights of
citizens as the constitution and the laws forming the state. Arndt felt that
transparent state buildings would fulfill this function by making government
accessible to citizens and open to participation and regulation, at least ideally.

Transparent glass architecture is often equated with other transparent materials that are highly prized, such as diamonds and crystal. Myths
associating such architecture with political utopia and preciousness appeared
beginning in the late nineteenth century but were based on ideas already in
circulation a century before. Enlightenment views of a world founded on
rational thought that would bring about greater societal order and harmony

sparked reconsideration of every aspect of society and its institutions. By the eighteenth century, a series of reform-minded thinkers and visionaries like Jeremy Bentham in England, Cesare Bonesana Beccaria in Italy, Antoine Desgodets in France, and Leonhard Christoph Sturm in Germany, began to propose ways of improving conditions in public institutions like hospitals, workhouses, orphanages, schools, and prisons.[21] They were concerned with a litany of problems from overcrowding and filth to ineffective reform programs, and hoped to apply rational methods to improving the architecture and thereby the function of these institutions. They worried about the proper architectural form that would maximize institutional efficiency, provide adequate observation of inhabitants whether prison inmates or the ill, and induce moral and ethical well-being. One key concept for improving the function of many institutions was tied to surveillance, otherwise known as the inspection principle, the notion that many institutional ills could be cured by proper, effective surveillance. The architecture developed to serve this principle had various forms: a model consisting of a central space with radiating arms was one, and a series of concentric spaces opening onto a central room was another. These forms worked with visual access and visually transparent space to enhance supervisory powers of authority.[22] Although the buildings were usually not materially transparent in these ideal schemes, the obsessive interest in observation, in making the actions of workers and others as visible as possible, prefigures later interest in material transparency and visual access and control (see Chapter 8).

Already in 1797, Bentham had proposed the centrally organized Panopticon as a building type that would facilitate communication between the interior spaces, especially visual communication. Although Bentham's Panopticon today is best remembered as a model for prison architecture, Bentham proposed it for numerous building types including factories, hospitals, and even an office building for government ministers where, in his opinion, supervision was key to the efficient function of the place.[23] Bentham proposed placing the prime minister's office at the center of a circular arrangement where offices for the other ministers sat on the outer perimeter facing inwards. The prime minister's office was in the position from which he could best view the others and what they were doing! Perhaps even more striking was Bentham's optimistic belief in the power of architecture to affect people: "Morals reformed – health preserved – industry invigorated – instruction diffused – public burthen lightened – Economy seated as it were upon a rock – the Gordian knot of the Poor Laws not cut but untied – all by a simple idea of Architecture!"[24] Besides institutional buildings, reformers proposed ideal communities whose building and street layouts used rational planning techniques similar to those employed for individual buildings. Authors of such schemes included Robert Owen in Scotland and Charles Fourier in France. Often the designs for such communities were centrally focused enclosed systems that simultaneously shut out the rest of the world and created an introspective, highly visible inner sanctum. One emblematic scheme was Thomas Stedman Whitwell's design for Robert Owen's New Harmony, Indiana settlement. Similar to the Panopticon in its centrally focused planning, the buildings form the perimeter for the village that surrounds a botanical garden whose center is occupied by a conservatory constructed, naturally, out of glass.[25] Fourier's plan for a City in the sixth Period is similarly organized about a central building. Although glass was not a key element in the concentric plan, unimpeded views were: the city was designed to afford views along main avenues to civic monuments at each end and along rows of buildings laterally.

The movement from schemes based on visual access to those based on see-through architecture was gradual but by the 1850s, when Joseph Paxton completed the Crystal Palace in London, transparent glass architecture was being used in utopian projects (see below for a more detailed discussion). By the 1920s, transparent glass architecture was associated with the progressive Neues Bauen architecture, with modern constructive techniques and forward thinking design. Also by the 1920s, novelists and some architects began to realize the other side of transparency – the same transparent condition that seems to form utopia makes dystopia – transparent architecture can be oppressive in its openness. Transparency is as much the agent of surveillance as it is that of honesty. But in West Germany after the war, transparency retained mostly positive connotations.

Finally, transparency of meaning plays a role in the West German projects. In *Words and Buildings* the architectural historian Adrian Forty suggests that "transparency of meaning" is a key aspect of transparency that has yet to be probed.[26] Although Forty does not explain exactly what he means by "transparency of meaning," the French philosopher Philippe Junod describes transparency of meaning as the clear mirroring of past formal solutions in contemporary work.[27] When known forms are repeated, the viewer can read the maker's intentions immediately. Alternatively, transparency of meaning could refer to the clear readability of conceptual meaning in an artifact. That is, if an art or architecture object communicates meaning without specialized codes, symbols, and icons it can be described as transparent. Indeed, by using notions current in architectural discourse, the West German projects discussed here all attempt to make meaning transparent in that they try to make their meaning legible to a wide, non-specialized audience. The use of transparency, whose many metaphoric and analogical uses are commonplaces of daily language, makes the buildings' meaning even easier to read. Literal transparency is only a vehicle for making meaning clear, however. In the West German culture of openness and egalitarianism, art and architecture that is easily read by any citizen regardless of class, background, and education, would be considered supremely democratic.

III

German fascination with transparent construction dates to the nineteenth century, to the greenhouses, exhibition pavilions, and floras constructed out of glass and steel.[28] The explosion of glass building types at this time is related to new material developments and constructive techniques, firstly the development of iron frame construction systems that were steadily improved over the course of the nineteenth century and secondly, the improvements in glass production, especially the invention of flat glass. Technical improvements were driven by horticulturalists' demands for glass and iron systems whose transparent surface to opaque surface ratio was improved so that the heating of the air inside the greenhouse, conservatory, and flora could be more efficient.[29] The first greenhouses were constructed with cast iron load-bearing frames and glass infill; by mid-century, new rolling techniques made wrought iron available for use. The wrought iron performed better in compression than cast iron and could be rolled into thinner profiles making for a lighter, more delicate frame. Superior production techniques for glass, especially the introduction of large sheets of flat glass, further facilitated the construction of larger, lighter glass structures. For all their technical inventiveness, from the beginning these structures were part of utopian visions, some social, some political, and some purely spatial and architectural.

The earliest glass houses were private greenhouses and conservatories designed to preserve nature in a manmade environment. Their presence was a sign of exclusivity and wealth, since the heating and upkeep made them very expensive to own. The artificial environments inside the greenhouses were private utopias, gardens planted with exotic non-native plants that needed the protective structure to survive. Thus, the first greenhouses were commonly called "winter gardens" because they permitted vegetation to flower during the normally barren winter months. The glass buildings were similar to other nineteenth century structures designed to accommodate a growing popular interest in classification and collection. As such, the greenhouses were giant display cases filled with life-sized specimens. The greenhouses were also conceived as retreats from the real world – micro-utopias. While the small greenhouse was a private utopia, utopian and democratizing intentions often drove the design and construction of larger public structures as well: the exhibitions were designed as "people's palaces" to bring modern technology to the masses, the floras were miniature gardens of Eden which, like the exhibition pavilions, were accessible to a broad public.[30]

In Germany, rapid industrialization after 1850 helped fuel an interest in social responsibility, whose ideals were first widely disseminated under the Gotha Program. The 1875 Gotha Program united the different German

Socialist factions under one common banner in an attempt to consolidate opposition to Bismarck and the Prussian regime. Among its causes in the name of the working man were universal suffrage, and safety and hygiene in the work place. In an attempt to thwart the mounting pressures from German socialists, and to win support from the working class, Bismarck introduced a number of progressive reforms in the 1880s. The most important innovation was state-funded insurance that protected workers against sickness, accident, and old age.[31] The new social climate engendered during this period also encouraged other transformative programs such as green ways, public parks, "people's palaces," and "floras" to help improve the public realm for the workers. Cities such as Berlin and Cologne made older private parks and hunting grounds public and razed the remaining city walls and fortifications, replacing them with green rings. Glass-enclosed conservatories and botanical gardens were constructed; floras were designed to combine the exotic green-house with other recreational facilities such as restaurants. The Cologne flora, built in 1864, for example, housed a glass-covered palm court together with a restaurant to form the height in leisure architecture designed for the people. Thus, transparent glass construction was the stuff with which utopia could be realized.

The architectural interest in transparent buildings coincided with a visionary and literary one. From 1893 onward, the German author and mystic Paul Scheerbart began to write obsessively about glass, helping to fuel an intrigue with the material that continued to develop during the next one hundred years. For Scheerbart, glass was the consummate modern material, it could transform the built environment, and thereby change the way people live. He glorified glass in a vision both utopian and prescient. It was Scheerbart who equated the glass house with the Garden of Eden and living in paradise.[32]

> The face of the earth would be much altered if brick architecture were ousted everywhere by glass architecture. It would be as if the earth were adorned with sparkling jewels and enamels . . . We should have a paradise on earth, and not need to watch in longing expectation for the paradise in heaven.[33]

Scheerbart saw the precious, crystal-like quality of glass as one of the reasons glass structures should be revered and embraced since they were akin to dia-monds in their brilliance.[34] Scheerbart foresaw the revolution in urban construction glass and steel would eventually effect.[35]

Scheerbart's vision had an undeniable influence on the first genera-tion modernists practicing in Germany between the wars. Bruno Taut collaborated with Scheerbart on the Glashaus design for the 1914 Werkbund exhibition in Cologne, a building that featured a series of rhyming couplets

2.1
**The Glashaus
designed by
Bruno Taut
sporting rhyming
couplets by
Paul Scheerbart,
Deutsche
Werkbund
Exhibition,
Cologne,
Germany, 1914.**
Akademie der
Künste, Sammlung
Baukunst, Berlin.

2.1
**The Glashaus
designed by
Bruno Taut
sporting rhyming
couplets by
Paul Scheerbart,
Deutsche
Werkbund
Exhibition,
Cologne,
Germany, 1914.**
Akademie der
Künste, Sammlung
Baukunst, Berlin.

written by Scheerbart extolling the virtues of glass (Figure 2.1). These included: "Happiness with out glass, how crass!/Without a glass palace, life becomes a burden/Light permeated the Universe, it comes to life in the crystal/Glass opens up a new age, brick building only does harm."[36] Taut was an active member in the Arbeitsrat für Kunst (Council of the Workers of Art), a group of avant-garde architects residing in Berlin who formed immediately after, and in response to, the November revolution in 1918; the Zehner Ring; and the Gläserne Kette (Crystal Chain), where Taut introduced Scheerbart's ideas.[37] The Crystal Chain group was a diverse fraternity led by Taut, who imagined new glass architecture in a series of letters that were often grounded in the mystical and fantastic rather than the real (Figure 2.2).[38] The members shared an interest in glass as a symbol of purity and perfection, light and goodness, and a material that can affect social change. "No material prevails over other materials so much as does glass," wrote the art critic Adolf Behne.

> Glass is a completely new, pure material in which matter is melted down and recast. Of all the materials we have it works in the most elementary way. All other materials next to glass are derivative and like leftovers. . . . The European is correct when he surmises that glass architecture must be uncomfortable. Absolutely true. It will be so. And that is not its narrowest advantage. The European must be extracted from his comfortableness . . . Only when comfort

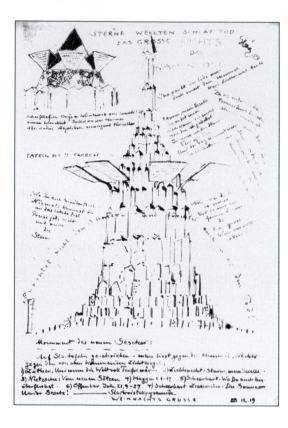

2.2
"Monument to the new Laws," one of Bruno Taut's letters to the Crystal Chain, December 25, 1919.
Akademie der Künste, Sammlung Baukunst, Berlin.

ends does humanity begin. Glass architecture lifts the spiritless inertia of jelly-like comfort in which all value becomes dull and weak, and sets in its place the state of light consciousness, a wild activity and the attainment of ever newer, ever more beautiful values. . . .[39]

The Crystal Chain group was corresponding during the period immediately after the First World War when there was almost no work for architects in Germany. Their writings ranged from visionary architecture proposed by Hans Scharoun, to the wildly fantastic and mystical writings by Hermann Finsterlin. Taut published some of the Crystal Chain ideas in the revolutionary magazine that he founded and edited, *Frühlicht* (*Dawn*), but most of the musings remained private, distributed to the members but not disseminated beyond.

Besides the Crystal Chain correspondence and his work with Scheerbart, Taut authored several utopian fantasies that included the *Kristallhaus* (*Crystal House*) and *Alpine Architektur* (*Alpine Architecture*). These short novels elaborated some of the points made in Scheerbart's *Glasarchitektur* by imagining glass cities whose mythic organization would reconcile the separation between body and spirit, sacred and profane.[40] Taut's first utopias were cities entirely constructed of glass whose beauty would be so great as to inspire peace and contentment, including political satisfaction, in all people.

> Merely to desire the useful and the comfortable without higher ideals spells boredom. Boredom brings quarreling, strife, and war; lies, robbery, murder and wretchedness, blood flowing from a million wounds . . . All men will serve the one concept, Beauty – as the image of the Earth that bears them – Boredom disappears, and with it strife, politics, and the evil spectre of War. . . . THERE WILL ONLY BE CEASELESS AND COURAGEOUS WORK IN THE SERVICE OF BEAUTY, IN SUBORDINATION TO HIGHER THINGS.[41]

Taut's Alpine cities were, in part, a reaction to the devastation experienced in Europe during the First World War and the hope that followed for a new world. These designs are based more on fantasy than on pragmatism or reality. It is nevertheless important that Taut chose glass construction for his Earthly paradise – clearly his choice because of the reference to crystals, naturally pure, precious glass-like objects.[42]

Scheerbart and Taut were also interested in transparent glass because of its mystical light-transmitting properties. They were particularly fascinated with transparent colored glass, tracing the use of glass in architecture to Gothic antecedents where colored light was thought to be God's manifestation on Earth. Colorless glass seems to have appeared in German visionary architecture slightly later in Mies van der Rohe's skyscraper projects of 1920 and 1921, for example, although it was used in built work as early as 1903 at the Steiff factory building in Munich (Figure 2.3), and at Gropius' and Meyer's Fagus Works of 1911 (Figure 2.4), both of which pre-dated the Werkbund Pavilion. Further, the Gropius and Meyer model factory constructed for the 1914 Werkbund exhibition near the site of the Taut/Scheerbart pavilion used colorless transparent glass, as did Walter Gropius' Bauhaus building of 1926 (Figure 2.5).

Taut's work undoubtedly influenced postwar West German notions of transparency because he equated glass architecture with political utopia in two of his visionary books, *Alpine Architektur* (Alpine Architecture) and *Die Auflösung die Städte* (Dissolution of the Cities). Taut did not, however, draw parallels between transparency and democracy, he only pointed to the mystical potential of glass construction to generate positive social and political change. "The new glass environment will completely transform mankind, and it remains only to wish that the new glass culture will not find too many opponents," Scheerbart had written.[43] His and Taut's beliefs were similar to

2.3
The Steiff factory building in Munich, 1903. The identity of the architect is unknown.
Photographer: Axel Föhl.

2.4
View of the transparent glazing at the Fagus Works in Alfeld a.d. Leine, 1911–25.
Walter Gropius and Adolf Meyer.
Bauhaus Archiv, Berlin.

2.5
View of the transparent stair towers flanking the entry of the office building for the factory complex at the *Werkbund* Exhibition in Cologne, 1914.
Walter Gropius and Adolf Meyer.
Akademie der Künste, Berlin.

ones appearing in futuristic literature at the time, in novels by H.G. Wells and Yevgeny Zamyatin, for instance, in which glass buildings form the architecture of a futuristic political utopia. In both cases, in Wells' *A Modern Utopia* and in Zamyatin's *We*, utopia and dystopia are synonymous. What at first appears to be a better world, an ideal political state, turns out to be evil and destructive.[44] The pristine, crystalline clarity of glass architecture turns out to be oppressively open. Bentham's inspection principle is carried to the extreme in *We* – the only time transparent glass buildings can be closed to view is when couples are having intercourse! But, of course, as soon as the blinds are drawn, every neighbor knows exactly what is going on behind them so that there is no privacy, even in the most intimate relations. The ironic potential in their utopian notions seems to have been lost on Scheerbart and Taut, however, whose writings remained optimistic. The notion that glass architecture could transform the political arena, coupled with the general belief held in the German avant-garde of the 1920s that art and architecture ought to be political, lays the ground work for the belief that transparent glass architecture represents the positive political attributes of a democratic state.

IV

Transparency was not only a key element of interest in early twentieth-century German architecture, but in art as well – it figures in Cubist formal strategies, in the Elementarist experiments, and in the atmospheric canvases of Paul Klee. But no one worked with transparency as the central aspect of his or her research program except Lazlo Moholy-Nagy. A close friend of Sigfried Giedion's, a teacher at the Bauhaus who later directed the Chicago Design Institute (what Moholy-Nagy called "the new Bauhaus"), Moholy-Nagy began his explorations into the painterly, sculptural, light and spatial potential of transparency in 1919 soon after he moved to Berlin.[45] Moholy-Nagy was systematic and committed in his work, combining his explorations into an influential teaching program in Germany, then in the United States. The sheer range and scope of his explorations is impressive. His work included paintings, photograms, photomontages, collages, mechanized constructions, and sculptures probing material and spatial transparency and several articles about his work. Perhaps even more importantly, transparency continued to be Moholy-Nagy's central interest for close to 30 years.

Lazlo Moholy-Nagy's "transparent paintings" and "transparent architecture" prefigure some of the whimsical experiments with overlapping transparent material, text inscribed on see-through surfaces, and open space found in the Behnisch Bundeshaus. Moholy-Nagy's first experiments with surface transparency date to the teens when he, by his own admission, first began to understand the implications of Futurist, Expressionist, and Cubist work. He points to a drawing entitled "Epits!" (in English, Build!) from 1919 that crystallized his understanding of the potential inherent in linear drawings. The piece shares the fractured divisions of a Cubist or Expressionist drawing suggesting multiple points of reference simultaneously presented on one surface. The word "epits" is scrawled in numerous places and in many different orientations relative to the paper's edge and the other images, helping to reinforce the sense of an aperspectival composition. Perhaps most indicative of Moholy-Nagy's future interest, the layered elements defy conventional spatial organization.

Beginning in the 1920s, Moholy-Nagy realized that light was a key element to the development of any new spatial representation.

> I suspect this is why my work since those days has been only a paraphrase of the original problem, light. I became interested in painting with light, not on the surface of canvas, but directly in space. Painting transparencies was the start.[46]

His paintings from the 1920s, with titles like "Glass architecture" and "Transparency," are made with layers of transparent color affixed to opaque or transparent surfaces. Overlapping figures do not optically obscure one another, but permit the simultaneous viewing of different geometric shapes. Like "Epits," there is no clear foreground in these paintings but rather an oscillating fore- and back-ground caused by the transparency interacting with the different light and dark values of the colored paint. Moholy-Nagy worked with simple geometric forms and color only in an attempt to reduce the paintings to the most objective (*Sachlich*) minimum possible, to move away from the representation of nature, which he believed disturbed the clarity of the work. In other words, Moholy-Nagy used transparent geometric figures to reduce painted expression to "pure relationships" and emotion.[47] Moholy-Nagy extended his work with paint to photograms and photomontage, techniques that relied directly on light and exposure to light for their effect (Figure 2.6). He then moved to three-dimensional work out of wood, glass, nickel-plated metal, and other materials where the bent linear and planar forms appear to be arcs of motion frozen in time. Given Moholy-Nagy's interest in space–time relationships (an interest he shared with Giedion), these sculptures can be understood as plays with transparency, spatial relationships, and the fourth dimension as engaged by the viewer. Many of the sculptures (*Transparency*, 1940; *Dual Form*, 1946) are reminiscent of the qualities Giedion praised at the Eiffel Tower where structure is linear and see-through permitting the simultaneous visual occupation of multiple points in space and the dissolution of boundaries between inside and outside.[48]

2.6
**Fotogramm,
Lazlo Moholy-
Nagy, 1943.**
Bauhaus Archiv,
Berlin.

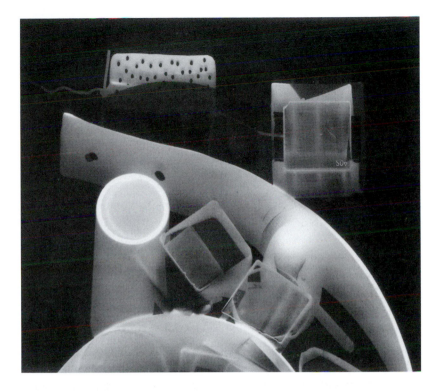

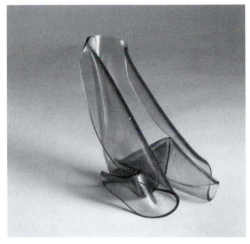

2.7
**Light-Space-Modulator, Lazlo Moholy-Nagy,
1922–1930. (Reconstruction 1970).**
Bauhaus Archiv, Berlin.
Photographer: Günter Lepkowski.

2.8
**Plastic Space Modulator, Lazlo Moholy-Nagy,
circa 1945.**
Bauhaus Archiv, Berlin.
Photographer: Markus Hawlik.

Painting with light reached its highpoint in Moholy-Nagy's work with the Light-Space-Modulator, fabricated between 1922 and 1930, a motorized construction assembled from concentrically arranged transparent plastic, glass, wire mesh, lengths of wire, metal plate, and lattice mounted on a revolving disk that, when set in motion, projected light and shadow into and out of the space framed by the structure to create an animated play of visual effects (Figure 2.7).[49] The machine was a transparent construction in that its many layers were see-through. At the same time, it was a device that made ephemeral paintings with light and shadow.

Among the many experiments with transparency and light that have implications for architecture were a series of sculptures in which Moholy-Nagy played with spatial possibilities inherent in transparent and translucent materials such as Plexiglas. Here, Moholy-Nagy was possibly at his closest in his interest to the postwar architects of transparent parliamentary buildings. The so-called "space modulators" manipulated the transparent medium light as it passed through and bounced off surfaces (Figure 2.8). The plastic forms, distorted planes bent into folds and waves that wrapped around each other, were as much about space as light. "The distorted shapes of my 'modulators' . . . were partly made of transparent plastics, with emphasis on the edges, partly of wire and air 'walls,' which were 'more transparent' than transparency itself."[50] Like his earlier three-dimensional pieces, the space modulators were essays in using transparency to create a physical model of the space–time Giedion wrote about.

> There the free "motion" forward and backward of color prepared a new type of spatial perception. This was in clear opposition to the renaissance method of producing illusionistic space by the illusionistic relationship of volumes . . . a new space articulation, trying to define intuitively and to satisfy more adequately the specific need of our time for a vision in motion.[51]

Thus, Moholy-Nagy used the see-through properties of Plexiglas as a means to an end; transparency was the medium with which he explored ways to represent relative perspective and the fourth dimension in static objects.

Moholy-Nagy's influence on German architects cannot be understated. Through his position as a professor at the Bauhaus, his published writings, and the example of his artistic production, he reached a large audience in Germany. His work was widely disseminated in the interwar period, especially in Berlin, the center of German art during the 1920s and 1930s. *The Abstract of an Artist* (*Vom Material zur Architektur*), based on his lectures at the Bauhaus, was first published in German in 1928, then translated into English, first in 1930, then in eight subsequent editions, the last of which appeared in the US in 1967. From 1947, *The Abstract of an Artist* was coupled with *The New Vision*, Moholy-Nagy's explication of Bauhaus teaching methodology and the new art for a North American audience. The sheer number of reprints testifies to the book's importance and widespread influence. Importantly for postwar architecture, Hans Schwippert was in Berlin at the same time, active in several groups of avant-garde architects, and certainly familiar with Moholy-Nagy's production. Schwippert was friendly with Walter Gropius, who was a co-member of the Zehner Ring. It is therefore likely that Schwippert even knew Moholy-Nagy personally.[52]

V

In the same way that Moholy-Nagy promoted transparency in art circles, Arthur Korn and Konrad Werner Schulze were active in architectural ones. Schulze and Korn each took up the notion of glass construction as the consummate progressive approach to design, coincidentally publishing separate books in 1929. Schulze's book was titled *Glas in der Architektur der Gegenwart* (*Glass in Contemporary Architecture*) while Korn titled his volume *Glas im Bau und als Gebrauchsgegenstand* (*Glass in Building and as Commodity*). Korn's was ultimately the more influential because it was published in German then appeared in English translation only two years later. It has also been reprinted several times. But in Germany in the 1930s, both were probably widely read. The two books share their belief in glass as the modern material of choice but the books diverge in their central thrust. Korn's book has only a brief introductory text by the author and six short pieces on different types of glass by other writers. Most of the space is given to images of projects, 187 in all. Schulze's book, by contrast, has copious text accompanying the projects. Where the images in Korn are large, often close to full page, the images in Schulze are small. The emphasis here then is on the textual argumentation; Schulze's book presents a detailed and reasoned argument for glass construction. It appears to have a broad audience in mind, one that may not be familiar with Neues Bauen philosophy or the genealogy of glass architecture. While the tone of voice is not that of a manifesto, the nature of the content makes it clear that it was written in order to convince its audience to build with glass. It is important to note that Schulze's book ends with an appendix filled with advertisements from glass manufacturing companies such as Luxfer, fabricators of glass prisms, and Heinemann & Schwarzmann, makers of crystal-mirror glass.[53] On the other hand, Korn's brief text seems to assume his audience is already convinced of the importance of glass construction and looks to his book as a catalog of important new projects using the method. There is a great deal of overlap in the projects presented by the two authors, a fact that indicates the extent to which a canon of glass lineage had already developed at the time.

Schulze's book is interesting because it offers insights into the reasoning behind the use of glass construction in the 1920s. Organized into two sections of three chapters each, the first section reviews the history of twentieth-century German glass architecture and the second section looks at technical innovations in glass.[54] His argument can be reduced to one basic principle: because glass construction represents the most modern in construction and material developments, it is the way rational contemporary buildings should be made. He dismisses esthetic reasons for using glass. Although he begins his history in the same way that we would present the subject matter today – Paul Scheerbart is held up as the spiritual father of glass ideology and Bruno Taut as the father of glass architecture – this aspect of the text is less than a page in length.[55] His comment under the image of Taut and Scheerbart's Glass House for the 1914 Deutsche Werkbund Exhibition reads, "This building heralds the pure experience of a building artist, that has less to do with function than with the essential meaning of its materials: glass, light, and color"[56] (Figure 2.1). Schulze quickly moves on to the practical, functional, and rational reasons for building with glass, however. He points to the transparent aspect of the pavilion as one of its most striking and memorable qualities showing how important transparency was already in 1929. The second project he discusses is Walter Gropius' office building for the same Deutsche Werkbund exhibition (1914) that he extols for its "functional clarity" as opposed to its esthetic (Figure 2.5). Both Schulze and Korn use the same photograph of the Werkbund building, an oblique corner shot showing the extreme transparency of the glass stair towers and a long view of the entry façade.[57] It is Peter Behrens' AEG Building in Berlin from 1909, however, that Schulze cites as the first glass and steel construction in the new spirit because of the contradiction between the building's outer appearance and actual constructive system.[58] The walls are not load-bearing but, like the glass surfaces, they are infill. Although it seems to be constructed with heavy, brick piers, the building is actually supported by reinforced concrete shells. Schulze ends the first chapter of his book by tracing the history of glass construction and architects' understanding of glass from the Roman period, through the Gothic, to the Baroque, and finally to the present. He explains the changing attitude towards the outer wall, light, and space as one that moves towards dematerialization of the wall and the extension of space both internally between separate spaces and externally beyond the boundaries of the building. Importantly, Schulze dates the beginning of the glass revolution to 1851 and Paxton's Crystal Palace.[59] Schulze concludes his history by arguing that glass construction combines engineering and esthetics, the rational approach to design with the intuitive, using the latest technical innovations and industrial production methods to produce buildings that are emblematic of the spirit of the age.

In the second chapter Schulze draws a parallel between the path towards enlightenment in the sciences and humanities and the development of a rational, functional approach to designing buildings.[60] Schulze also ties the movement towards lighter and lighter construction methods to clearer, more enlightened thinking overall.[61] In this way he is suggesting that rationally thinking architects will naturally prefer glass construction for their projects.

> Are the technical codes for the use of glass, the modern laws of hygiene, the new construction possibilities and materials like reinforced concrete and steel; or is it the esthetic program of a group of architects that makes glass meaningful for the future of building?[62]

Schulze concludes that all these factors operate in a complex way together but that no single one is more important than the others. Schulze begins the third chapter with the quote, "Form is the visible appearance of the essence."[63] Rather than the façade, he writes, the new architecture begins with what the façade encloses, space.[64] Because glass is see-through, it best embodies the spatial continuity that lies at the heart of early twentieth-century design.[65] More importantly, because the choice of glass is not necessarily an esthetic one, it does not signal allegiance with a specific architectural school or movement.

Korn was, like Bruno Taut and Moholy-Nagy, Berlin-based and an active member of the Neues Bauen. Unlike Scheerbart and Taut, however, Korn was taken with the *"Es ist da, und es ist nicht da"* (it is there, and it is not there) property of glass, a property he referred to as the unique one glass possesses.[66] In the introduction to *Glas im Bau*, Korn describes the illusory qualities of transparent glass surfaces and how they can be exploited architecturally. He also recognizes the tremendous consequences glass and steel construction have for the design and function of exterior walls. Transparent glass permits architects to dissolve the division between exterior and interior by making the outside walls appear to be invisible. In this new construction system, wall is membrane, or surface, rather than substance, with the ability to "close and open and not only in one, but in many directions."[67] Writing fully 12 years before Siegfried Giedion first published *Space, Time and Architecture*, Korn already recognizes the importance of Gropius' buildings and Mies' built and un-built work. Further, he sees in transparent glass construction the potential to realize spatial continuity, multiple viewpoints through a building, and a new kind of perspective made possible by the depth of view transparent façades permit. Korn was also clear about the ways in which transparent glass architecture could exploit light by bringing it into the very heart of a building through glass walls and partitions, and by emanating light at night. Unlike Taut, whose books idealize glass in a mystical way but never attempt to address the practical or pragmatic, Korn intended his book to be a resource for practicing architects. Korn's book is at once a catalog of transparent glass projects deemed important to publicize to support his views, a treatise on new glass products available in 1929, and a manifesto for transparent architecture.

The projects Korn chose to include in his volume include built and un-built work although the majority is built, no doubt to reinforce the argument since it would be much more difficult to convince contemporary architects to follow a course that was still untested. Korn chose architects from throughout Europe, the United States, and the Soviet Union, to convey the international nature of this new constructive phenomenon. Korn was also incredibly inclusive in his selection including works of many different esthetic styles, from Erich Mendelsohn to Jan Duiker, Mies van der Rohe to Werner Moser. As Rosemarie Haag Bletter points out in her introduction to Adolf Behne's *Modern Functional Building*, such an approach was typical of the German attitude towards contemporary architecture in the 1920s but very unlike the approach taken by others such as Hitchcock and Johnson for the *International Style* book and exhibition. German books tended to be broadly based, focusing more on ideology than on appearance.[68] The un-built projects are: Mies' glass skyscraper project (1920–21), the Adam Building (1928), the Office Building for Friedrichstrasse (1919), the Bank Building, Stuttgart (1928), and the Glass Skyscraper (1922) (Figure 2.9), Le Corbusier's Centrosoyus Building (1928), three projects by Moishe Ginsburg, a business center by Korn, and two housing projects by Alberto Sartoris. The built work ranges from storefronts to single family homes, from factory buildings and skyscrapers to industrial glass products. Perhaps the one glaring omission from the collection is Bruno Taut's pavilion for the 1914 Cologne Werkbund exhibition. Taut's building was a pioneering example of glass architecture but was not concerned with the dematerialization of the exterior envelope. Korn must have believed that, for this reason, it did not belong in his catalog.

Mies' visionary designs demonstrate the potential inherent in transparent skins – visible depth, reflective surfaces, and dematerialized volumes. Built work such as Walter Gropius' Office Building for the 1914 Werkbund Exhibition and the Workshop Wing of the Bauhaus bring Mies' visions into reality. The famous corner photograph of the Workshop Wing that Giedion used in *Space, Time and Architecture*, is included here too to provide concrete evidence of the extreme see-through quality transparent exterior glass walls make possible. In this particular shot, the concrete columns and slabs behind the glazing are so dark that they seem to be the dominant elements, along

2.9
**Glass Skyscraper
Project, 1921–22.**
Ludwig Mies van
der Rohe.
Bauhaus Archiv,
Berlin.

with the radiators, while the glass and steel façade system is almost invisible. Through the corner, it is possible to see the administrative wing and the bridge building beyond. As shown in Figure 2.5, the photograph of the Werkbund Office Building taken at an oblique angle to the transparently glazed stair tower works the same way – the concrete stairs are clearly visible behind the skin as is the concrete support around which the stairs wind. The steel mullions are so thin they read as a delicate lattice curled around the stairwell, rather than a steel and glass façade.

Night photographs of J.W.E. Buys' De Volharding building in The Hague, Richard Döcker's Shop and Offices for Luz Electrics in Stuttgart, and Karl Schneider's Hammerschlag Store in Hamburg show the radiant luminosity created when totally glazed storefronts and buildings are lit after dark. Glass cupboards, tables, shelving systems, glassware, light fixtures, and bulbs represent the variety of interior domestic fixtures made from glass. Korn also includes images of scientific instruments to illustrate the diversity of glass uses and to help reinforce the notion of glass as progressive technology. Korn concludes his book with a photograph of Naum Gabo's set for a ballet by Serge Diaghileff, Director of the avant-garde Ballets Russes de Monte Carlo. The set is constructed of transparent Plexiglas pieces cut into simple geometric forms such as circles and squares, layered spatially in relation to the audience (from downstage to upstage) and in relation to the floor. Like Moholy-Nagy's Plexiglas sculptures, the edges reflect light to form delicate linear traces in space, while the Plexiglas forms partially transmit and reflect light making the various spatial positions simultaneously visible. Some pieces are clearly meant as sets for the dancers, still others are bent and rendered as furniture and ramps thereby inviting human interaction. Unlike many of the architectural projects Korn published in his book that exemplified one or another aspect of transparency, Gabo's construction embodies the full range.

VI

Transparency in West German state architecture has a metaphoric and analogical lineage as well as a material and formal one. More confusing, these histories are difficult to disentangle from one another since the use of material transparency almost always signals analogical transparency. Two projects from the 1920s used transparency as an analogy for democratic, open government: Hannes Meyer's competition entry for the League of Nations building (1927) and Mies van der Rohe's Barcelona Pavilion (1929) (Figures 2.10 and 2.11). Meyer's design for the League of Nations is the first German proposal on record to associate transparent building with open, honest government. Meyer's design was an agglomeration of glass and steel volumes whose unusual materiality Meyer defended with the words, "No more back corridors for backstairs diplomacy, but open glazed rooms for the public negotiations of honest men."[69] In this pithy statement, Meyer aligned transparency with many of the qualities still associated with transparent architecture today: openness, honesty, and light.

In 1928, Mies van der Rohe was selected to design the German buildings for the 1929 International Exposition in Barcelona. The project included exhibition halls and the *Repräsentationsraum*, a small pavilion that, as the German term suggests, was for ceremonial occasions rather than exhibits. Furthermore, the name of the building, *Repräsentationsraum*, could also be interpreted to mean the place in which to create a positive image. And, in the eyes of those granting Mies the commission, Mies' architecture for the exposition was just that – a building with which the Weimar Republic would demonstrate who and what the new Germany was – namely, democratic, modern, progressive, and open. "We wished here to show what we can do, what we are, how we feel today and see. We do not want anything but clarity, simplicity, honesty."[70] Here, the transparent qualities of clarity and honesty are attributes explicitly connected with German democracy.

2.10
**Exterior view of
the German
Pavilion at the
Worlds Fair in
Barcelona, 1929.**
Ludwig Mies van
der Rohe. Bauhaus
Archiv, Berlin.

2.11
**Interior view showing the transparent aspect of both glass surfaces and the open plan of
the German Pavilion at the Worlds Fair in Barcelona, 1929.**
Ludwig Mies van der Rohe. Bauhaus Archiv, Berlin.

Transparency at the Barcelona Pavilion occurred in several different guises: material, spatial, and formal. The Pavilion's form was open, borders between inside and outside were intentionally obscured so that in drawings it is almost impossible to distinguish built form from garden space, inside from outside. A series of parallel planar elements made from differing materials sit atop a continuous plinth that extends from the exterior to the interior without interruption. Overhead, a continuous slab forms the roof extending outwards on all sides to engage the surrounding space. The planes slip and slide against each other to demarcate edges and spaces without making closed forms. The geometry delineates a series of overlapping spatial zones whose borders and transitions are never clearly marked. The glass panels Mies used for the pavilion are colored light green, but are transparent. The color renders the surfaces alternately see-through and reflective so they perform in a manner similar to the water in the reflecting pools that are also integrated into the design. Here, Arthur Korn's principle of *da und nicht da* (there and not there) can be applied almost universally to the structure. The shifting reflections on the façades and in the ground plane make surfaces appear both there, and not there, while the fluid boundaries between spaces even call into question the material existence of the building.

Honesty and clarity operate selectively. The forms of the individual elements such as walls, roof, and floor are simple and clear, and there is no applied ornament, but Mies goes to great lengths to create the constructed illusion of pure form. The marble partition walls that appear to be massive are not solid stone but sandwich panels with thin cladding on the visible exterior; connections between elements are buried (the column/beam connections and wall beam connections, for example). Thus honesty applies to the architectural image but not to the means by which this image is achieved.

The Weimar Republic did not last long enough, nor command the economic means, to sponsor a substantial federal building program beyond public housing projects, thus the Mies project stands alone. The next federal buildings constructed where transparency can be read as an analogy for democracy, progressive attitudes, openness, and honesty were built after the end of the Second World War. State buildings constructed during the 12-year long National Socialist regime varied in their material and stylistic approach from the Neoclassicism favored by Hitler and his personal architect Albert Speer, to more contemporary designs for buildings such as the Luftwaffe headquarters, but did not work with transparency in the way that Mies had or others later would.[71] Hans Schwippert's 1949 Bundeshaus was the first major West German federal project built after the war in which this discourse was adopted. Although transparency was by no means universally present in West German state architecture in the post-Second World War period, there were a series of important projects that used transparency as Schwippert had, and whose architects made claims in similar terms to Schwippert's. The projects share certain formal, spatial, and stylistic characteristics: open forms, open plans where programmatically possible, and extensive use of transparent glazing. Four prominent West German architects designed the most important buildings in this group: Egon Eiermann, Sep Ruf, Paul Baumgarten, and Günter Behnisch. The projects divide into two categories: those constructed abroad and intended for international consumption such as the German Pavilion Eiermann designed for the 1954 Triennale in Milan, the German pavilions designed for the World Exposition in Brussels (Eiermann and Ruf, 1956–58), the Chancellor's Bungalow for the West German Embassy in Washington, DC (Eiermann, 1958–64), and the West German Embassy in Moscow (Eiermann, 1969); and those constructed at home and intended for West German consumption like the "Lange Eugen" federal building in Bonn (Eiermann, 1965 69), the Chancellor's Bungalow in Bonn (Ruf, 1963–64), the first renovation of the Reichstag in Berlin, and the new Law Courts in Karlsruhe (Paul Baumgarten, 1961–70).[72] These buildings share an architectural language often reminiscent of Mies at the Barcelona Pavilion – they are all primarily transparent glass and filigree steel construction, with exposed structure, overlapping floating planes, open plans, and often open form. An explication of several examples should serve to illustrate the common design approaches.

The 1958 World Exposition in Brussels presented West Germany with an opportunity akin to that presented to Weimar by the Barcelona exposition in 1929 – the chance to present the new West German national identity to an international community. Architects Egon Eiermann and Sep Ruf were selected to design the 18,000 square meter pavilion while Hans Schwippert served as consultant for building technology. From the start, West Germans were aware of the difficulty of choosing an appropriate architecture to represent the country given its recent history.

> How difficult it was to represent Germany at a world exposition in 1958 . . . only with tact and even modesty [would it be possible] to overcome other people's resistance and resentments . . . The architects resisted any symbolism or kind of pomp . . . did without, and built simply and functionally, and have therefore built in accordance with these facts.[73]

The design opportunity was equally recognized as acknowledgment that West Germany had re-entered West European society.[74] Some saw the transparent architecture to be appropriate because it was apparently simple, straightforward, and unpretentious – all qualities espoused by the nascent republic. But just as many contemporaries criticized the transparency because it made the pavilions unable to accommodate the exhibitions easily.[75] Both

Eiermann and Ruf were already known for their Miesian glass architecture when they were selected for the commission, but at the Brussels pavilions they attained a new level of precision, clarity, structural integrity, and attention to detail.

The two architects initially disagreed over the best design strategy for the project but ultimately were commissioned to construct Ruf's pavilion system, eight square-shaped structures arranged around a large garden court-yard. The three-story glass pavilions were connected by a system of bridges and walkways that allowed the visitor constant contact with nature. Writing 30 years later, Schneider described the Eiermann and Ruf building:

> The Pavilions show themselves in full transparency . . . through the lateral glazing like a crystalline building form, in which geometry is increased through the linear system of the steel skeleton and the ordering of the individual pavilions that expand the landscape's effect.[76]

Hans Schwippert cited the Brussels project many times in his speeches from 1958 onwards as:

> the most beautiful buildings . . . in which the present human condi-tion is perceptible . . . the glass walls of the new buildings, the new lightness of the offices, the atelier, the factory, the graceful look of the new furniture, the friendliness of living in green . . . are every-where a superb attempt at resistance against threats, darkness, and the lurking chaos. The German contribution to this movement towards openness and lightness is historic and has international recognition.[77]

Contemporary photographs of Ruf and Eiermann's complex show the clear, prismatic building forms wrapped by the darkly colored lines of the floor slabs, and framed behind an exterior cage of filigree white, vertical steel supports. Everything is light and weightless – the buildings seem to float above the ground, as do all connecting walkways, exterior stairs are suspended between floor plates so they appear to be hanging on air. The building façades are not single tight skins but a series of planar and volumetric layers that begin with the white steel supports that flank an outdoor circulation space. There is nothing between these elements on the plane of the façade except void. A meter or so into the circulation space hangs a grid of even thinner cables that support an exterior sun-shading system. A meter beyond the grid of cables is the transparent glass façade whose joints are virtually impossible to discern, making the distinction between interior and exterior extremely difficult to identify. The glass panels are inserted into the ceiling and floor where concealed hardware holds them in place. The glass façades are see-through but also highly reflective, rendering the pavilions a superb illustration of the here/not here quality of transparent glass surfaces. The surrounding landscape is simultaneously visible through the buildings and reflected on them while the depth of successive spaces is overlaid with these exterior images. Here, the transparency connects the interior space with the surrounding landscape in a virtually seamless space.

The Federal Chancellor's Bungalow in Bonn (1963–64) could be compared to the White House in the United States or 10 Downing Street in Great Britain, in that it was to be both the real and ceremonial home for the West German Chancellor (Figure 2.12). As such, the house would be a symbol both at home and abroad. The house was commissioned during Konrad Adenauer's last year in office. As at the Bundeshaus, a stylistically modern architecture was chosen perhaps because of a general feeling that a contemporary style would be best accepted abroad. Ruf worked together with Hanns Oberberger and used many of the same techniques he and Eiermann had employed in Brussels: floor-to-ceiling transparent glass sheets that virtually disappear, flat roofs delineated as a dark-colored horizontal line, the seamless connection between interior and exterior space articulated by continuous floor and ceiling planes and nearly invisible outer walls. It is composed with two adjoining square structures, each of which encircles an inner courtyard. Supported on thin steel columns, the massive roofs of each pavilion hover

2.12
The Chancellor's Bungalow in Bonn.
Sep Ruf.
Bundesbildstelle Bonn.

2.13
View of the Bonn Bundeshaus with Egon Eiermann's "Lange Eugen" in the background.
Bundesbildstelle Bonn. Photographer: Julia Fassbender.

over the transparent base, only occasionally interrupted by some other, opaque planar element. When viewed from the front, the compositional strategies using overlapping and extending planes are strikingly similar to the Barcelona Pavilion. The free-standing columns take the same cruciform shape Mies invented for his pavilion while the flooring material is Travertine![78] According to Hans Wichmann, from the start, the building was intended to be "a modern building . . . Ludwig Erhard wanted, with this building, to show the world [that West Germany had] a cosmopolitan, quality-conscious architectural cast of mind."[79] It is the larger of the two wings, the one housing most of the public functions, that is almost entirely clad in transparent glass. As one writer pointed out, the transparency "made the building somewhat cheerful, open, the opposite of what was the usual fortress-like protection of representational buildings."[80] The official publication on federal buildings, *Bauten des Bundes*, describes the Chancellor's Bungalow: "The building has style. The possibilities of modern technology are exhausted. Through its weightlessness, spaciousness, and openness it appears cheerful in spite of a strict order."[81] Although written 16 years after the building was completed, the text demonstrates the importance of openness to the federal building program.

Egon Eiermann's "Lange Eugen" skyscraper (1969) constructed near the Bundeshaus in Bonn is a highly visible project largely because of its great height. The building towers over the surrounding landscape and over the neighboring buildings as well (Figure 2.13). At 29 stories, it was for many years the dominant visual element in the government complex. Eiermann clad the tower in a layered system akin to that of the Brussels pavilions although without achieving a similar degree of transparency. The outermost layer is made from a grid of filigree white steel elements that support sun shading devices behind which is a void layer that, in its turn, sits in front of a glass façade. "These elements give it a play of light and shadow together with the chosen materials – steel, wood, and glass – a lightness, that makes it appear transparent. The building has become a true sign of the Capital city."[82] The lightness that is apparent on the exterior is everywhere in the building: transparent glass partition walls and screens serve to separate spaces while handrails are made from steel and cable so they are reduced to almost nothing.

Paul Baumgarten designed two important federal projects in the 1960s, the renovation of the Berlin Reichstag in Berlin and the Federal Constitutional Courts in Karlsruhe. In both cases, transparent glass surfaces are key to the architectural resolution of the building, as is the notion of seeing through. "Karlsruhe will not be blessed with a 'palace of justice' of the old mould, instead it receives a highly transparent building mass, that one can very well take as the symbol for the transparent decision-making of the supreme court."[83] At the Constitutional Courts, Baumgarten used floor-to-ceiling transparent glass panels to create the illusion of continuous space (Figures 2.14 and 2.15). The reflective floor surfaces mirror the natural context outside with plays of light and images of leaves and trees. Whereas the transparency at the Federal Courts was largely at the building envelope, transparency at the Reichstag project was entirely an interior condition. The West German government decided to restore the Reichstag in order to be able to use the building, which had stood empty since 1945. The exterior was restored as much as possible but the interior, where the greatest damage had been done to the building during the Second World War, was completely redesigned. Baumgarten's strategy was to make the interior as lightweight and transparent as possible considering its placement inside a massive stone shell. In order to achieve his goals, he removed many of the large stone columns Wallot had constructed, replaced others with thin steel supports, replaced stone partition walls with see-through glass and steel ones. Baumgarten inserted a new glass-enclosed plenary chamber into the existing structure. He enlarged the plenary chamber substantially and moved it from its original location towards the rear of the ground floor at the center.

> Here is everything contemporary: material, construction, space, concept and form all the way to the installations made by artists. The large plastic, almost cold exterior form is answered on the interior with a spiritually disciplined architecture that in its simplicity, delicacy, clarity and almost ascetic severity is an appropriate contemporary picture of representation in spite of the excessive scale . . . The generosity of the contiguous spaces, with their transparency (*Durchsichtigkeit*) and distance is impressive. . . .[84]

Photographs used to publicize the project show the many spatial layers visible through the transparent glass partition separating the plenary chamber from the entry lobby. Two large steel sculptures are suspended from the wall; they are striking for their asymmetrical and dynamic composition. Looking from the chamber either east or west in the visible distance, light pours into the lobby. Stairs, handrails, balconies, indeed visible structural and space-making elements, seem to be as finely crafted as possible. Material is used sparingly, a design decision that heightens the sense of dematerialized structure inside the space.

The importance that many of these projects had to contemporary architects is borne out by the numerous references to the work in later literature, in histories of architecture, discussions of West German parliamentary and state architecture, in reviews of the three parliaments, and in essays and speeches authored by Schwippert, Behnisch, and Foster. This holds especially true in West Germany and for architects educated there, although many of the

2.14
**View showing the
transparent quality of the
glass façades at the Federal
Constitutional Courts in
Karlsruhe.**
Paul Baumgarten. Akademie
der Künste, Sammlung
Baukunst, Berlin. Photographer:
Foto Orgel-Köhne.

2.15
**View of the
transparent
walkway and
bridge at the
Federal
Constitutional
Courts.**
Paul Baumgarten.
Akademie der
Künste, Sammlung
Baukunst, Berlin.

buildings and writings discussed here were published widely abroad. Schwippert cites the Barcelona Pavilion on numerous occasions as an example of correct, even revolutionary, contemporary design, and openness, and lightness in architecture. In the folder marked "Glass" in the Schwippert Archiv are photographs of the World Exposition of 1937, the Van Nelle Factory, Paxton's Crystal Palace, and Gropius' Fagus Works. Schwippert also referred often to the 1958 Brussels World Exposition, a project he considered exemplified transparent architecture. In his clearest debt to Bruno Taut, Schwippert penned an essay entitled *Glück und Glas* ("Happiness and Glass" – see Appendix 4), a paraphrase of Scheerbart's rhyming couplet for Taut's 1914 Werkbund pavilion that read, "Happiness without Glass – how dumb is that?"[85] Behnisch cites Adolf Behne, the art critic who vocally supported the German avant-garde in the 1920s and 1930s, refers to Mies' work, and Eiermann on occasion as well. Behnisch draws parallels between what he calls "Modern Architecture" of the 1920s and 1930s and the qualities that he wishes to create at the Bundeshaus.[86] In one article, Behnisch specifically acknowledges his debts to Schwippert.[87] Because he is British and not German, Foster is probably only familiar with some of the precedents whereas Schwippert and Behnisch would have known them all. However, Foster worked intimately with German thinkers, architects, engineers, and parliamentarians in order to develop the Reichstag design. The German architect, Mark Braun, was project architect on site and the German professor of philosophy, Wilhelm Vossenkuhl, consulted with the Foster team about concepts for the project. Through them, German notions of transparency, openness, and democratic design filtered into his thinking as well so that even if his knowledge of certain ideas is sometimes secondhand, it nevertheless exists.

Chapter 3

The quest for an open society

It is certain that the cloak of silence in which, for political reasons, Nazism was enshrouded after 1945 has made it impossible to ask what will come of it in the minds, the hearts, the bodies of the Germans. Something had to come of it, and one wondered with some trepidation in what shape the repressed past would emerge at the other side of the tunnel: as what myth, what history, what wound?

Michel Foucault[1]

From the start in 1945, transparency had different connotations depending on whether it was interpreted literally, metaphorically, or analogically. The architectural profession repressed the Third Reich as a subject, making that period in German history temporarily invisible though always palpably present. In external politics the construction of West Germany as a modest, unassuming, almost invisible entity in the heart of Europe was a form of transparency; and in internal politics the movement towards a pluralistic, participatory representative democracy – an open society, with an open government, accessible representatives, and a free market economy – was another. But in spite of the importance Arndt accorded transparency, perfect transparency was never a goal or even a real possibility under the West German system. The Weimar Constitution was, in fact, more "transparent" than the Basic Law whose statutes provide for a balance between the freedoms implicit in a democratic society and controls deemed necessary either for the public good or to prevent the kind of political stalemates that recurred during the Weimar era. The framers of the constitution recognized that increased transparency in government and civil society was necessary especially given the transgressions of the

Third Reich but, at the same time, they understood that transparency had to be regulated and that a democracy could not function in a state of perfect transparency. Thus, from the start the West German parliamentary democracy was based on a balance between parliament's responsibilities to communicate with and to the public, and its responsibility to control the workings of the state.[2]

Direct democracy, arguably the most transparent way of involving the general public in running the state, was never a part of the West German system. Until recently, even elections for the chancellor were indirect. The people elected members of parliament who, in turn, elected the chancellor. Except in three elections, 1949, 1961, and 1969, the general public knew whom each party would choose to serve as chancellor so that to some degree the vote cast was for MP and chancellor alike.[3] But the chance always remained that some backroom deal or unforeseen circumstance such as an unexpected governing coalition would cause a different candidate to be chosen chancellor. Thus, forces containing the drive towards greater transparency were always present, operating in tandem with those forces pushing transparency forward.

Transparency in 1945 had other implications too if it is interpreted as an analogy rather than a real condition. Externally transparency suggested a modest, reserved West German regime that was well integrated into the rest of Western Europe, so well integrated that it abrogated self-interest for greater European interests. By 1989, however, West German democracy was successfully established. Although not perfectly transparent, the openness in the 1980s far exceeded that of previous German regimes. At the same time, crises of doubt over the extent to which the parliament and its workings had failed to achieve transparency had already precipitated debate over possible procedural reforms in parliament.[4] The country was considered a "model democracy" and an "economic miracle" both at home and abroad, achievements that owed their successes to greater transparency in government and in society on the one hand, and greater transparency in the economic system on the other hand, at least until the 1970s. Thus, at this time the transparency analogy in architecture can be linked to the crystalline utopias and notions of preciousness and worth as well as to fragility and vulnerability. The ideology of transparency was firmly implanted by this time too but, paradoxically, the successes and maturation of the West German state caused both greater transparency in some arenas and a slow retreat from transparency on many other fronts: in public accessibility to members of parliament, in the Bundestag's effectiveness at communicating its intentions and decisions to the German public, in public participation in decision-making, and in the operation of the political parties.[5] The internal structures that tended to hinder transparency had strengthened: the power of political parties, governing coalitions and individual politicians, the size of the federal bureaucracy, the power of special interests and private lobbies.

After unification in 1989, transparency can be seen to take on another set of subtle analogical meanings based on the circumstances that existed before and after unification occurred. The two halves of Germany literally turned (*Die Wende*) to face one another directly for the first time in over half a century. For many, the experience was akin to looking at oneself through the transparent surface of a mirror and seeing one's other self in the reflection for the first time. Unification also rendered the divisions between the two Germanies transparent, that is, the opaque separations that veiled the true identity of East and West dissolved leaving each side revealed. Thus, the understanding of transparency after 1989 extends the notions of a pluralistic, open, participatory democracy to include a self-reflective confrontational condition that reveals the underlying tensions between East and West.

"No experiments!" was Konrad Adenauer's famous postwar quip – a phrase that is emblematic of West German attitudes from 1945 to the early 1970s. By this Adenauer meant that Germany should concentrate on rebuilding itself; should not stand out in any unusual way; should maintain the status quo; should conform to the Allied requirements; should enter the West; and even quietly dissolve into the middle of Europe for a time. It was almost a wish to be rendered inconspicuous, invisible, transparent, to do nothing that would call attention to the Federal Republic. Domestically, West Germans turned to the task of reconstruction but turned away from discussions about the Third Reich in a national act of memory suppression. (The silence caused a national eruption in the 1960s when a generation of young West Germans rebelled against the silence of their elders eventually calling for an *Aufarbeitung der Geschichte* – Working through of History). In this sense, West Germans made the Third Reich invisible, imperceptible, an 11-year period through which people looked as if it had never occurred. In architectural terms, the desire to be inconspicuous translated into forms of memory suppression and selective memory when architects advocated forgetting the Nazi period and connecting their new work to the renowned achievements of the Weimar era, American, British, and French architecture from the 1930s and 1940s, and work by German ex-patriot practitioners during the interwar period. While transparency may have connoted the wish for anonymity in the immediate postwar years, transparency in another sense was also one of the founding concepts for the reconstruction of the West German political system. The new constitution, the Basic Law (*Grundgesetz*), contained the framework to make West Germany into an open society, a pluralistic, participatory representative democracy whose government is elected by the people and in ideal terms is responsive to their wishes and open to their visual and regulatory control.

Transparency was a fundamental quality the new nation strove to embody in its society through any number of means: the construction of the Basic Law; the reconstruction of its political system as an open democracy;

3.1
Portrait of Konrad Adenauer in 1960.
Bundesbildstelle Bonn. Photographer:
Georg Bauer.

the reconfiguring of its society as an inclusive community; the restructuring of its education system to promote unfettered, uncensored dialog; and the establishment of a press unconstrained by censorship of information or the printed word. The move towards transparency occurred because of the confluence of many forces but three, more than any others, were responsible for the new direction West German politics took: the political goals the Occupying Powers had for Germany, the essence of the Basic Law, and the personality, prejudices, likes and dislikes of the first Federal Chancellor Konrad Adenauer (Figure 3.1). Adenauer was such a forceful presence in postwar West German politics, partly because of the length of his tenure in office and partly because of his strong personality, that he played a part in most major political decisions between 1948 and 1963. He was also instrumental in the rebirth of political parties and the institution of the democratic process in West Germany.[6] He served both as a founding member of the Parliamentary Council, the elected body that drafted the Basic Law, and as its President. Although Adenauer was not the sole author of the new constitution, he did have strong opinions, was an astute political operator, and as president of the Council, had a position that bestowed him with more than ordinary influence.[7] Thus, Adenauer had a hand in writing much of the Basic Law along with many of the provisions for enacting the new constitution.

The relationship between the German *Länder* (states) and the Occupying Powers in 1948 and 1949 was yet another factor that profoundly influenced the writing of the Basic Law, and the notions of democracy embedded in it. Although the Ministers President of the *Länder* were ostensibly given freedom to craft the new constitution, they began their work with

3.2
**Portait of the
three Military
Governors,
General Pierre
Koenig (France),
General Sir Brian
H. Robertson
(Great Britain),
and General
Lucius D. Clay
(US), on May 12,
1949, the day the
Basic Law was
approved.**
Bundesbildstelle
Berlin.

a set of explicit "guidelines," drafted by representatives of the occupying powers at the London Council in 1948, as to the content the new document was expected to have. Moreover, the final draft had to have the approval of the representatives of the three occupying powers before it could be adopted (Figure 3.2). Just as importantly, so much of the internal German politics of the period was entangled with British, American, French, and Russian interests either as a rejection, adaptation, or modification that it is impossible to discuss one without at least briefly looking at the other. The Basic Law is important because it describes the fundamental nature, functions, and limits of the West German government. By studying the articles included in the Basic Law, as well as its general structure and intentions, it is possible to extract an image of West Germany as the members of the Parliamentary Council envisaged it as well as the way the occupying powers imagined the new state. In addition, the Basic Law is revealing because of the ways in which it responds to history – to the first German democratic constitution written for the Weimar Republic; to the weaknesses in that constitution that permitted Hitler's ascension to power and his eventual dissolution of the democracy. Interestingly, the Federal Republic of Germany is unusual in Western history because it is the only democracy whose members had the opportunity to rewrite their constitution a second time, making specific provisions and structural arrangements to correct constitutional weaknesses they discovered in the first document. One of many major innovations written into the Basic Law that had not existed in the Weimar Constitution was a bill of rights modeled after the American one whose articles cannot be amended by any governmental body.[8] Finally, since politics is the science of government, the structure of the government reveals the expected nature of political interactions within the state, how openness is to be instituted and preserved, and even the degree to which actual openness is desired.

I

Late in 1947 it became apparent that the Russians were backing out of some of the terms stipulated in the Potsdam Agreement negotiated by the three Allied Powers and France between July 17 and August 2, 1945. In Potsdam, President Truman, Prime Minister Attlee, and Marshal Stalin agreed to the four-way division of Germany during the occupation period. The primary goals for the occupation were: to prepare the eventual reconstruction of German political life on a democratic basis and to integrate Germany into the international community of nations in a peaceful manner. The Russians, Americans, and British also agreed that German government should be decentralized with the exception of individual administrative departments in a kind of weak federal system. The clearly stated objectives for the occupation were reconstruction and return to self-determination and self-rule. By early 1947, it became apparent that the Russians were hedging over the restitution of German self-rule. Worse, the British, Americans, and French began to fear Russian ambitions to form an empire of its own by annexing East Germany, West Germany, Poland, other countries in Central and Eastern Europe, if not beyond.[9] In March 1948, the Russians walked out of the Allied Control Council, making their position against the other three nations totally clear. Great Britain and the United States, and eventually France, therefore decided to work together on a tri-zonal plan for the remaining three occupied sectors, with the goal of establishing political autonomy and a new democratic government as quickly as possible. In June 1948 the three powers, together with Belgium, Luxembourg, and the Netherlands, issued the London Recommendations, a document that outlined the steps the Germans should take towards writing a new constitution and founding a federal republic. The Recommendations specifically called for a federal form of government, similar to that of the United States. Under the federal model, the *Länder* and the local communities would reserve certain political rights, jurisdictions, and autonomy, so that political authority could not be centralized as it had been during the Reich.[10] These recommendations helped assuage fears all six nations had of a resurgence of German nationalism and military power by dispersing political power widely rather than concentrating it in one person or institution. The London Recommendations suggested that the Ministers President of the *Länder* convene their legislative bodies in order to select representatives to a

Parliamentary Council whose responsibility would be to draft a new constitution whose contents were subject to Allied approval. Sixty-five representatives were duly appointed, including the future Chancellor, Konrad Adenauer.

The United States was fairly clear from the signing of the Potsdam Agreement what its objectives were for the occupation and the eventual new German state. Although there were differences at times, Great Britain and France eventually acted in concert with the Americans. Furthermore, the policies adopted in the American Zone were similar, if not identical, to those adopted in the British and French Zones. But because the Americans were so insistent on the restoration of German self-rule and the re-institution of democracy from the start, the American example was likely the most influential on the new West German government.[11] If the State Department and the President wavered from time to time, the Military Governor General Lucius D. Clay rarely did. Again and again, Clay urged a speedy return to German self-determination and self-rule arguing that this was the most effective way to guarantee the establishment of a strong democracy. During the London Council of 1947, for instance, Clay wrote Lewis Draper to strongly urge the swift conversion to German self-government.[12] Clay was afraid of the threat posed by the Soviet Union and of the threat internal dissatisfaction could pose if the Germans were deprived of self-rule for too long.

One of the ironies of the new Federal Republic was that the occupying powers insisted that the West Germans adopt a democratic system, that is, the German people had no choice in the matter. Furthermore,

3.3
The street signs pointing visitors and delegates the way to the Parliamentary Council meeting place in Bonn, 1948. The humorous juxtaposition between the signs and the cows shows the rural nature of the city at the time.
Bundesbildstelle Berlin.

the occupying powers dictated the outline for the type of decentralized federal democracy they felt West Germany had to adopt. Even more ironic, although according to the preamble of the Basic Law, all power of the state emanates from the people and the people have "given the strength of their constitution giving power to this Basic Law," the German "people" had no part in writing the constitution! Only a small group of elected officials participated in the process and they had little freedom to write the document as they saw fit.[13] By a democratic regime, American diplomats and military officials had certain specific notions in mind. First and foremost, the new democracy had to be participatory, one in which the political authority of the government clearly emanated from the German populace, rather than residing in the hands of an elite ruling class. In an article entitled "Democratizing Germany," published in the *Information Bulletin* on April 20, 1948, Dr Harold W. Landin, Chief of the Democratization Branch of the Civil Administration Division, explains the American goals, the rationale behind them, and the obstacles to realization.

> Freedom and democratic responsibility, which go hand-in-hand, have to be fostered and strengthened among this vanquished people for some time to come. But it is not enough for the United States to encourage the Germans to seize the opportunity to enjoy this new freedom and embrace this new responsibility. The German people must learn to cherish, defend, and preserve these objectives . . . A zeal for knowing liberty, and a will for achieving liberty, which are inseparable, must be the dynamic force generated out of the spirit and passion of the people.[14]

Landin's essay goes on to recognize how difficult it will be to transform the attitudes and behavior of an entire people, especially in a country with a long history of authoritarian rule. Landin emphasizes the need to focus not only on the education of individual Germans about democracy, but also the need to reform the civil service if democracy is to take hold. Ironically, as numerous historians have pointed out, neither the civil service nor the judiciary were reformed in the immediate postwar years. Only the highest placed former Nazis, those responsible for the most heinous crimes against humanity, were barred from returning to public service. Most of the former civil servants were rehired after the war; it would have been impractical, if not impossible, to rebuild the civil service from scratch. The silence relative to the National Socialist period was present here too – few appointments were challenged, few people discussed the past involvements of colleagues who had been active in the National Socialist party apparatus. Paradoxically, the seamless continuity in the civil service and judiciary probably contributed to the rapid recovery experienced in the West German economy. Real reforms of these two branches of government only began a generation later after the turmoil of the 1960s and after the war generation retired.[15]

In addition to being participatory, the Allies insisted that the new West German government be open to dissenting opinions and tolerant of difference whether religious, racial, or otherwise. Clay promoted this idea of the open society by setting an example: he broadcast his instructions to subordinate command over normal AM radio channels, so that both Americans and Germans might be informed. General Clay recognized the need for the Military Government to regulate the media for a time after the war, but as soon as he felt able, he moved to establish a free press and to teach about tolerance for difference by example.[16] Clay exercised his policy of openness with regular "open, no holds barred, press conferences with representatives of the local press – a lesson both for the press . . . and for a new generation of German politicians."[17] But the policy of openness was tempered by exacting control over the media; transparency was tolerated as long as it presented different facets of the American position – right-wing propaganda was not tolerated. The Americans alone published five German language newspapers to disseminate information and propaganda; controlled all the West German radio stations, newspapers, journals, and theaters in the American zone; and published several magazines and journals of their own. For several years after the war, the Allies also supervised the license granting operations to West German-run newspapers, magazines, and radio stations. The aim was to ensure the democratization of the German media, the conversion to an open, free press by supporting the democratically inclined press and suppressing the right-wing and reactionary press.

To ensure the democratization of the West German education system, the Americans created a German education reconstruction program under the direction of Dr Alonzo G. Grace. Initially, Dr Grace's Education and Cultural Relations Division worked to eradicate nationalism from the curriculum and to insert democratic values instead. The Division then worked to help German educators rewrite their textbooks, train teachers in the social sciences, revive German educational journals, and sponsor exchanges between the United States and Germany.[18] Integral to the democratization effort was a program directed at the grass roots of West German society where the Americans encouraged the foundation of, and participation in, community-based organizations in order to teach West Germans about participation in a democracy. The American military government actively promoted the Town Hall meeting as a model for popular political participation. The Americans also encouraged the reconstitution of the labor unions and employers' associations that Hitler had dissolved. American publications from 1945 to 1949 are filled with articles about public education programs which included ones for the young to help develop leaders among West German youth and to counter the defunct Hitler Youth movement. The stated goal for the education programs was to teach Germans to be a "free people in a free society." The expression of dissent, existence of and support for a free press, guarantee of free speech and peaceful assembly, "is not only a moral or ethical right but also a practical means for attaining honest government."[19] The hoped-for result was an open society run by an honest, open government where differing factions and versions of the truth could be aired.

Not only did the United States have definite programs for the occupation period, it had clear ideas as to the way the new constitution ought to be crafted and how the new government should be structured. Clay summarized the most critical objectives for the United States occupation and an eventual independent West German government in his letter of July 19, 1946 to Major General Oliver P. Echols, who was head of the Internal Affairs and Communications Division of the military government.

> The United States believes that this constitution must contain the following minimum essentials of democracy:
>
> A. All political power must originate with the people and be subject to their control.
> B. Programs and leadership must be referred frequently to popular election.
> C. Elections must be held under competitive conditions in which there are at least two competing parties.
> D. Political parties must be democratic in character and clearly distinguished from governmental instrumentalities.
> E. The basic rights of the individual must be defined in the constitution and preserved by law.
> F. Government must be exercised through rule of law.
> G. The powers of the central government must be limited in the constitution to those agreed by the several states composing the central government.[20]

Clearly, Clay and his associates were looking at the United States Constitution as a model for a document supporting a successful democracy. Although many of the guarantees come from the American Constitution and Bill of Rights, others respond to Germany's recent past by attempting to create a system in which National Socialism, or any other radical political ideology, could never rise to a position of power again. They also respond to the failures of the Weimar Republic. Thus, Clay insists on government through the rule of law, on a decentralized federal authority, on frequent elections, and on a system with a minimum of two political parties.

II

The Ministers President of the 11 *Länder* proposed the name of the constitution, the Basic Law (or Provisional Law), when they accepted the Allied Control Council's terms for drafting the document (see Figure 3.3). The Ministers were reluctant to write a permanent constitution that could not be ratified by all Germans. They did not want to appear to be creating a permanently separate West German state. They preferred to draft a provisional constitution until such time in the future when the Soviet Zone could be integrated into the rest of the German nation. Thus, the notion of West Germany as a temporary creation was present at the very founding of the Federal Republic.

With the adoption of the Basic Law on May 23, 1949, the Federal Republic of Germany was created. The new republic merged the three former British, American, and French occupation zones which included the following *Länder*: Baden, Bavaria, Bremen, Berlin, Hamburg, Hesse, Lower Saxony, North Rhine Westphalia, Rhineland-Palatinate, Schleswig-Holstein, Württemberg-Baden, and Württemberg-Hohenzollern. The government was organized as a "democratic and social federal state" whose "authority emanates from the people."[21] Like the constitution of the United States, and other democracies, the Basic Law opens with a list of fundamental rights shared by all citizens. Freedom of speech, press, education, religion, and assembly are all guaranteed in the Basic Law, as are equality under the law, and the equality of men and women. Other rights necessary to an open, free society expressly protected by the Basic Law, that respond to the National Socialist experience, are the right to political dissent and the right to complain! However, in seeming contradiction to the move towards a more open society, the parties of the extreme right were banned from meeting, disseminating information, and from fielding candidates for office.

In a move clearly designed to appeal to the Allied Control Council and citizens of the Allied countries, as well as to affirm West Germany's commitment to European union, the Basic Law opened with the statement, "Conscious of its responsibility before God and mankind, filled with the resolve to preserve its national and political unity and to serve world peace as an equal partner in a united Europe. . . ."[22] With the opening phrase, the German Federal Republic asserted its new Westward orientation. The opening statement was directed to West Germany's immediate neighbors, especially the French, who even to this day, harbor deep-seated suspicions about German political and economic aims.

The clauses most indicative of the new spirit of open government are contained in Articles 42, 43, and 52 which establish a transparent government structure. Article 42 requires all meetings of the Bundestag be public (*offen*), while Article 43 provides for internal transparency between the different branches of government by guaranteeing the right of any member of the Bundesrat or federal government to attend any meeting of the Bundestag. Article 52 requires all meetings of the Bundesrat to be public except when the body votes to meet privately. It is these three articles that German parliamentarians like Adolf Arndt and architectural historians like Heinrich Wefing have credited with inspiring the notion of transparency in state buildings. The idea of openness in particular merits some further discussion because it is key to any understanding of the project. While the term "transparency" does not appear anywhere in the language of the Basic Law, the German word for "open," "*offen*," does. In German, "*offen*" also means "frank and candid," and "openness" is "*offenheit.*" "*Offen*" is also a synonym for "transparent, obvious, and clear," in the sense of "honest," while "*offentlichkeit*" is the word for "public." Therefore the notion that a public building should be open and transparent is, to some degree, a double-entendre, a layered word play.[23] Transparency was only a partial goal of the Basic Law: the lack of direct democracy, the checks and balances between chancellor and parliament, Bundestag and Bundesrat, federal and state governments, even the simple fact that only certain sessions were meant to be open to public view and could be closed by a vote, belies transparency as a goal. Rather, the Basic Law describes a partially open system, a practical working democratic order, but not an ideal.

Accessibility to the decision-making process should also mean the openness of the system to service in parliament and in government. The use of government funds to finance political campaigns was intended to help make access to political office more open and less dependent on party affiliations and personal wealth as it is elsewhere. But as Heinz Laufer and Ursula Münch point out, a professional political class emerged in West Germany after the war just as it had existed in Wilhelmine Germany and during the Third Reich.[24] Politicians tend to be careerists; state positions lead to federal ones and vice-versa but it is rare for a neophyte to be able to secure important political office except through appointments that are invariably tied to party politics. Again, accessibility is limited.

Other aspects of the constitution help ensure some transparency, at the same time making full transparency unlikely – at least in the relationships between governmental branches and agencies, and between government and the people. The Basic Law instituted a system with three branches: the legislative, executive, and judicial. Similar to the American model, each branch is endowed with individual responsibilities and with the power to check and balance the actions of the other two branches. The Basic Law also introduced a federal constitutional court that, unlike the American Supreme Court, is not the highest court in the national system, but a separate court that only hears cases with constitutional implications. It also serves as the final arbiter of disputes between the various branches of government and the *Länder*. Most importantly, the court has developed into an activist institution. Certain court decisions over the years have placed it squarely in the middle of the political debate – decisions over immigration law, for example, helped move the FRG to more egalitarian policies for foreign workers.[25] Article 20 establishes West Germany as a "democratic and social federal state" distinguishing it from the start from its American model by guaranteeing that the federal government has a greater stake in each citizen's life. The same article includes a provision requiring political parties to account publicly for their financial sources and assets – an attempt to keep the political machine as transparent as possible. As the Kohl scandal of the late 1980s demonstrates, however, these provisions have not been adequate to guarantee transparency. The Christian Democratic Union managed to funnel millions of Deutsch Marks into its coffers without accounting for either the sources or the expenditures. More scandalous, in a breach of transparent policy, neither Chancellor Helmut Kohl nor senior members of the CDU were ever prosecuted. The full truth of the abuses is still not known. Article 23 contains the provisions for joining a European Union. Thus, the Westward thrust of West German international policy was enshrined in the constitution itself. Article 146 makes the Basic Law provisional. It will cease to exist on "the day on which a constitution adopted by a free decision of the German people comes into force."[26] That is, it will be replaced after East and West Germany unify. Although the Basic Law describes a parliamentary democracy whose government is elected by the people and open to their observation and regulatory control, the transparency described is always conditional, never perfect.

In order to further encourage open government, and to help avoid another swing to a totalitarian regime, certain control instruments were incorporated into the Basic Law. Fiscal authority was dispersed. The Bundestag was given the authority to keep constant watch over the federal budget; even though it does not propose budgets, it must approve and then regulate them. If there is suspicion of individual indiscretions on the part of parliamentarians, either the majority or the minority may convene an investigative committee. The provision allowing the minority party to form such committees, rather than rely on a majority vote, was intended to protect against abuses by the majority.[27] One of the structural weaknesses of the Weimar government had been the ease with which governments could be dissolved and toppled. They rarely lasted more than two years, making it impossible for the central authority to accomplish anything of substance. Article 67 provides for a "constructive vote of no confidence" which means that if the Bundestag wishes to replace the Federal Chancellor because of a loss of confidence, it can do so only if it can elect a successor with a majority vote. This has only occurred once since 1948 when Helmut Kohl was elected to replace Helmut Schmidt. The article also stipulates that 48 hours must elapse between the motion of no confidence and the actual vote for a new chancellor. In this way, the members of parliament benefit from a period in which they can reflect over the pros and cons of replacing the chancellor, making it far less likely that they will be swayed by the heat of the moment or inflammatory rhetoric.

Finally, the decentralized structure of government further diffuses power, which helps to ensure openness but can also create a kind of opacity in both intergovernmental affairs and external public communication. The reason for dispersing political power so widely was that it made it less likely that any one person or institutional body would be able to abuse it. Furthermore, the larger the number of people and institutions that are involved in the political realm, the more information must be distributed and shared in order for government to function. At the same time, however, the often-confusing distribution of power over a wide field often makes it difficult to assign responsibility for specific events or to negotiate agreement between the various governmental units. Regional interests often contradict national ones. The *Länder* were accorded important powers over policy and administration of policy; they control education, cultural affairs, radio, television, law enforcement, environmental policy, the bureaucracy, and the regulation of local government and the administration of governmental policy, while the federal government makes the laws, negotiates treaties, sets foreign policy. The upper house of the government, the Bundesrat, is composed of representatives from the *Land* governments appointed to serve, rather than officials elected by popular vote, whose presence at the federal level is supposed to bridge the divide between regional and national government. The decision to institute a Bundesrat was largely based on the conviction that the indirectly elected body would have strong ties to the state governments but weak ties to the national parties. It would therefore be less likely to mirror the power structures in the Bundestag and thus bring a different view to debates. But the reality is more complex since the state governments are composed of members of the same parties that hold national office and therefore owe some allegiance to national interests as well as regional ones. The Bundesrat's role is to guarantee cooperation between the central government and the states, and to provide veto power over any policy decisions that go against regional interests. Thus, the Federal Government is forced to work through cooperative means, to be somewhat transparent in its aims, or its policies can be overridden. But as a succession of chancellors have shown, beginning with Adenauer, transparency in aims does not always achieve political success. Adenauer was a master political operator whose true goals were usually obscured.

III

Although Konrad Adenauer was not the founding father of modern Germany, he is as close to a founding father as there is. Historians agree that the German Federal Republic owed much of its shape to Adenauer and his vision – even if his manner was sometimes authoritarian and drew as much criticism as it did praise. In fact, today, many historians credit Adenauer and his authoritarian ways with firmly establishing democracy in Germany. His forceful personality and independent mind offered the strong leadership Germans seemed to want and need to make the smooth transition from totalitarian to democratic government. He was Chancellor when Hans Schwippert received the commission to design the renovation and addition to the Pedagogical Academy in Bonn. While Adenauer does not seem to have influenced the design for the Bundeshaus, he did help shape the structure of the West German democracy and write the blueprint for that structure. Schwippert adopted the transparency analogy because, in his opinion, transparency best reflected both the structure of the state and the ideals of democracy, as well as West Germany's status in the world in 1948 and 1949.

By all accounts, Adenauer was a shrewd political operator. He consolidated political control in Cologne during the prewar years when he served as *Oberbürgermeister* (mayor), prompting criticism that he was authoritarian and dictatorial. Then, he prompted similar criticism during the 14 years he was Federal Chancellor because he often acted more like a dictator than an elected representative.[28] In his critical biography, the British journalist Charles Wighton recounts the story of a new bridge Adenauer's regime commissioned for the Rhine River in Cologne, to demonstrate how Adenauer got his way.[29] Apparently, Adenuaer and the design committee did not agree about which design had the most merit and ought to be built. The committee majority (seven people) favored a bridge with arched supports proposed by Krupp while Adenauer and one other favored a suspension bridge scheme. After efforts to sway the jury to his beliefs failed, Adenauer hired an engineer who assessed the soil conditions of the riverbank and claimed that the preferred design would fail because the soil could not support it.[30] Adenauer therefore prevailed and had the suspension bridge built. Criticism notwithstanding, the consensus today is that Adenauer's authoritarian ways ultimately, even paradoxically, formed an easy bridge between the authoritarian Wilhelmine empire, the totalitarian Third Reich, and successful democracy.

Adenauer determined from the first to anchor his new democracy in Western Europe. The German city-states and principalities historically had been the buffer between East and West, a weak center, with no preferential political or economic ties to either. After the First World War, the Allied Powers forced Germany to sign such an adverse peace treaty at Versailles that they effectively isolated Germany from the West. Isolation contributed to Germany's economic collapse, the general anti-Europe sentiment rabid in Germany between 1919 and 1939, and the extreme nationalism that aided Hitler's rise to power. Adenauer was convinced that his country needed strong ties to Western Europe in order to avoid political collapse or the repetition of the events between the world wars. Adenauer's Westward focus was undoubtedly inspired by pragmatic concerns as well. The three occupying powers retained tremendous political control over West Germany. Adenauer realized that he would only win political autonomy for his country by adopting policies that reassured Western Europe about West Germany's intentions.

Adenauer had an abiding interest in America and France that was apparent throughout his political career. The sympathy for France very likely came from his Catholic upbringing. Much of France was, after all, Catholic and the German Rhine Land had been part of France under Napoleon. Between the wars Adenauer pursued what has been termed a "cold separatist" policy, attempting on at least two occasions, in 1919 and in 1923, to create a separate West German Republic in the Rhine Land. Although it is not clear how aggressively he pushed for separation, it is certain that Adenauer was sympathetic to the notion. Later, as Federal Chancellor he was responsible for the first rapprochement between Germany and France, for cooperative economic policies, and the birth of the European Union. Adenauer also greatly admired the great French Catholic statesman of the postwar period, Charles de Gaulle who was also a charismatic, authoritarian leader.

Adenauer had an equally high opinion of America and Americans. His second wife was half American; Adenauer visited the United States for the first time with her. But, most importantly for Adenauer, the Americans liberated West Germany and reinstalled Adenauer in his prewar post as Oberbergermeister of Cologne, a favor he would not forget. Furthermore, much as Adenauer esteemed the Americans and the French, he disliked the British. Almost from the beginning of the Allied occupation, Adenauer had problems with the British High Command who were responsible for administering North Rhine Westphalia. British Brigadier Barraclough removed Adenauer from his position as Oberbergermeister on October 6, 1945, citing the lack of progress on reparations and Adenauer's inability to fulfill his obligations. Point 10 in Barraclough's letter read, "You will not indulge either directly or indirectly in any political activity whatever."[31] Besides losing his position, Adenauer was barred from entering the city of Cologne. Adenauer believed the British were slapping his wrists for being too outspoken and for beginning to organize politically against the British command. Ironically, Adenauer's removal turned out to be fortuitous since it allowed him to turn his attention away from parochial Cologne politics to national ones, and left him free to play a major role in the establishment of the new West German state.

Whatever his manner as Chancellor may have been, Adenauer was committed to the idea of democracy but had a fear of it as well. In his speech on October 1, 1945, he said,

> It is in accordance with the principles of democracy that the will of the majority should decide matters. But . . . let me insert the words "in the last resort"; it is in the last resort that the will of the freely elected majority should decide. The principles of democracy also demand respect for and confidence in the man of different political views; they demand an effort to enter into his thoughts and his reasoning and to reach an understanding with him; they require that the ultimately coercive act of voting someone down should be resorted to only when all else fails.[32]

Adenauer was eager to establish West Germany's place in the community of West European democratic nations while making an unequivocal separation between it and both East Germany and the Soviet Bloc. The turn Westward would, in his opinion, only strengthen the new West Germany's image as a committed democracy. When Bonn and Frankfurt came under consideration as potential capital cities for the Republic, their proximity to the West and distance from Berlin and the East made them both attractive. A German Federal government located in either city would underscore the new Westward orientation of the FRG.

Dr Hermann Wandersleb was the first to suggest Bonn for the new capital. He knew the city and its environs because already in 1945, he had installed the *Verwaltungslehrgang* from North Rhine Westphalia in the Bonn Pedagogical Academy building. The building was outside the city center, in the suburb of Bad Godesburg, directly on the Rhine promenade. Although Wandersleb thought this sleepy university town on the banks of the Rhine would accommodate the parliament well, the majority of cabinet ministers were apparently skeptical about the choice of Bonn as Capital City because they saw the location as a political advantage for Adenauer and the CDU. Adenauer's political base was in Cologne and the new Christian Democratic Union, an inter-denominational party that replaced the prewar Catholic Center party, formed there. Adenauer's support for a capital in the southwestern part of Germany is certain; his support for Bonn per se may have wavered. He certainly used the promise of Frankfurt as future capital to win the support of the Hesse CDU.[33] Countless historians and journalists covering the Adenauer era have suggested that the decision to move to Bonn was purely mercenary on Adenauer's part.[34] Not only was Bonn only minutes from Adenauer's political base but, it was across the river from his home in

Rhöndorf! Conveniently, Adenauer could militate against any opposition to the move to Bonn with assertions that the relocation was only temporary. He was confident that Germany would, in short order, reunite and return the federal government to Berlin. Adenauer certainly harbored the Rhinelander's traditional distaste for, and mistrust of, things Prussian, hoping the new capital would be as far from the former Prussian capital, Berlin, as possible.[35] Bonn was a quiet city of only 50,000 when the German government decided to establish itself there. Located in bucolic rolling hills on the banks of the Rhine, filled with quaint nineteenth-century architecture largely left intact during the war, the city suggested anything but monumental authoritarian government.

The choice of Bonn was only one part of a committed West-leaning policy based on transparent domestic politics as well as transparent foreign relations with West Germany's neighbors. Already by the spring of 1946, Adenauer realized that Germany's geographic position between the area of Soviet domination in the East, and the Western powers, gave Germany two options: to remain neutral, or to choose a side.

> There was only one way for us to save our political liberty, our personal freedom, our security, the way of life we had formed in many centuries and which was based on the Christian and humanistic ideology: we must form firm links with the peoples and countries that shared our views concerning the state, the individual, liberty and property. We must resolutely and firmly resist all further pressure from the East. The fundamental precondition for this, in my view, was a clear, steady, unwavering affirmation of identity with the West. The orientation of our foreign policy had to be clear, logical and open.[36]

Indeed, if Adenauer were alive today, he very well might have used the fashionable word "transparent" instead of "clear" and "open." Equally apparent in his comments is the awareness of the importance of constructing identity for West Germans and West Germany. Furthermore, in the excerpt above, identification with the West is partly based on transparency. Adenauer repeatedly called for a union of European states to strengthen both the economic potential as well as the political might of the West.

Adenauer's priorities in 1949 were to gain West German political autonomy and to begin the transition to full political sovereignty. To the extent that transparency could aide his cause, he embraced it. He certainly pursued transparent relationships with the three occupying powers and the emerging instruments of West European union. In Adenauer's hands, at least in the early years, transparency meant choosing a course that the Americans, French, and

British would support. Practically, this necessitated substantial dialog between the West German and Allied governments. Adenauer was shrewd enough to realize that if the West Germans conformed to the policy expectations of their conquerors, West Germans would likely win sovereignty more quickly than if they followed an independent course. Although Adenauer has been sharply criticized for kowtowing to the Americans and British, his foreign policy agenda can also be described as brilliant. Within a year of the establishment of the West German state, the country was admitted into the European Coal and Steel Community and the Council of Europe. Shortly thereafter, in the early 1950s, West Germany joined the North Atlantic Treaty Organization (NATO). In the domestic arena, Adenauer supported the democratization of West German society, which meant the gradual transformation to a more transparent society. By the time he left office in 1963, his country was on the way to stable democracy, a more open society, a successful economic recovery, and close relations with its neighbors.

IV

Whereas in 1948 and 1949, West Germans and representatives of the occupying powers could only hope that democracy would take hold in the new Federal Republic of Germany, by June 1987, when the full session of the Bundestag met to ratify Behnisch & Partner's final design for the new Bundeshaus, West Germany was a successful democracy considered a model both at home and abroad. The phrase, Modell Deutschland (Model Germany), was coined in the 1970s to describe the transformed economic and political system. More than anything, the fact that West Germany could be referred to as a model reflects the dramatic changes since 1949. To begin with, the democracy was 50 years old. It was almost three times the age of Weimar when that regime collapsed, and four times the age of the Third Reich at the end of the Second World War. Whether because of provisions in the Basic Law, the generational changes, or because of other factors, certain transformations had occurred in German society and the culture of everyday politics that created a more transparent society and parliamentary system as well as a stable democracy. These included the accomplished fact of a strong and vocal free press; political opposition in the form of a multi-party system; freedom of expression in the arts; and a more pluralistic society. Participation in the political process was more open and inclusive when compared with previous regimes, at least for those with German citizenship. This is not to say that West Germany achieved a completely transparent government or society, but merely that in 1989 Germany was palpably more transparent than it had ever been before. At the same time by the 1980s West Germans were concerned about the lack of transparency in their political system, the rise of special interests, the power of the political parties and coalition members over the opposition, and the dearth of real public participation in the workings of parliament. By the 1980s literature on the subject referred to the lack of "transparency" as a problem that needed serious consideration.[37] That is, the understanding of "transparency" as a metaphor for openness, accessibility, and inclusiveness in German political discourse was the dominant one by 1989 in spite of the fact that transparency only existed in a conditional, partial fashion.

West German political identity in 1989, then, was partly defined by its successful transition to social democracy. But this was only part of its identity. It had established itself as a phenomenally strong economy, the largest in Western Europe and third largest in the world, a model welfare state, and a responsible member of the European and international communities. The move towards greater transparency had occurred in almost every area of society and government: institutional, societal, and cultural transparency operated primarily in the domestic arena, and openness to the international community operated in the area of foreign affairs. To the architect Günther Behnisch and his contemporaries, the ideology of transparent government architecture was possible only because of the success of the post-Second World War West German state. Yet even as Behnisch embraced this ideology, he remained skeptical of it, remarking in a recent interview that, "transparent buildings do not ensure transparent government."[38] Moreover, from the beginning of Willi Brandt's term as Chancellor, West Germany embarked on a new course in its relations with the East. Dubbed Ostpolitik (East Politics), the phrase referred to the thawing in relations between West and East Germany. The change was predicated on one major shift in attitudes on both sides of the Berlin Wall – mutual acceptance of the right to exist which implied transparency to the other state's sovereignty. By accepting that East Germany had a right to exist, West Germany was also on the path to abandoning hope for an eventual unification between the two, which meant that Bonn would no longer be the provisional capital of a provisional state, but the permanent capital of a permanent one. Transparency in this context was more than an analogy for openness, accessibility, and honesty in government; it was an analogy for worth, as in the crystalline Tautian utopias. By 1989 transparency was even more clearly an ideology based in myth rather than reality. The very transformation to a functioning, mature democracy made real transparency in the political realm impossible. In spite of Hannes Meyer's and Günter Behnisch's disdain for backroom deals, this is the stuff of democracy without which the compromises needed to make policy change would never occur.

The Green Party learned this lesson in the 1990s. The Greens were the party that most loudly advocated increased transparency in German government, so after it joined the government in 1996, the party decided to make all of its party meetings public. But the members discovered that when all their meetings were public, they had no bargaining power in parliament because their positions were known. They soon retreated from holding open public meetings!

An article entitled "National Representation through Federal Buildings" published in the Bonn SPD party newspaper *Vorwärts* (Forwards), in 1973, that outlines the "political ideas and values" that might be incorporated into federal architecture, typifies the mainstream adoption of transparency as the appropriate analogy for open government in West Germany.[39] The article was published after the first national competition for new designs for a federal quarter in Bonn, but before the succession of redesigns that continued until the 1980s. *Vorwärts* enumerates several basic qualities that the editors thought should be in any project:

> Openness, popular appeal, the transparency of parliamentary and government decision making, ready accessibility to the parliamentary and government areas. The new federal buildings ought, in their connection to one another as well as individual buildings, reflect the fact that parliament and federal government are fulfilling their responsibilities to the democratic public.[40]

The article calls for state architecture to be a reflection both of the legal rights enumerated in the Basic Law and the governmental structure. By 1989, the articles published expressing similar notions are too numerous to be enumerated.

The impression that West Germany was a privileged place, a utopia of sorts, was fueled by the high standard of living and the largesse of the welfare state with its generous unemployment, retirement, and health care benefits, all of which were seemingly made possible by the phenomenal postwar economic expansion. While economic stability alone cannot account for West Germany's democratic stability, it certainly contributed to it. The economic system built after the Second World War relied on four basic policy principles: economic stability at home, competitiveness abroad, steady growth, and full employment. The successful implementation of this program depended on a broad consensus between labor, industry, and the political parties. As many economic historians have pointed out, the consensus remained until the end of the twentieth century even as governments changed.[41]

The economic reconstruction of Germany involved the adoption of a new system that struck a balance between unregulated market competition and total government planning. In order to succeed, the West German government pursued a path based on moderation, incremental growth, export-driven production, and consensus building.[42] If transparency in government describes openness, accessibility, and unimpeded popular participation, in economics it could describe open and free markets, cartel-free industries, and shared decision-making between management and labor. While some aspects of the new economy in the Federal Republic could be described as transparent, or more transparent, in relation to what had been before, Germany never adopted a totally free market system. Rather, it steered a middle course between the laissez-faire free market economics of the American model and the centrally controlled economic policy of the Soviet model. The special circumstances of German history in the twentieth century taught Germans to be cautious about leaving monetary policy to politicians and about permitting government too much economic control. The Weimar government had attempted to eliminate its war debt by printing more money, a policy that helped fuel the disastrous German economic collapse in the early 1920s. The National Socialists, on the other hand, regulated more and more aspects of the economy in their efforts to fuel the war effort and impose a "New Order." By the end of the war in 1945 Germany's economy was virtually closed to individual initiative or market forces. In contrast, by 1989, the economy was a moderately regulated but decidedly free market.

The new institutions established under the Basic Law to help safeguard and operate the democracy themselves proved to be stable. The violent upheavals of the late 1960s and early 1970s, that included kidnapping, murder, and other forms of terrorism, some fears notwithstanding, did not result in a return to authoritarian government. Even repressive legislation enacted in the 1970s to combat terrorism did not lead to a repressive authoritarian regime as similar events in Peru did.

By 1989, the makeup of German society as a whole had changed substantially. More and more, West Germany was becoming a country of immigrants, a pluralistic society. This change is due, in large part, to two factors: the economic boom which necessitated the importation of unskilled laborers to fill the gaps as West Germans restricted themselves to the more skilled and better paid positions, and to the policies written into the Basic Law guaranteeing asylum to political refugees who were threatened by persecution in their mother countries.[43] The first wave was Italians, Portuguese, and Spanish, the second wave was Turks, and the third wave was Africans, Vietnamese, Bosnians, and others from the former Yugoslavia. Under Article 16 of the Basic Law, West Germany grants asylum to all foreigners who apply on the grounds of political persecution at home. Until 1993, when the law was revised, it was easy for immigrants from the Eastern bloc to enter West Germany, and difficult for the state to control the numbers entering the country. Ironically, the fear that the health of the welfare state would be jeopardized by an over-abundance of new immigrants was the catalyst for revising the liberal law of asylum.[44] In 1960 only 1.2 percent of the total population was made up of foreigners, by 1983 that figure had jumped to 7.4 percent. By 1992 the numbers had reached 8.4 percent in the West German *Länder* and 0.8 percent in the East German *Länder* and by 1996 there were 10.5 percent foreigners in the former West Germany and 2.1 percent in the former East Germany.[45] While Germany has nowhere near the minority population that the US has, by 1989 it was looking more like a pluralistic society than ever before but the change has not been universally embraced. A persistent problem with violence against foreigners underscores the coexistence of intolerance with openness in German society. Since unification, anti-foreign aggression has included East German attacks against West German citizens traveling in the eastern part of the country, especially in the new *Bundesländer*!

Another area in which West Germany moved towards greater transparency after 1949 was in its international relations. Here, transparency can be seen as the open dialog West Germany established with its West European neighbors and the political integration effected by establishing the European Union. Before Hitler's ascension to power, Germany was the "weak middle" of the European continent, a political and military buffer between the West and the East. Under Hitler Germany was transformed into a strong center that stood alone. By contrast, by 1989 the FRG had transformed into the economic and political engine driving West European political and economic unity, a strong center with committed ties to the West. Today, Germany is still a strong center, albeit somewhat weaker than in the 1980s, with connections to both East and West. Unlike Great Britain, where the majority of citizens remain "Eurosceptics" even today, a majority of West Germans have supported integration into a European federation since 1948. According to a survey conducted by OMGUS in 1948, 82 percent of respondents were in favor of unification and 96 percent considered the chances of success to be very high in spite of the skepticism on the part of Adenauer, the Americans, and the French.[46] Between 1962 and 1980 support for West European Unification barely wavered, holding steady at around 78 percent even though it had dropped as an overall priority by 1988.[47] But strong support for the EU does not mean that Germany is willing to relinquish all of its power as a sovereign nation, to become totally transparent to the rest of Europe. In recent years, Germany has demonstrated that if necessary, it will pursue an independent economic policy in order to try to solve domestic economic problems even if this means flouting EU regulations.[48]

V

The movement towards greater transparency has always been balanced by its opposite, a movement towards opacity, towards less real popular involvement and more backroom deal making, a condition common to mature democracies.[49] Transparency of access has been a myth from the beginning. Although there was an "open house" in September 1949 which any interested German citizen was able to attend, this was a tour of the parliamentary complex, not a parliamentary session. From the first session, public attendance has been controlled both in numbers (seats are limited), and in spontaneity (the guest had to apply in advance for permission to attend a parliamentary session). In 1952 access was formalized with the establishment of an "Office for Visitor Group Services." This agency changed over the years but always existed in some shape or another. In sheer practical terms access had to be restricted because of the limited number of seats available to the public in all three versions of the plenary chamber. According to Detlef Lenz, member of the Bundestag police force, the vetting process for visitors to the parliament has also changed over the decades, especially after the rise of the Red Army Faction in the late 1960s and early 1970s, and after the terrorist attacks on the World Trade Center in New York on September 11, 2001.[50] Today, the private police force performs stringent background checks on anyone who wishes to observe a parliamentary session with the exception of visitors personally brought into the building by the MPs themselves. The heightened security, which translates into limited access and less transparency, is deemed necessary given the realities of contemporary society.[51]

The parliament has had a mandate to communicate openly with the German public from its inception (Article 42 of the Basic Law). In 1949, the "Press and Information Office of the German Bundestag" was formed to handle public dissemination of information about the parliament. In 1953 the office expanded its purview to include newsprint, radio, and television but in 1957 it was dissolved in favor of an "Office of Press Technical Opportunities." This too, in turn, was abolished and replaced in 1970 by the "Press and Information Center of the German Bundestag" after members of parliament complained that the Bundestag was not adequately fulfilling its mandate to inform the public. The new agency was divided into three sections responsible for: press/radio/television, parliamentary correspondence, and visitor services in Bonn. September 15, 1970 witnessed the first publication of "Today in the Bundestag": November 1971 was the date of the first issue of "Parliament Today." Other reforms included: the "Youth Question Hour" in the plenary chamber of the Bundestag begun May 21, 1981, the 1980 reform of the rules governing public access to plenary debates designed to help improve parliamentary consideration of the public voice, the 1993 "Citizens' Telephone," a hotline to MPs open between 16:00 and 20:00 to any citizen with questions (but the line had only been opened 10 times between 1993 and 1997), the 1995 "plenary core time" television broadcast on Thursday mornings; and the establishment in 1996 of a website, www.bundestag.de, with all the minutes of parliamentary discussions as well as information on numerous aspects of the parliament.[52] But public access is still controlled. Access to the website depends on having access to a computer and being informed enough to know that the site exists. The same is true for the Citizens' Telephone for which access is even more restricted. It is not possible to simply decide to attend a meeting and arrive. Worse, most members of the public who attend parliamentary sessions are actually invited guests with some personal or business interest in the discussion, not disinterested outside parties! To gain access to the Reichstag, for example, it is necessary to write in advance for permission to attend a session but the department in charge of answering such requests has a spotty record of timely responses.

The Bundestag has also grappled with the idea of a parliamentary television channel and over the years the freedom of television channels to film the parliament at work has vacillated back and forth between restricted and less restricted access. The first live television broadcasts took place in the 1950s but after a live debate over the reunification of East and West Germany was broadcast in 1957, President Eugen Gerstenmaier decided to abolish live transmissions except in exceptional circumstances. In 1958 the Ältestenrat decided that television should not record working sessions where parliamentary arguments were evident, but document decisions after they were taken.[53] Thereafter the norm was to film clips of debates for evening newscasts. In this way, of course, parliament could control the information being disseminated. The debate over television access accelerated again in the 1960s but in 1966 the Ältestenrat decided to allow special broadcasts and clips only. This decision too has changed over the years so that the press has been able to decide what it wanted to film or broadcast rather than being told what it would be permitted to cover. Nevertheless, the real limitations of broadcast time mean that nothing more than snippets of parliamentary debates are shown. Thus, the public has access to only a tiny portion of the actual parliamentary discussion. The percentage of actual coverage has varied from 2 percent of the time parliamentarians debated in one election period to as much as 27.1 percent.[54] One hundred percent has never been covered, nor do television journalists cover the thousands of hours of party and faction meetings, committee and commission meetings. In other words, a tiny fraction of the actual political discussion is available to the public through television coverage. Since 1997 the "Phoenix" channel has broadcast some parliamentary debates in their totality but again, the reality is that there is not enough broadcast time to carry them all on television so the ones that are broadcast tend to support the positions of the governing coalition members at the expense of the opposition.[55] Worse, when the MPs realize that they will be broadcast, they jockey for prime speaking time. Again, because of the structure of parliamentary procedure, coalition members tend to receive the better time slots. In other words, the methods designed to improve transparency are themselves fraught with problems; no system of perfect information transmission exists. Transparency remains a desire, a myth, rather than a reality.

Chapter 4

Looking in the mirror
Transparency after 1989

Nothing can remain as it was.

Willy Brandt – when the Berlin Wall fell[1]

the other
indifferent to himself
of whom I know nothing
of whom nobody knows who he is
Who does not move me
that is i

From "The Other" by Hans Magnus Enzensberger[2]

When the first East Germans freely crossed from East to West marking the beginning of the end for the Berlin Wall, it seemed as if a huge, impenetrable, physical barrier between the two worlds was disappearing forever. "Now Show Openness!" screamed a contemporary headline in *Der Spiegel* (*The Mirror*), the West German weekly magazine.[3] But the openness, or transparency, many expected to result from the destruction of the wall has yet to fully materialize. As numerous writers have pointed out, the "wall in the head" is still there.[4] In other words, after 45 years of separation into two states, the Germans feel "unified but not united."[5] Political unity may have been the result of unification, insofar as East and West are now part of the same political system, but this is not the same as social, cultural, or psychological union. In 1996, 74 percent of all Germans believed that the majority of their countrymen identified more as East and West Germans than as one people.[6] After only 14 years it is still too soon to properly assess the many changes set in motion by the events of November 9, 1989, but it is possible to point to some trends and to speculate on their significance. Transparency in the aftermath of unification is still a metaphor for openness, accessibility, and honesty in government, as well as an analogy for the same qualities in state architecture, evidenced by the rhetoric accompanying the renovation of the Reichstag. But transparency can also be interpreted differently as a metaphor for openness to the past, and the other conditions brought on by the razing of the Berlin Wall.

Transparency has certainly played a part on the political scene, perhaps not always in the ways one might have expected, but it has played a part nevertheless. Removing the Berlin Wall, then the other border checks controlling movement between East and West Germany, offered the first promises of greater transparency in many areas of East German life: political, economic, social, cultural, and psychological, in the form of a more open and liberal society. But these conditions already existed for West Germans before 1989. What, then, would transparency signify to all of newly united Germany? Removal of physical and legal impediments to free circulation between the two Germanies were certainly common forms of increased openness, and represented the first steps towards greater freedoms for both sides. Although the lifting of barriers also marked the beginning of greater openness between the two societies, real transparency in East–West relations and in the politics of unification does not exist.

In the euphoria following the fall of the Berlin Wall, there was talk about greater political and economic transparency, about the benefits of rejoining the two halves of Germany, but few considered the tremendous economic costs of unification, or the social, cultural or political challenges to integrating two very different societies. East Germany was very rapidly absorbed into the Federal Republic in a way some refer to as "annexation."[7] The Bundestag used Article 23 of the Basic Law to approve the incorporation of the five eastern *Länder*, and Berlin, into the FRG rather than write a new constitution and have all the states, east and west, ratify it as the authors of the Basic Law had intended in Article 146 (see Chapter 3). Using Article 23 was swift and expedient. This method avoided lengthy debate and potential political hurdles pushing through legal unification while the popular mood was still heady. The old East Germany therefore had become so transparent to its Western counterpart it had literally dissolved into the existing political framework of the Federal Republic and disappeared for all time. But for West Germany, and for East Germany as well, unification has not been the seamless melding of two states into one nation. Rather, unification replaced the physical separation made by the Wall, and the metaphysical separation formed by the "Iron

Curtain," with a clear view of the "other," a phenomenon that is rather like looking at one's image in the mirror for the very first time. And like looking at one's reflection, the image is deceptive. It looks familiar; it resembles something well known; but only the surface is perceptible. The image is illusionary. It appears to contain depth of space but these depths are impenetrable, opaque to the viewing eye.

The immediate effect of unification was to join together two states whose historic development over 45 years after the Second World War had been radically different. The union placed East and West Germany, for the first time since 1948, in direct confrontation with one another. Pursuing Ostpolitik had, of course, included making contacts between the two countries, but only in the superficial ways accorded diplomatic relations. After 1989, East and West Germany, and East and West Germans, found themselves looking at each other without any of the protective devices that had hitherto been in place: the geographic separation afforded by the Wall, veils of differing political systems, closed and monitored communications, and adverse or positive propaganda. Germans in both the East and the West refer to the period from November 1989 to actual political unification in 1990 as "*Die Wende*" (The Turn). As Charlotte Kahn puts it, "East and West Germans simply turned – towards each other."[8] The new condition could be described as facing the other and looking him or her in the face. Alternatively, because Germany had once been a single nation that was separated into two, unification was akin to looking at part of oneself again, albeit a part long obscured and ignored. Or, the experience could be compared with confronting one's double. East and West were parallel German states formed for people with the same historical consciousness, cultural identity, and experience before 1945. The separation into the Federal Republic and the German Democratic Republic therefore created states whose political, economic, social, and cultural systems were developed completely differently from a common origin. "Unification in the center of Europe immediately creates a new perspective on the histories of the two Germanies and the ways in which they constructed their identities."[9] The experience is like catching a first glimpse of oneself in the mirror – a moment that is at once pleasurable, shocking, and disturbing since the one thing people can never see without an external aid is their own image. Looking in a mirror, one sees through the transparent glass surface to the reflective material of the image beyond. Transparency after unification, then, signifies both transparency to the "other" and the re-examination of self precipitated by that newly present image.

The transparent surface of a mirror is an apt metaphor for Germany after unification for many reasons. To begin with, the mirror and its reflective properties have long been associated with crises of identity and self-image. The reflection in the mirror forms the split of the subject into two – subject and

89

object – a division that can cause a range of emotions from pleasure to anxiety to terror. Interestingly, the German Romantics used the mirror as a metaphor for the dark and melancholic double. In her book on the history of the mirror, Sabine Melchior-Bonnet describes the strangely alienated state we encounter when looking at our reflected image. "Man's relationship with his reflection is conflicted. Forced to let his image enter the mirror, he is revealed – visible, naked, vulnerable, subject to the sight of himself as others see him."[10] Viewing one's own image is fascinating and alluring as well as frightening and disconcerting. People think they know themselves well until they look at that reflection in the mirror – the image that reveals all the nuances that are normally invisible. Worse, confronting the image is "to come up against one's limits, to see time work its destruction, to fear painful or disturbing evidence that the subject shelters from itself. . . ."[11] Both East and West Germans have experienced some of the same anguish looking at their own images as well as at one another. Unification has forced a self-reassessment on both sides of the former Iron Curtain as well as new assessments by citizens of each former republic of their old images of one another. Friedrich Nietzsche once wrote, "the question 'what is German' never dies out among them."[12] Indeed, at the core of the new political order is the reframing of the German Question in new terms.

Not all aspects of West German, or German, life have been called into question since 1989. Unification was partially predicated on acceptance of the political system already established in the Federal Republic, and of the GDR's integration into the FRG's version of market economics. Indeed, by 1999, Chancellor Gerhard Schröder connected the ten-year anniversary of unification with the 50-year anniversary of the founding of the FRG, as one celebration of the success of the Republic. But integration has forced radical rethinking of many assumptions comprising the pre-1989 German Model – most notably those assumptions that applied to one part of divided Germany, but not to the other. For example, integration forced both the government of the Federal Republic, and its citizens from East and West, to confront the real economic crisis that existed in the East, the dilapidated state of East German industry and infrastructure.

Furthermore, as many analysts have noted, unification created a strange doubling of German history. In the most curious way, West Germans seemed to be either glancing in a mirror that reflected the past, or standing transported back to 1949. Where the separate Germanies struggled with the moral dilemma of how to remember one dictatorship with its oppressions, repressions, and outrages, now united Germany has inherited a second dictatorship, a second set of perpetrators and victims, and many of the same dilemmas associated with exorcising the ghosts of National Socialism have reappeared. "Let us declare this century's most important lesson for us

Germans – never again dictatorship!" declared Rainer Eppelmann, a former East German dissident, "Whatever the label it may carry – national, religious, National Socialist, Socialist or Communist – never again dictatorship!"[13] East German abuses included a closed political system and the Stasi, the State Security police, who spied on a third of the 18 million East German citizens and kept copious files on their subjects. Even worse, the Stasi used friends to spy on friends, neighbors to spy on neighbors, wives to spy on husbands, brothers to spy on sisters. Because it was impossible to be certain of the trustworthiness of anyone, no matter how close they seemed to be, most East Germans lived a "schizophrenic life."[14] This usually meant presenting one face to the world at large and another one to family and close friends. True beliefs were repressed in favor of the "party line." Unification has forced Germans to come to terms with the former police state, to find ways to reveal the truth about life in East Germany without destroying the social peace.

Unification caused deeper existential crises for many Germans from both sides of the Wall. For many left-wingers in the West, the revelations of the true failures of the GDR were a bitter disappointment. Before unification they could at least deceive themselves into believing that the Communist state had something positive to offer, especially in its refusal to espouse the Western capitalist model.

> In the aftermath of unification there is an ideological vacuum. The collapse of Communism, the electoral defeat of the SPD and the demoralization of the Greens, overrun by a process that they neither expected nor wanted, means that for the first time since the French Revolution the Left is no longer the party of hope. The continuing traumatic legacy of the Third Reich means that the integral nationalism of the traditional Right also remains at a discount.[15]

In other words, old definitions of Left and Right no longer seem valid.

What has been called into question since unification goes beyond the political realm to the very heart of Germany past and future: German national identity, Germany's role in Europe as a nation-state, and Germany's place in history.[16] More precisely, unification refocused debates over German national identity, in the face of differing historical experiences, by framing the question about what residents of the two Germanies had in common. Could national identity be defined in terms of cultural similarities like common language and literature, ethnic similarities, or should it be defined in terms of citizenship and place of residence? Debates over the identity of Germany as a nation-state center around its identity as an economic and political power and its place at the center of Europe as well as the notion of the normalization of Germany after unification. Finally, the question of the existence of a German

Sonderweg, a unique historical path to modernity colored by responsibility for two world wars, the Holocaust, vehement fascism in the form of National Socialism, and the unusual division into two states after the Second World War, is once again being posed. Can Germany finally become a "normal" state, with a normal past? These are questions that, even at the time of writing, 14 years after unification, are still present in contemporary German debates.

As Ralf Dahrendorf has pointed out, nationalism and the question of national identity reared their heads already in October and November of 1989.

> The sudden transition during the Monday demonstrations in Leipzig last November, from "*Wir sind das Volk,*" "We are the people," to "*Wir sind ein Volk,*" "We are one people," is not just one from democracy to nationalism. It also uses "people" in two very different ways, as a society of citizens first, and as a somewhat mystical community second, *demos* and *thymos*, perhaps, *Gesellschaft* (society) and *Gemeinschaft* (community) certainly.[17]

In other words, unification brought old notions of German identity to the fore including the question of who is German. The linguistic shift also signaled the new identification between East Germans and their relations in the West as one people – the start of the next wave of German confrontation with questions of identity and nationhood. Wolfgang Schäuble, Kohl's successor as majority leader of the CDU/CSU coalition in the Bundestag, observed that 1989 left the Germans with no identity and disoriented by political change.[18]

The disorientation has, in some ways, been profound. As David Schoenbaum and Elizabeth Pond point out, before unification Germany was described as "One nation, two states." Unification now seemed to have turned it into "One state, two nations."[19] Unification seems to have caused the paradoxical widening of the gap between East and West even as it joined them together. Today, residents on both sides of the former iron curtain still identify themselves as "East" or "West" German. The response to the question "do you believe that Germany will grow together or remain forever two separate states?" has fluctuated. In the wake of post-unification optimism in 1990 the majority believed they would grow together (58 percent). By the middle of 1992, when differences between the two peoples had begun to surface, only 35 percent believed this was possible with 45 percent doubtful. In 1994, 51 percent were again optimistic and 32 percent pessimistic, but by the beginning of 1997 pessimism was more prevalent with 40 percent doubtful and only 37 percent positive.[20] East Germans resent the wealth possessed by West Germans; West Germans see the East Germans as lazy opportunists who want something for nothing. East Germans find "Wessis" arrogant and pushy, West Germans think the "Ossis" are lazy good-for-nothings. Fourteen years after, "Ostalgie," nostalgia for the old East Germany, is widespread. "Memory, of course, is selective, and what is remembered now is this: there were jobs for everyone [in the GDR] even if they did not amount to much, time for friendships and a sense of solidarity, of community, of a life beyond 'me'."[21] Unification exchanged a society based on conformity and security, albeit in the most uncomfortable of conditions, for one based on risk. The privileged position the former East Germany held within Comecon, the Council for Mutual Economic Cooperation that arranged trade between communist countries, no doubt made the transition even more painful for many.

In 1990, the Dutch historian Maarten Brands remarked that, "the unification of Germany . . . removed the embargo on the notion of nation."[22] Brands meant, of course, that with the unification of the two Germanies, a new nation was formed, a condition that would free its citizens from some of the burdens of history allowing them to consider the meanings of nation, national identity, and nationalism for Germany in the new millennium. As Brands predicted, the German media have been full of editorials grappling with these issues. A nation consists of men united in a political system, residing in a circumscribed geographic area, who share culture, language, and history.[23] Most important to the construction of the abstraction "nation," and the sense of national identity that comes with it, is a sense of collective consciousness of belonging to a larger entity.[24] Until 1989, Germans east and west of the Wall shared some history, some culture, and language, but not the political system of the last 40 years. National identity is constructed in one of two ways, the first is as a myth, evoking "ethnic identity, language, culture, literature, tied to a romantic feeling of *heimat*. The other is founded on political institutions."[25] Before 1989 the myth of nation connected East and West, after 1989 the fact of political unity connected them. But unification revealed the real differences as opposed to the mythological similarities. The challenge facing the Germans today is how to construct a common sense of community from two sets of people whose historical and political consciousness differs, as well as their emotional attachment to the Republic. Some suggest the new Germany must abandon the traditional German definition of nation based on ethnic, linguistic, and cultural commonalities in favor of the model based on shared political institutions. In time, this may be possible. Before unification most West Germans shared "*Verfassungspatriotismus*" ("Constitutional Patriotism" – patriotism founded on pride in the Basic Law and the economic and political successes of the FRG), a feeling that defined national pride and identity. But former East Germans do not yet have the historical experience that would allow them to feel *Verfassungspatriotismus*.[26] Others, like the writer Ian Buruma, revisit European integration as the solution to the German identity dilemma.[27] According to this view, the nation-state must give way to a new political order based on a sense of pan-Europeanism, and post-unification

Germany is uniquely poised to lead the way. Whatever the solution proposed, most Germans agree that unified Germany needs to develop a new sense of identity that those east and west of the former Iron Curtain can share.

Prior to 1989, East Germany was considered the economic miracle of the Eastern bloc, a kind of mirror image of West Germany in the East. Like its sister state in the West, the East successfully rebuilt its industry after the Second World War, to become the most industrially developed country in Eastern Europe, second only to the Soviet Union in Comecon, after the postwar *demontage* and reparations payments. But the standards of production that were acceptable for export to the East were not acceptable for Western markets. Not only were factories in East Germany producing inferior products but also their machinery was outdated and their profits were subsidized by the state so the factories were shielded from true market pressures. East Germans were largely unaware of the looming economic crisis they were facing before unification. West Germans were likewise unaware of the true condition of East Germany's economy and they were ill prepared for the fiscal measures they would need to adopt in order to rescue it.[28] The economic measures taken to remedy the problems in East Germany have, in turn, weakened the West German economy. For the first time in decades, the certainty of economic stability, that is so closely tied to political stability, is threatened, as is the efficacy of Modell Deutschland. For example, West German economic success was predicated on a free market economy in which the government safeguarded the competitiveness of the market, but rarely interfered directly. But in order to ease the transition from a socialist economy, where all industry was state-owned, inefficient, and largely out-of-date, as well as heavily subsidized, the Federal government enacted a system of transfer payments to the East that, in effect, were replacements for the former state subsidies in the pre-unification era. These payments have, in turn, drained West German resources forcing substantial cutbacks in the beloved social benefits. Resentment over transfer payments to the East exists although West Germans do not seem sure of their feelings. Their responses to a series of questions regarding transfer payments and related issues posed in 1996 demonstrate the mixed feelings. In 1996, 44 percent of West Germans agreed with the statement, "I find it bad that so much is invested in the new *Bundesländer*. They develop new services, new work places, while the West suffers."[29] Not surprisingly, 88 percent of East Germans surveyed at the same time found the transfer payments fair and proper. Strangely, when asked directly whether they found the payments irritating or not, only 35 percent of all West Germans found the payments an annoyance.[30] On the other hand, 69 percent of West Germans believed that East Germans did not recognize how hard the West Germans had struggled after the War before they achieved economic affluence. The subtext here is that the East Germans must also work hard if they wish to become prosperous, they cannot expect to have prosperity handed to them by their wealthier West German cousins. Finally, in what is perhaps the most revealing question as to the attitudes many West Germans hold on the subject of economic aid to the East, is the statement, "Certainly one must show solidarity to the people in East Germany and financially support the reconstruction of the new *Bundesländer*. But at the moment we can do more, if we support West German industry. Now help must be cut back somewhat."[31] This statement was posed to West Germans with the question whether or not they agreed; 63 percent responded that they did. The statement is interesting because it is equivocal in nature – it allows the respondent to be both for and against financial support for the East at one at the same time. More than anything, the response demonstrates the extent to which many West Germans were still ambivalent about the financial aspects of unification in 1996.

Opinions over the successes and failures of making the transition from a socialist to a market economy differ significantly in the East and West. Interestingly, the overwhelming majority of East German respondents to questions about the trusteeship agency's (Treuhandanstalt) efforts to privatize former state industry viewed the efforts as unsuccessful and generally benefiting the West over the East.[32] West Germans, on the other hand, did not have much of an opinion either way. And when asked if the monetary transfers were an annoyance or not, West German respondents were divided along Left/Right political lines with only 29 percent of CDU/CSU finding transfers an annoyance but 43 percent and 52 percent respectively from the SPD and FDP finding it a nuisance.[33] Even more telling, when asked whether more was being done than the West German economy could withstand, 75 percent in the West answered "yes" in 1996, while only 15 percent in the East answered "yes."[34] The Allensbach Institute's findings support the contention that many West Germans were neither ready for, nor willing to, embrace unification and its challenges. Rather, ". . . the FRG public wanted unification without cost," a fact supported by political rhetoric immediately preceding unification when politicians presented the imminent act as something only positive.[35] Moreover, unification has encouraged many Germans to begin to question both the importance of economic stability to political stability, as well as the means used to achieve economic stability.[36]

Until 1989, economic stability was based on limited federal involvement, free market economics, and a stable currency. Maintaining low unemployment and avoiding deficit spending were additional tenets of the Model Germany approach. Yet the realities of post-unification Germany have led the federal government to operate with large deficits – a radical departure from Modell Deutschland economic orthodoxy.[37] Kohl had initially hoped to fund unification through growth-related tax revenue increases. But these did not materialize. The federal government was then forced to choose between taxation and borrowing. Because increased taxation would be both politically unpopular and economically detrimental to the strong West German economy, the government has opted for deficit spending. In his 1995 book *Founding of the Berlin Republic,* the publicist Johannes Gross pointed to the "normality of instability" as the identity of post-unification Germany, replacing the stability of the old FRG.[38] Gross's statement is more than oxymoronic – it underscores the contradictory nature of post-unification Germany and its two-sided identity. By 1999, instability was as stable as stability had been before!

By 1999, the tenth anniversary of unification and the fiftieth anniversary of the Federal Republic, *Der Spiegel* could write, "It is becoming ever more difficult to find 'typical German' characteristics. Globalization has also affected the character of the folk. But the question remains, what is German?"[39] In his article, Henryk Broder points to the paradoxical situation Germany now finds itself in: a series of conflicting demands for the new German identity. On the one hand Germany is unified; on the other, internal divisions persist. Germany's allies demand the country assume a stronger role and more responsibility in international affairs, yet warn against the dangers of enlarged power and a "fourth Reich."[40] Many Germans deny their country's status as an immigrant nation, yet over 8 percent of its resident population is foreign born, and it has the highest rate of immigration in all of Europe. Even the choice of capital city is fraught with double entendres – Berlin is both the former capital of the Prussian empire and the Third Reich as well as the new capital of a successfully democratic Germany. "The inner contradiction of the historical moment was already there to follow. So true was the happiness and the fear men have from the rumblings of change."[41] Germany is being asked to be itself and its opposite. The two-sided pull on German identity is a form of self-reflection and confrontation.

The construction of national identity had been a dilemma before unification. The extreme nationalism that accompanied National Socialism effectively made issues of national identity delicate, to say the least, especially in the West. The decades of integration with the West were meant to counter nationalist tendencies and to act as a substitute for them by providing West Germans with a strong European identity.[42] By the middle of the 1980s, a dispute erupted among German historians over German identity in a divided Germany. The so-called Historikerstreit was a debate essentially divided into two camps: one that argued for the "normalization" of German history, meaning the absorption of the 13 years of National Socialist rule into a larger historical perspective that viewed National Socialism as a brief and isolated incident, an aberration, rather than the defining moment in the past. The opposing view argued for a continuous confrontation with the past and acceptance of responsibility and culpability during the Third Reich in order to strengthen the democratic project. Unification has shifted the grounds of the debate once again.

A series of articles in *Die Zeit* entitled "What's Left," in 1992, and a second series in the *Frankfurter Allgemeine Zeitung* entitled "What's Right," in 1994, point to the confusion of ideological fronts since unification. As the terms of the Historikerstreit made clear, before unification both the Right and Left defined themselves by particular views of West German, and German, history, especially the catastrophes of the twentieth century. The Right supported unification and a return to the nation-state. The Left, on the other hand, viewed separation as just punishment for German crimes – the two world wars, the Holocaust, etc.[43] Today, German conservatives rationalize unification and the return to a nation-state by describing a condition of German "normalization" which sounds very like the argument for normalizing German history that conservatives were promoting in the 1980s. According to this view, unification finally has placed Germany in a position where it can normalize its society, its sense of identity, and therefore its view of history. The conservative Hans-Peter Schwarz claims that Germany has finally become a proper nation-state thereby achieving political normalcy. In an opposing view, the progressive philosopher Jürgen Habermas calls Schwarz's view the basic lie of unification.[44] In October 1998, the writer Martin Walser caused a furor when he said that Auschwitz should not become a "routine threat, a tool of intimidation, a moral cudgel or just a compulsory exercise." Walser's remarks were particularly troubling because they came from the Left, not the Right, in one of many post-unification demonstrations of shifting ideologies. In his defense, the writer Monika Maron suggested that the new generation did not need to carry the shame of its ancestors because enough historic time had intervened between the Third Reich and the 1990s. Maron asked how "we can convince other countries of our normality if we ourselves deny that claim?"[45] The normalization controversy is a debate over which sense of self should prevail in the unified Germany as much as which view of history. As Konrad Jarausch asserts, the current debate is a "battle for the authority to interpret the past," proof positive that Germans are looking at the past, yet again.

I

Even the choice of words to describe the events of 1989–90 is rife with historical implications. Deciding to refer to the union of West and East Germany as "unification" suggests the creation in 1989–90 of a new condition with little or no connection to the pre-Second World War past. Unification implies a first, a new joining of West and East Germany in which the post-Second World War histories and identities determine the new configuration of the Federal

Republic. "Unification" describes the subsuming and incorporation of five new *Länder* into the FRG's successful market-driven, liberal democracy.[46] Whereas "reunification" suggests an historic continuity with the Third Reich, Weimar Republic, Wilhelmine Germany, and the 200 years of debate over German nationhood and identity.[47] Choosing the word reunification, therefore, permits commentators to claim both the positive and the negative aspects of German history, the great achievements of German culture in the eighteenth and nineteenth centuries as well as the devastation of the Second World War.

  Unification has complicated any assessment of the past, however. Now both Germanies must confront the legacy of National Socialism and the added burden of 40 years of Communism. The challenge is further complicated by the differing memories of the past developed in each country; the FRG and the GDR had developed differing memories of National Socialism, a condition the historian Jeffrey Herf describes as divided memory, and certainly had diverging perspectives on the era of separation as well. The two forms of memory were affected by the ideologies that emerged after the Second World War along with the international alliances formed by each state. As mentioned above, West German memory also divided according to Left- and Right-leaning belief systems. The tension between the two extremes on the Right and the Left created "tension between memory and justice on the one hand and democracy on the other."[48] However, the equation "more democracy necessitates more memory" did not emerge in West Germany until the 1960s. Because the Nazis had persecuted the Socialists and Communists along with the Jews, Gypsies, homosexuals, and other groups they perceived as "deviant," the Communists and Socialists did not suffer the same moral degradation either in the eyes of foreigners or in their own self-esteem during the Third Reich. In post-Second World War East Germany the tendency was to use the memory of Nazi crimes in order to legitimize the Communist state.[49] The abuses Communists had suffered under the National Socialists including expulsion from government, purges, imprisonments, exile, and liquidation, made membership in the Communist Party heroic. Furthermore, the Communists used the historical record to present themselves as strident anti-fascists. The Communists also moved quickly after the war to make clear the distinction between National Socialism and Socialism. National Socialism was linked to imperialism and capitalism and shown to support the propertied classes over the working classes. National Socialist connections to the Junker class and prominent German industrialists were used to support this case. According to Herf, *Die Legende vom Deutschen Sozialismus* (*The Legend of German Socialism*), written by Walter Ulbricht and later republished under the title, *Der Faschistische Deutsche Imperiliasmus (1933–1945)*, with a circulation in the hundreds of thousands, was the authoritative text presenting the East German view.[50] Interestingly, the logic employed by Ulbricht was almost the same as that used by the West German Left to justify the permanent partition of Germany.

II

Equally fascinating is the fact that a debate similar to the one over remembering National Socialism and the Holocaust has now erupted over the Communist legacy. The argument divides along the same Left/Right ideological lines – with those on the Right advocating forgetting the past and those on the Left advocating remembrance and penitence.

Fifty years after the Holocaust, Germans are still struggling with how to remember the event and whether to remember it. "Auschwitz is and remains the most meaningful German construction of the twentieth century,"[51] wrote Henryk Broder of Germany's identity crises. ". . . the French have 1789, the British have their long democratic tradition, the USA for 200 years . . . the Foundation of our unique identity is Auschwitz," wrote Arnulf Baring.[52] On April 27, 1995, federal president Roman Herzog made a speech at Bergen-Belsen in which he reminded the world that the lesson of the Holocaust was "Human dignity is inviolable." He goes on to admonish his countrymen, ". . . there may be new forms of exclusion and *Gleichschaltung* (forcing into line), of selection and totalitarianism that we cannot foresee today. We must therefore remain vigilant. To do so we must preserve memory. Only those who remember can ward off future peril."[53] Herzog continues by admitting that he is not sure the Germans have yet discovered the correct forms of remembrance. In an era when, for a third time, there is a generational shift under way, how to remember is even more significant. The more distance there is between existing generations and the perpetrators, the more challenging it becomes to remember.

In his speech to the Bundestag on January 19, 1996, the Day of Commemoration for the Victims of National Socialism, Herzog acknowledges the temptation to bury the past. Indeed, the other face of remembering is forgetting. Herzog reminds his countrymen, however, that remembering does not constitute forever assuming guilt and responsibility for the misdeeds of the past but, rather, assuming responsibility to prevent the repetition of totalitarianism and racism in the future. He refers to Ingeborg Hecht's *The Rise of Invisible Walls* (or transparent) as one guide to recognizing the appearance of totalitarianism. Herzog emphasizes the necessity of sharpening young Germans' vision so they can perceive potential danger even in its most nascent form, use an understanding of history in order to overcome it.[54] Most important, Herzog wishes the new Day of Commemoration for the Victims of National Socialism to be a day for "reflection and contemplation" rather than a holiday, because he believes that a holiday can easily lose its meaning and force by deteriorating into a pro forma day off from everyday tedium. What Herzog desires is one day a year on which Germans reflect about themselves and their past in a serious way. He acknowledges that by choosing to call this the "Day of Commemoration for the Victims of National Socialism," he is "well aware that many, in a broad interpretation of this expression, will include the victims of the National Socialist war and in the period after the war, the victims of flight, expulsion and abduction."[55] But Herzog feels that the broad implications and possible interpretations of the name are its strength for they allow as many Germans as possible to identify with the occasion and to find something meaningful in it to contemplate. For Herzog, then, remembering the past and contemplating it, as well as using the lessons of the past to create a better future, constitute German responsibility.

Unified Germany has as much to contemplate in the East German past as it does in the National Socialist past. The new transparency to conditions in the former East Germany prompted questions about the GDR's political system, added a new set of victims for Germans to be concerned about, and fostered the first probes into the truth about Stasi, the former East German secret police. Of all the different ways in which the "Wende" promoted facing the "other," unveiling the truth about the totalitarian state and its secret police were the ones most fraught with pain and controversy. In confronting the other, Germans soon discovered the multi-layered complexity of the double image. Not only was East Germany a parallel German society but, within that society, double life was the status quo for many citizens. In the transparent society of unified Germany all the secrets of the former GDR were to be bared; the difficulty was how to achieve this without creating irreparable lesions in German society. The double speak of official propaganda had to be unmasked in a constructive manner so that Germans could learn from their past experience.

Soon after unification, the Federal Republic established a commission to investigate the political abuses of Communism. Headed by Rainer Eppelmann, the legislative commission was charged with reviewing vast numbers of government and private documents in order to issue a report on the ways in which the Communists wielded and retained power. Eppelmann cited the production of "a judgment on Communism and its methods" as his goal. Gerd Poppe, a former East German human rights activist and member of the commission said, "We are going to investigate all the repressive tools of the old regime starting with the open ones like imprisonment and expropriation and going through the various forms of indoctrination and social pressures. We are going to leave something valuable for history, and it will be written from the point of view of the victims."[56] The commission's purpose was to create a kind of anti-propaganda, to expose the truths about the former

East German state in order to help its former residents exorcise their past so they could move into the future. At the same time, a clear picture of the GDR would help to eradicate "Ostalgie" by rendering life in the totalitarian regime in its true colors. Among the many revelations were the numerous groups of potential enemies of the state listed in the Stasi files: "spies, agents, subversives, saboteurs, and political criminals" and those whose views might be understood to be negative in relation to the state.[57] The first four categories of enemy are typical of any regime, the last two of a politically repressive one. The potential treatment Stasi had at its disposal, revealed during investigations, ranged from observation by spies, to internment, to "liquidation."

Once again faced with the dilemma of how to punish the crimes committed by residents of a totalitarian state, the Federal government decided to prosecute certain figureheads leaving most former citizens untouched. The pattern mirrored the postwar treatment of Nazi officials. Prosecutions targeted leading members of the former East German government and Stasi including former chief of police Erich Mielke, former spy master Markus Wolf, former East German leader Erich Honecker, former head of state security Egon Krenz, and former lawyer Wolfgang Vogel. But the decision to only prosecute high-level members of the former East German government is fraught with difficulty. Who determines where the line lies between high- and low-level party and government members? Does guilt for a crime lie only at the hands of the person with whom an order originates or does the person executing an order also share responsibility? So many East Germans were complicit, in the same way that so many Germans had been complicit with the Nazis, that prosecution threatens to undermine any chances of re-establishing civil society. Worse, it is often difficult to differentiate between those who were "perpetrators" under the totalitarian regime, and those who were "victims."[58]

The federal constitutional court eventually ruled that trying East Germans for actions they committed when the GDR was a separate state could only proceed if their actions were not legal in the former Communist republic.[59] The ruling conforms to international law, Article 7, Paragraph 2 of the European Human Rights Convention that forbids retroactive punishment. Beyond the legal issues involved, the moral ones proved to be extremely complicated. Many East Germans found the singling out of leaders unjust. "The trial is a very convenient way of fixing responsibility on one man, or one group of men, for injustices we all contributed to."[60] Thus, by November 1999, of the 854 suits filed claiming government criminality or *Justizunrecht*, only 106 judgments had been made against perpetrators with 24 judgments stating *Haftstrafen ohne Bewährung gekommen ist* (suspended sentences which under German law means that there is no imprisonment but the perpetrator is placed under observation).[61] The paltry number of judgments is partly due to reservations many Germans have towards prosecuting the crimes of the DDR and partly due to the normal workings of democratic justice systems. Proving guilt "beyond a shadow of a doubt" is more important than exacting some form of abstract justice or revenge.

In addition to the legal actions and Eppelmann's commission, the Federal government established an agency to manage public release of the Stasi files since there was a call for opening the files. Headed by the former East German dissident minister Reverend Gauck, Federal Deputy for Secret Service Documents, the agency was charged with releasing files to Stasi victims who wished to see them. Again, the hope was that by enabling people to read their files, the government would promote understanding and closure without exacting revenge. The Stasi had kept files on 6 million of the 18 million East Germans as well as prominent West Germans. The sheer volume of paper used to record people's lives and secrets was astonishing – "over 125 miles of shelf space, with each mile containing about 17 million sheets of paper and weighing nearly 50 tons."[62] The legislation opening the Stasi files was controversial and many argued that the explosive nature of the files made them more destructive than constructive. Nevertheless, Members of Parliament from East Germany felt that opening the files would deliver a kind of justice, and help to cleanse the historical record, so they persuaded the Bundestag to declare each Stasi file the property of the person on whom it was kept.[63] The type of transparency resulting from this action was soon undermined by the court decision in the case of ex-Chancellor Helmut Kohl that prominent persons' files have to be closed to the public and to further inquiry. In other words, even in the case of the Stasi record transparency was to be partial only.

The eerie aspect of confronting the "other" is most deeply felt when examining the role of the Stasi. East Germans were well aware that the Stasi was dangerous, but the extent and nature of their operations were largely unknown. "I am coming out of a labyrinth where there is hardly any light, only blackness, foul smells, and filth piled upon filth," says poet, folk singer and former dissident, Wolfgang Biermann, "The Stasi's methods were unbelievable. If I had known this when I lived in East Berlin, I would have gone mad."[64] The Stasi used agents to try to break up marriages, indoctrinate children, destroy careers, even sap the physical and mental health of people thought to be dangerous to the state. Writer Lutz Rathenow points to the omnipresent "other" in East German society in his book *Berlin-East: The Other Side of a City*. Paradoxically, the Stasi once upbraided Rathenow for using the notion of the "other" in a satirical way. "I forbid you to write poems with double meanings!" an officer shouted at Rathenow. "Also poems with triple meanings! We have experts who can decipher everything."[65] The disclosures reveal another ironic aspect to life in the former GDR – the ever-present double. People in every society have a public face and a private one, but in the

Die Kluft zwischen Ost und West:
die bipolare Welt
Karikatur von Bruce Russel, 1945,
für ›Los Angeles Times‹

4.1
Clipping from a
contemporary American
newspaper illustrating
the degree of separation
and hostility between
the East and the West.
Photographer: Axel Föhl.

GDR, the difference between public and private faces was often extreme. Worse, the private face was not always benign; it may have been an instrument of the Stasi.

Revelations from the Stasi files can destroy a person's future even though they do not take into account the degree of complicity or the pressures exerted on former East German citizens to inform on one another. Moreover, many are painful and not necessarily constructive. Marriages, friendships, and trust have all been broken by archival revelations.[66] CDU leader Lothar de Maizière was forced to leave politics after his dealings with the Stasi were made public; bobsledder Harald Czuldaj continued with his sports career but had his name dragged through the press; while writer Sascha Anderson's career and friendships have been ruined by public exposure. MP Gerhard Riegge hung himself on February 16, 1992 after it was reported that he had been a Stasi collaborator.[67] Many East Germans

are still grappling with the competing desires for retribution and moral accountability versus the pain and havoc opening the files can cause. In addition, East Germans are suffering from the same kind of amnesia that afflicted West Germans in the aftermath of the Second World War. West Germans spent 20 years after the war avoiding a full confrontation with the truth about National Socialism. A real examination of the issues occurred only after the generational shift of the 1960s when young West Germans began to demand information from their parents and grandparents. Interest in investigating the past is likewise accelerating 10 years after unification as the passage of time puts distance and allows historical perspective. Applications to see Stasi files rose to 15,000 a month in 1999 from a mere trickle when they were first opened. "It's the same story as in 1945, partial amnesia is followed by awakening. I believe the real wave of interest and generational conflict are still to come."[68] At the moment, East Germans are on the path to confronting their past. The assessment and coming to terms with that past is going to be essential to building a common future.

4.2
Clipping from a contemporary American newspaper illustrating the fears of the Eastern bloc.
Photographer: Axel Föhl.

III

International interpretations of German political identity after unification were no less complicated than those at home. In a now infamous discussion between former Prime Minister Margaret Thatcher, Foreign Minister Douglas Hurd, and well-known historians such as Gordon Craig and Timothy Garton Ash, over how the British should respond to imminent German unification, the British laid bare their conflicting feelings. Advisers were torn between historical memory of Germany's ugly past and Great Britain's suffering at Germany's hands, and the memory of West Germany's successes over the intervening 50 years. In the end, the council advised support for German unification, with reservations:"... we should be nice to the Germans. But even the optimists had some unease, not for the present and immediate future, but for what might lie further down the road than we can yet see."[69] Many of the French criticized Chancellor Kohl for the way he pursued unification without, in their view, properly consulting with his French neighbors. Some articles in the French press warned of the return of "the Boche," the imperialist German of the past. French political scientist Alfred Grosser pointed to the source of French fears and resentments – on the one hand, a memory of Germany's past transgressions, on the other, French distress at the prospect of losing its political importance in the wake of a stronger Germany.[70] In an article for the *New York Times* written in March of 1990, correspondent Alan Riding reports French and British concerns about their diminishing political influence in the face of a unified Germany.[71] Riding also discusses the reactions of other German neighbors both to the East and West that initially opposed unification, but already by spring of 1990 had come to accept it. These include the Netherlands, Belgium, and Italy. Contrary to France and Great Britain, who saw German unity as a potential threat to their national political power abroad, some of the smaller states saw the return of a strong Germany as the only guarantee against further political destabilization in the East. The divisions so apparent in German society, then, have their parallels elsewhere – unification is both bad and good.

Transparency in the aftermath of unification is two-sided: on the one hand it reflects the positive achievements of German democracy since 1948; on the other, it reveals the tensions of the new society. Transparency to history is neither wholly embraced nor wholly possible after unification. Although both East and West Germans have examined some of the past, that examination is limited and will probably continue to be so until another generation or two intervene between the present and history. Nevertheless, transparency is a metaphor for the openness to the historical truth unification made possible as well as for the openness to the "other." In architectural terms, the metaphor translates to an analogy with similar connotations at Norman Foster's Reichstag, a building whose most interesting aspect is its confrontation with history, both political and architectural. Like transparency in its earlier iterations, however, transparency after unification is a myth; it represents a desire for conditions that do not, and most probably cannot, exist.

Chapter 5

A metaphor for the new Germany

"Germany Builds!" And just behind that lurks, rarely concealed, the question, "But how?" And the answer can, yes it must be open: here wonderfully, there questionably!

Theodor Heuss.[1]

On September 21, 1949 the German Parliament moved into its newly reno-vated provisional home at the old Pedagogical Academy on the campus of Bonn University. In a scant nine months, the architect for the project, Hans Schwippert, had managed to fully renovate the old part of the building, and construct an addition to house the plenary chamber (Figure 5.1). Schwippert boldly declared his building the "first modern parliament building" explaining the transparency he used throughout the project as reflective of the goals of the new West German democracy.[2] Seen in the light of Adenauer's famous mantra, "No Experiments!" Hans Schwippert's project for the first plenary chamber at Bonn Pedagogical Academy can be read as the attempt to realize an invisible, self-effacing building metaphorically tied to West Germany's psyche in 1949. The Bundeshaus can also be read as an audacious experi-ment, as the first architectural attempt to assign meaning to the new regime – by constructing an analogy for democratic government as open, accessible, honest, fragile, egalitarian, and above all, transparent. Ultimately, the project is the first to demonstrate the mythological nature of transparent ideology for in spite of its use of material, spatial, and formal transparency the building is still very much physically present and perceptible while transparency in the political realm was limited at best. Transparency exists intermittently but is never whole or perfect.

5.1
**View of the
completed
Bundeshaus from
the Rhine River,
1949.**
Schwippert Archiv,
Germanisches
Nationalmuseum,
Nuremberg.

Schwippert was not the only one to recognize the uniqueness of his achievement; writers for the international architecture press as well as for the Allied military governments extolled the project's appropriateness. The *Picture Post*, the official paper of the British military in Germany, described the Bundeshaus as "the outward and visible token of a fresh start. The visitor's first impression is reassuring. Here, he feels, is a complete break with Nazi and traditional German architecture, a total rupture of the heavy brigade tradition."[3] The *Picture Post* suggests a close correlation between the new political order in Germany and Schwippert's transparent architecture. At the same time, the article posits the German parliament as a symbolic antithesis to the negative aspects of German history. The *Picture Post* caption appears beneath a photograph showing the members of the newly convened Bundestag in their chamber. In the background stands a tremendous, transparent, floor-to-ceiling glass wall – the courtyard and greenery beyond are clearly visible. The delegates appear diminutive in comparison to the scale of the wall, almost insignificant. The image makes the German landscape in the background, and the glass partition separating inside from outside, appear more important than the elected officials themselves. That is, the see-through wall is as physically present as any other wall would be except that in this case, it is possible to see the landscape through it while perceiving its mass and presence. Strangely, while Schwippert's notion of transparency reflects many of the stated goals of the three occupying powers and the German Parliamentary Council for the new government, Schwippert was the first person to use "transparency" to

107

describe the new German democracy, or to adopt transparency as the analogy for the new political system and for the new German political identity.

I

How did Schwippert develop his approach to design, one that was stylistically so close to the Neues Bauen, but ideologically original? Educated first at the conservative Technical University in Darmstadt, and then at the Technical University in Stuttgart, his first real exposure to innovative design came when he worked for Erich Mendelsohn in Berlin between 1924 and 1925. Interestingly, Schwippert took Richard Neutra's place in Mendelsohn's office when Neutra left for the United States.[4] While no essays or letters survive from the period, it is obvious from Schwippert's sketching style how profoundly impressed he was with Mendelsohn's ideas and design approach.[5] Schwippert's drawings assumed the dynamic aspect of Mendelsohn's expressionist sketches using the same thick, broad, sweeping strokes, impressionist and minimalist technique. It was during the same period that Schwippert met and befriended a group of avant-garde Berlin architects including Mies van der Rohe, with whom he maintained a lifelong relationship. For Schwippert's seventieth birthday *Festschrift* Mies wrote,

> Naturally this understanding (between Schwippert and Mies) deepened over the years more and more. It was the attention to mutual efforts; to clarify the situation and to discover a passable way from which new building developments could unfold; that always reinforced our relationship. At the end it was the deep conviction based on a mutually high sense of architectural responsibility in these times that connected us so closely.[6]

From Mies' letter, and from comments Schwippert himself made in several speeches over the years extolling Mies' work as exemplary, it is possible to infer that Schwippert owed a debt to Mies as well.[7] Schwippert's commitment to simplicity and straightforward massing and his fascination with steel and glass construction are just a few examples of concerns he shared with Mies. The other architect who clearly influenced Schwippert was Rudolf Schwarz, the distinguished German church designer. Schwippert worked for Schwarz for seven years between 1927 and 1934. Afterwards, Schwippert quoted Schwarz and referred to his ideas on many occasions. In fact, like Mies, Schwarz and his wife Maria remained lifelong friends of Schwippert. From Schwarz, Schwippert likely took an interest in the mystical side of architecture (something Mies also shared). Schwippert's design work from 1926 onward confirms his movement in a contemporary direction, building massing becomes increasingly simpler, material use tends more and more to white stucco, glass, and steel, and the space planning is more open, although plenty of his designs remain traditional looking. It is important to note, however, that Schwippert's full conversion to a contemporary esthetic is only fully evident after the Second World War when he became an outspoken champion for the new architecture.

Just what were the basic concepts informing Schwippert's esthetic views? To answer this complicated question with a simple answer would be dishonest since there is no single answer. To begin with, from the 1920s Schwippert's essays betray a belief in the necessity of art in life, and of its mission to improve the quality of life for all men. "Everyone in his work and also in the crafts must bring a high degree of performance to his work. (Artists) are an indispensable, highly responsible, but not privileged piece of the human society. . . ."[8] Further,

> I do not believe that Art is a special area of human work. I do not believe that Art is of a higher order than certain workaday presence, of certain human endeavors, or of certain areas of human work, but I do believe that we should use the title Art for all completed human work. We correctly speak of the art of cooking as we do of the art of painting, the sacred arts and diplomacy, and I am not for continuing the isolation that Art brought in the last century because man set it on a special pedestal . . .[9]

The speeches echo many of the ideas championed by the German avant-garde in the 1920s and 1930s, where art is no longer considered the special preserve of the elite, but rather for all people and all human endeavors. Schwippert's list includes some unusual entries: the healing arts, speech, play, and statesmanship, along with expected ones like building construction, painting, and music.[10]

Schwippert did not confine his thinking to the relationship between art and those making it, he also thought deeply about the meaning of art, the way it should be realized, and what it should embody. By the time he received the Bundeshaus commission, Schwippert had developed many of the concepts manifested in his mature architectural work. To begin with, Schwippert believed, as did Mies and Goethe, that "Visual artists do not speak or write."[11] Rather, the work should speak for itself; its meaning should be clearly embedded in its form and structure so that neither the artist's presence, nor his explication would be necessary to read the piece. Schwippert's down-to-earth, egalitarian notions of what art is are balanced by a mystical attitude that often equates artistic production with aspects from religion, especially from

Catholicism. In a letter to Hugo Kükelhaus, written before the Second World War, Schwippert identifies the artistic trinity: Material, Form, and Content as the foundation for the arts. He calls the trio the "mysterium trinitatis," a clear reference to the Holy Trinity that suggests the trio's importance. Following the general definition is a three-part list of the constituent parts of each category:

Material	Form	Content
Looking for Material	Looking for Form	Looking for Content
Energetic Order	Moral Order	Mystical Order
Father	Son	Ghost
Nonexistent	Becoming	Being
World	Man	God
Origin	Time	Eternity
Unsolved	Solution	Solved
Emptiness	Vessel	Fullness
Apprentice	Journeyman	Master
Learning	Understanding	Inventing
Persistence	Patience	Courage
Justness	Courage	Restraint
Love	Hope	Belief
Exit	Way	Goal
Not Become	Becoming	Become
Darkness	Chiaroscuro	Light
Childhood	Youth	Old age
Need to express material	Need to express form	Need to express value
Groping	Forming	Fulfilling[12]

Schwippert's list represents his attempt to order the creative world. Besides the obvious references to Christian ideology in the tripartite division of Schwippert's categories and naming of the "Father, Son and Holy Ghost," there are references to contemporary philosophy and architectural theory in such categories as "Material, Form and Content," "Nonexistent, Becoming and Being," and "Not Becoming, Becoming and Become." The synthesis focuses the creative act on making something meaningful from nothing. It presents art as the movement from dark and groping ignorance to fulfilling light, in a progression that suggests the long path to mature design. Importantly for the Bundeshaus project, the list posits light as the highest goal of artistic production.

In a series of notes made to himself dated Easter, 1943, Schwippert attempts to outline a broad philosophical basis for his work.[13] In an apparent contradiction with his later writings, Schwippert identifies art as the "absolute highest rank of human works, fixed through Form [and] Creative Character" and asserts that, "artists are the agents of the true world order."[14] Schwippert writes that Form is

> not the writing of pictures from "reality," but beyond (and the means to)
> appearance
> to make the original picture (archetypes) visible
> the eternal example.[15]

Schwippert's note could be interpreted to mean that the mission of form is to create an analogy to something outside and different from the form. This outside thing should be a universal concept, perhaps an original concept in the sense that Goethe and Wilhelm von Humboldt meant the term. To use Schwippert's phrase, the form should not be "pictures of reality, but beyond appearance." Equally important are Schwippert's phrases: "original picture (archetypes)" and "eternal example." By these, Schwippert seems to mean the essence of a form. That is, one purpose of creating form, of making art, is to reveal the essence of something, the inner life that is beyond the visible. When he writes, later in the piece, that one of his aims is "to make the cosmic structure visible, to make it realizable," Schwippert reaffirms the mission of art as making the unseen seeable.[16] Perhaps the most important clause in Schwippert's essay is the one in which he writes, "thinking in an artistic way is to: Show visually, visualize, be visually aware, have imagination, and see the connection between things."[17] For the first three characteristics, Schwippert uses the German words based on "*Bild*" – "*Bildhaftes Schauen*," "*Bildmachung*," and "*Bildbewusstsein*." In German, "*Bild*" means "image," "picture," or "representation."[18] Thus, Schwippert's dictum could just as easily be translated as "Thinking in an artistic way is to: show pictorially, make a picture (or image), be aware of an image, have imagination, and see connections between things." When taken together, the notes describe the belief that artistic production should be based in images, or in some invisible essence, and that it should be timeless. Schwippert may also be suggesting that artworks create analogies, ideal representations of the world, when they reveal the "connections between things."

Schwippert's later writing confirms his interest in image and analogy since it is the device he uses to structure entire texts. In 1943, five years before he received the Bundeshaus commission, Schwippert already tested his ideas about transparency using analogies he would shortly develop more fully. Schwippert established the relationship between glass and value, between transparency and architecture:

> As to glass: Glass is melted sand. More than that? One knows that sand is granulated crystal, often crushed granules of semi-precious stone, from which one finds the origins of clarity, transparency (*Durchsichtigkeit*) and the gleam of glass and every origin and quality that is an obstacle to extreme abuse.[19]

In 1952 he drafted a defense of the Bundeshaus project that was published in 1952/1953, largely based on analogical parallels.[20] The essay was entitled *"Glück und Glas"* ("Happiness and Glass"), a paraphrase of the poet and mystic Paul Scheerbart's famous rhyming couplets for Bruno Taut's Werkbund Exhibition Pavilion (1914) (see Chapter 2).[21] The title also comes from a German saying, *"Glück und Glas, wie leicht bricht das,"* (Happiness breaks as easily as glass). Thus, by using this title Schwippert simultaneously associated his argument with fragility and transparency. Schwippert's *"Glück und Glas"* was more than an essay, it was a manifesto for postwar architecture, in particular for his parliamentary project. In his piece, Schwippert uses a series of associations to enumerate the argument for transparency. Although *"Glück und Glas"* seems to be the only piece of this kind Schwippert ever wrote, Schwippert's work after 1950 continues to manifest the principles outlined in the essay. Furthermore, in numerous speeches he delivered from 1951 onwards, Schwippert returned to the transparency theme, albeit in a less dogmatic and less poetic manner.[22] While there is no documentary evidence to explain what prompted Schwippert to author *"Glück und Glas,"* it is probable that he felt compelled to defend the Bundeshaus (see Appendix 4). The international architecture press received the design with favorable reviews but the German architecture press was mixed. The more liberal journals, such as *Neue Bauwelt*, gave the project positive reviews echoing the architect's explanation for his design decisions.[23] But some architecture journals, like the conservative *Baumeister*, simply ignored the building or panned it for its technical shortcomings. Most of the reviews agreed upon the unique approach Schwippert had taken – an approach that demanded an explanation of some sort.

The architecture Schwippert argues for in *"Glück und Glas"* embodies the optimism and openness of both life and politics in the new German Federal Republic in a fragile, transparent envelope. "We love the other side – openness, sensitivity, transparency, want light not darkness, want freedom not frightened caution!"[24] The analogy calls to mind the political, economic, and social uncertainties of 1940s West Germany. Schwippert calls for glass walls, light construction of steel and reinforced concrete, cheerful design, buildings free from massiveness, darkness, and false decor.[25] His hope is that the awareness of the metaphors and analogies he uses, and their opposites, will have a positive effect on people.

Because our dream so desired it, we have won: [the freedom] to float on air, to hear distant voices, to see distant things, to construct filigree, to look through glass walls, to open doors without moving the hand . . . We will not stop living life because it dies; desiring happiness because it is fleeting; or building with glass because it breaks.[26]

Schwippert concludes his manifesto on a profoundly optimistic note: we can live with fragility.

II

It is not completely clear how Schwippert received the commission for the Bundeshaus. There is no surviving correspondence before the project began, and there was no public search for an architect or national competition as there was for both the 1980s Bundeshaus project and the 1990s Reichstag renovation, although the written contract for Schwippert's project dated November 3, 1948 survives in the Schwippert Archiv.[27] The contract is between Schwippert and the state of North Rhine Westphalia. The signatory for the state of North Rhine Westphalia is the Minister for Reconstruction, Konrad Rühl. According to the terms of the contract, Schwippert was to "plan the enlargement of the gymnasium at the Pedagogical Academy in Bonn as a provisional meeting room."[28] A second, later contract dated August 26, 1949 is even more specific about the work, naming the project the Bundeshaus.[29] Schwippert knew Adenauer, Wandersleb, and Rühl before he started work on the Bundeshaus.[30] He had met them during his stint as director of the Abteilung Wideraufbau des Oberpräsidiums Nordrhein Provinz (Department of Reconstruction of the High Presidium of North Rhine Westphalia), Düsseldorf in 1945, the position later assumed by Wandersleb.[31] Further, Schwippert came from a similar background to Adenauer, from a devout Rhenish Catholic family. As has already been mentioned, Schwippert had worked for seven years with the famous German church architect Rudolf Schwarz, and Schwippert's writing about architecture in the 1930s reflects the religious and mystical influences on his thinking. Although Schwippert remained in Germany during the National Socialist period, he did not join the party, and seems to have stayed remote from party patronage. Like most Catholics, he was probably deeply suspicious of the Nazis.[32] Also importantly, he had been a member of the Werkbund which he helped re-establish after the war. While it is not certain whether or not Schwippert's background helped him secure the job, it certainly did not hurt his case. Finally, some documents survive concerning the controversial Bundeskanzlerhaus commission for the

Palais Schaumburg renovation. Apparently the former Ministry Director Dr Wandersleb approached Schwippert on behalf of the government and made a verbal contract for the project.[33] Most likely it was Wandesleb who approached Schwippert and asked him to take on the Bundeshaus as well.

Although it is not certain why Schwippert was chosen over other architects for the renovation of the Pedagogical Academy, the decision to go ahead with a project was clearly a political ploy on the part of Wandersleb, Adenauer, and Karl Arnold, Minister President from Bonn. Beginning in 1948 the press is full of speculation as to which West German city will become the capital after a new government is formed. At one point, as many as five different cities were vying for the honor: Berlin, Bonn, Frankfurt, Kassel, and Stuttgart, but by spring 1949 only two were in serious contention: Bonn and Frankfurt. As early as January 1949 an article appeared in the *Rheinische Zeitung* under one of Schwippert's early sketch studies for the Bundeshaus.[34] The article's title reads, "Thus will the enlarged Pedagogical Academy appear . . . if Bonn becomes the Federal seat." Strangely, the article does not credit Schwippert or even mention him by name but it does suggest the behind-the-doors politicking that must have been going on. Having a building ready to receive the newly elected officials would no doubt strengthen the case for Bonn. And Frankfurt was engaged in similar activities readying buildings for the parliament in the event it became capital city![35] In December 1949 Wandersleb thanked Schwippert for his help securing the vote for Bonn, writing "that without your pragmatic help and readiness for work, the push for Bonn would never have been able to win. . . ."[36] The state government of North Rhine Westphalia paid the building costs with the intention of giving the Pedagogical Academy to the federal government in the event that Bonn became the capital city, otherwise the plan was to use the building for the state administration.[37]

It is equally possible that Schwippert obtained the commission by force of argument, by presenting Adenauer and Wandersleb with an image for the new seat of West German government that, at least partially, mirrored Adenauer's picture for the postwar West German state. The piece of the puzzle that is hard to grasp is how Schwippert's esthetic could appeal to Adenauer. Adenauer personally chose the building for the Chancellor's Ministry, picking the historic, neo-baroque Palais Schaumburg. During the highly public controversy over restoration of the Palais Schaumburg, Adenauer refused to let Schwippert install the contemporary furnishings he had chosen for the Palais, hiring an antique dealer instead to provide more traditional objects. According to an article in the *Kölner Stadt-Anzeiger*, Schwippert chose furniture he believed would be "to the entire world of experts recognizable signs of a healthy democracy."[38] The rhetoric was in keeping with Schwippert's claims for his parliamentary architecture and, esthetically, the furniture was similar to pieces Schwippert had already used for the Bundeshaus. In fact, this makes the event stranger still because by the time Schwippert was working on the Palais Schaumburg, his taste must have been apparent to Adenauer. Furthermore, as mayor of Cologne Adenauer had quite a number of "modernist" architects working for the city on public housing projects such as Wilhelm Riphahn so he certainly knew what the "modern" esthetic was.[39] Why did Adenuaer accept that taste for one project but not the other? Unfortunately, Adenauer's reaction to the furniture went beyond dislike, to hatred. He "did not feel the democratic symbolism, and found the things (Schwippert) obtained loathsome," so he sent them all back![40] Adenauer particularly objected to furnishing an older building with contemporary objects, something he felt was highly inappropriate. Adenauer had special objections to Schwippert's design for an executive desk, preferring his own, traditional, desk instead. In his letter to Schwippert explaining his position Adenauer wrote, "You are not responsible, but I am responsible. And when you believe that you cannot bring your conviction into harmony with my desires, then nothing remains for us but to find another solution."[41] Clearly, Adenauer wanted Schwippert to understand who was boss in all governmental matters, even esthetic ones!

Given Adenauer's conservative tastes, it is surprising that he would choose an architect firmly committed to contemporary design for the Bundeshaus project, unless he believed that in the case of a building so representative of the new Federal Republic's political and national identity, a non-traditional image was needed. Perhaps Schwippert's vision for the parliament was indeed the decisive factor in the Bundeshaus commission. Perhaps he was able to convince Adenauer and Wandersleb that a contemporary design was the only appropriate one to choose for the new Germany; that openness, transparency, and light were the proper analogies for the new democracy.

III

Schwippert's first task was to determine an appropriate image for the seat of the new German democracy. As his assistant and interior designer Wera Meyer-Waldeck pointed out, "Rebuilding does not mean building anew, but giving form to a new way of life and a new spirit."[42] Newness was as much in Schwippert's mind as otherness – an architecture that could not be associated with the Third Reich, reflective of a political system that could not be tied to Nazism. With the Bundeshaus, he wrote, "we have gone well beyond the Wilhelmine and National Socialism. It was important to find a new approach and to make rooms that in themselves allow most people to remain true to their essential drives."[43] In other words, this architecture was not supposed to force itself and a message on the visitor but to encourage the visitor to be open about his or her beliefs. Schwippert described the problem in terms similar to Hannes Meyer's description of his design for the League of Nations project: "politics is a dark affair. Let's see that we shed some light upon it."[44] Schwippert wrote that from the start he wanted to design a light-filled building in order to create an inspirational and uplifting environment for parliament, a place that was completely different from what he viewed as the dark state buildings of the past. Light-filled architecture meant using as much window surface as possible, hence the transparency. In his manifesto Schwippert also wrote that "We love the other side . . . light not darkness. . . ."[45] Light in art and literature is traditionally associated with goodness, openness, know-ledge, illumination, and enlightenment; while the light of the sun makes heat; associations that make light a positive attribute.[46] For those who might not accept the metaphoric associations between light and goodness, the undeni-able benefits of better natural light inside a building were a strong argument for Schwippert's approach. But material transparency alone was not the only goal; Schwippert wished to imbue his project with an exceptional, inspiring quality. "The walls and rooms should have neither sentimental nor political pathos but deepen the self-confidence and spirituality."[47] He hoped to do this using non-representational means, by designing an open, light-filled building whose spatial and formal qualities would be self-evident. Even the non-architectural press of the day seems to have understood and sympathized with his goals. The *Westdeutsche Zeitung* called the Bundeshaus "A building without deceptions or allegory. . . ." praising its lack of symbolism and iconographic program.[48]

Schwippert wrote that state architecture should demonstrate the openness and fragility of the state along with the fact that political power emanated from the people rather than the authority of one personality, all of which are principles embodied in the constitution, the Basic Law (see Chapter 3).[49] Schwippert's approach has, therefore, been read as a literal trans-lation of Article 42 of the Basic Law and another fundamental clause that defines Germany as "an open society of democrats."[50] In this schema, demo-cratic openness comes from free access to parliament and from the freedom to participate, to share one's views. Although access is not the same thing as transparency, access can facilitate transparency and certainly free access gives the impression of transparency by making it appear to be easy to approach and speak with MPs and participate in the parliamentary proceed-ings. The problem with this notion is that it represents an abstract ideal but not the reality of an everyday parliament. Neither access to parliament nor public expression of views during sessions has ever been possible in West Germany. With the exception of the open house in September 1949, which was an invitation to all West Germans to visit the parliament building but not a working session of parliament, attendance at the parliament has been by invitation and application from the start. Furthermore, attending a Bundestag session never meant the opportunity to speak out, or question the MPs, but silent and respectful observation of the proceedings!

Hans Schwippert's design for the Bundeshaus developed quickly during the nine-month period allotted for design development and execution. The program called for renovating, and adding on to, the old Pedagogical Academy of Bonn University sited near the Rhine between Bonn and Bad Godesberg. Since the government itself was provisional, the building had to be altered with future uses in mind, specifically the possible conversion of the plenary chamber into a congress hall or concert hall.[51] This approach necessitated a certain anti-governmental esthetic for the building otherwise it would not be suitable to receive another program later on. From the start, most of the elements used in the final version are apparent: the plenary chamber, restaurant, and office spaces for the delegates. The new plenary chamber sits in its own volume, an almost square form attached to the older building (Figure 5.2). In surviving three-dimensional study sketches, the additions have the signature glass façades on two sides of the chamber – the one facing the same inner courtyard onto which the restaurant opened and the other facing the landscape (Figures 5.3 and 5.4). In the earliest sketches from January 1949, these elements are drawn as a continuous extension of the existing structure, a kind of prosthesis reaching out into the landscape.[52] In the next set of sketches dating from February 1949, the extension is even longer since it has an office block added onto it. Another set of drawings from February 1949 shows the version Schwippert built, a grouping of additions to the older building, placed around an exterior courtyard on the Rhine side (Figure 5.5). The final version was a much more compact agglomeration of structures that skillfully combined the new construction with the existing building so that it was difficult, if not impossible, to see where the old ended and new began.

Most of the studies are remarkable for their ordinariness and lack of architectural distinction. Executed in thick lead and charcoal strokes similar to the sketches Schwippert had made years before while working for Mendelsohn, the drawings explore massing strategies, but not spatial qualities, nor do they investigate transparency, a surprising fact given the importance Schwippert assigned to transparency in his defense of the project after it was complete. In fact, the drawings make the initial schemes look quite solid and opaque, not transparent at all. The only concession to open form occurs in the compositions whose radiating boxes are decidedly Elementarist.

Schwippert did study transparency in the project, but from the inside, not the outside, in a set of interior perspective sketches but above all in one surviving sketch of the plenary chamber (Figure 5.6). Like his other

117

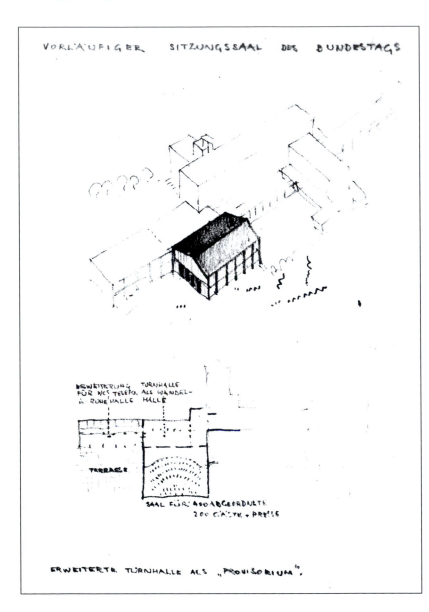

5.2
Early sketch study for the Bundeshaus.
Schwippert Archiv, Architecture Museum, Technical University (TU), Munich.

drawings, there is nothing remarkable about the style with which Schwippert executed his sketch, as in the drawings Mies van der Rohe began to produce in the 1920s. But, unlike his massing studies for the building volumes that were rendered in a monolithic manner, with heavy dark strokes, this sketch is drawn with filigree, barely discernible, pencil lines.[53] This conceptual sketch from the Schematic Design phase shows three walls that appear to be transparent.[54] One shows the repetitive mullion structure he used in the built version, while the other two walls appear to be giant transparent curtains, almost totally dematerialized surfaces. The illusion is created because the lines

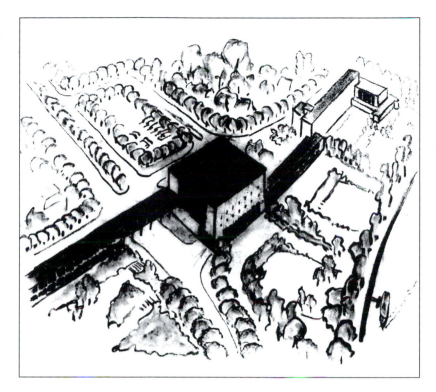

5.3
Massing study for the Bundeshaus.
Schwippert Archiv, Architecture Museum, TU, Munich.

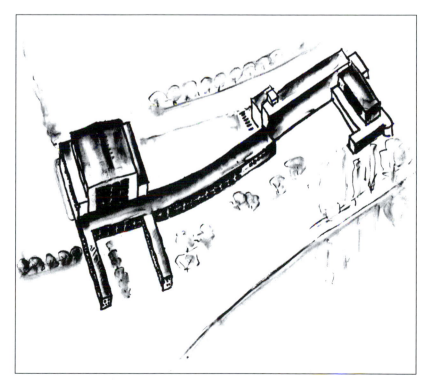

5.4
Massing study for the Bundeshaus showing a much more complicated arrangement of building volumes than earlier sketches.
Schwippert Archiv, Architecture Museum, TU, Munich.

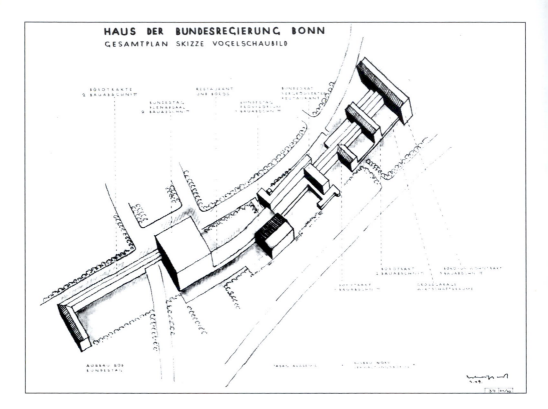

HAUS DER BUNDESREGIERUNG BONN
GESAMTPLAN SKIZZE VOGELSCHAUBILD

used to generate the free-hand perspective are visible through the sketch, the construction lines are preserved as extensions into the outside space and defining surfaces are all left white so that there is virtually no difference between interior space, surface, and exterior space. Schwippert's drawing technique uses delicate, sometimes barely perceptible, overlapping lines to enhance the illusion of transparency. The drawing makes the room appear light and weightless at the same time making the exterior seem to lack presence or personality. Enclosure is minimized. It may be that Schwippert did not intend these surfaces to be see-through at all but the way the drawing is made emphasizes the notion of the chamber as a light, almost invisible, space, making the sketch emblematic of the larger goals for the building. The transparent quality in the sketch makes the architecture dramatically less substantial than the actual building was.[55]

Schwippert's interpretation of openness to mean "transparency" has several nuances, some of which relate directly to material, spatial, and formal transparency. He was committed to an unpretentious, anti-monumental architecture that would seem common, and everyday, rather than grand, and pompous. Anti-monumentality was attractive because it was the natural opposite to the traditional monumental scale of state architecture and, for Schwippert's generation, the scale of many of the National Socialist projects.

5.5
The most complex surviving massing study for the Bundeshaus.
Schwippert Archiv, Architecture Museum, TU, Munich.

5.6
Sketch study of transparency in the plenary chamber.
Schwippert Archiv, Architecture Museum, TU, Munich.

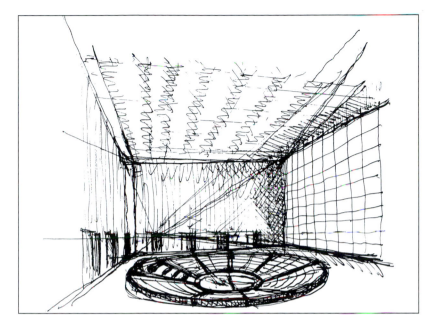

Even more, anti-monumentality implies a kind of open architectural structure, rather than a closed form, and would therefore support the Neues Bauen approach to design, over classical and neo-classical models. In the case of Schwippert's project, the building envelope was made open to views, and formally open, in the same way that the radiating forms of the Neues Bauen can be called open. The building volumes are articulated according to individual function and organized around the plenary chamber on the one hand, and the inner courtyard on the other (Figure 5.7). Buildings constructed with the fragile transparent material glass and covered with white stucco seemed especially anti-monumental in contrast with the stone typically used in monumental construction. Schwippert was also firmly against ornamentation, preferring to make a simple form whose construction materials and systems, combined with unimpeded visual connections with the surrounding German landscape, constituted the visual interest. The lack of ornamentation was in keeping with his belief in abstraction in architecture, in making architecture "beyond the writing of reality." Successful abstraction in art and architecture is transparent, that is open to interpretation, in that it is readable without any special knowledge, accessible to everyone.[56] Where he needed some embellishment, such as art works, Schwippert favored non-representational, abstract art. If openness is part and parcel of transparency, then egalitarianism can be equated with social transparency because it is a condition in which society is open to everyone equally. Schwippert manifested his ideas for an egalitarian architecture in his proposal for a circular, non-hierarchical plenary chamber; the use of pluralistic images; the avoidance of pomposity in art

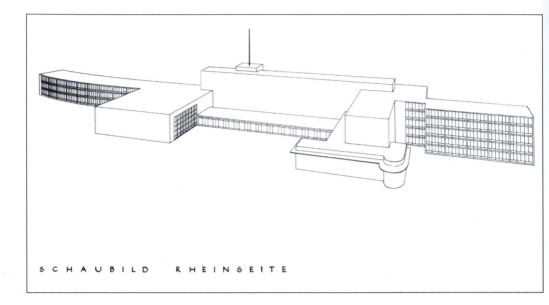

S C H A U B I L D   R H E I N S E I T E

objects decorating the landscape and architecture; informal promenade sequences; and simple furnishings. The chamber design was Schwippert's attempt to use architecture to correct some of the evils he perceived in the closed government by the few of the Nazi era by making the workings of government both visible and accessible. In other words, this architecture was not supposed to force itself and a message on the visitor but to encourage the visitor to be open about his or her beliefs. Perhaps most importantly, Schwippert recognized the importance of metaphor and analogy to architectural expression, using highly poetic and metaphorical language to defend his position. Taken together, the elements of Schwippert's state architecture begin to define a new national image – one of pluralistic, open, delicate, and fragile modern democracy. To realize his vision, Schwippert adopted the ideology of transparency as the guiding concept for his design.

In the constructed version of the parliament, Schwippert added to both sides of the old Pedagogical Academy Building, preserving the Academy intact. In keeping with the style of the original, Schwippert's additions are simple, rectangular forms, regulated by Golden Section proportions, with the exception of the square-shaped plenary chamber whose proportions are slightly more than a perfect square. Like Witte, Schwippert covered the solid building façades with white stucco, causing contemporary wags to refer to the new West German parliament as the "White House."[57] On one side, he appended a five-story office block to the foyer of an existing lecture hall. He used the restaurant as a connecting device between the old building on one side, and the volume housing the plenary chamber on the other. Then, he attached a second, lower, three-story office block to the other side of the

5.7
Axonometric drawing of the final design for the Bundeshaus.
Schwippert Archiv, Germanisches Nationalmuseum, Nuremberg.

plenary chamber. The large circulation spaces and spaces for social functions therefore act as the pivot points, or central spaces for the entire ensemble. Circulation both originates in these spaces, and culminates in them. Another way of reading the parti is to see the collective as the connection between branches of parliament and parliamentary functions. That is, in the schema, spaces for the collective are analogies for the West German public and are used as the focal points and references in a symbolic move that acts as a constant reminder that in an ideal democracy political power emanates from the people. The design represents the ideal and not the real because in the representative system, although the MPs rely on individual votes for election to office, power resides with wealthy interest groups and politicians in key governmental positions. A member of the general populace actually has very limited political power unless he or she is part of a larger group with financial resources and lobbying power.

5.8
**Entry floor
plan for the
Bundeshaus.**
Schwippert Archiv,
Germanisches
Nationalmuseum,
Nuremberg.

The composition forms an exterior courtyard on the Rhine side of the building (Figures 5.8 and 5.9). Because most of the volumes surrounding the outdoor space are glazed, the courtyard serves as the visual center of the building composition. In contrast with the later projects, the Bundeshaus by Behnisch and the Reichstag by Foster, where the visual center is the plenary

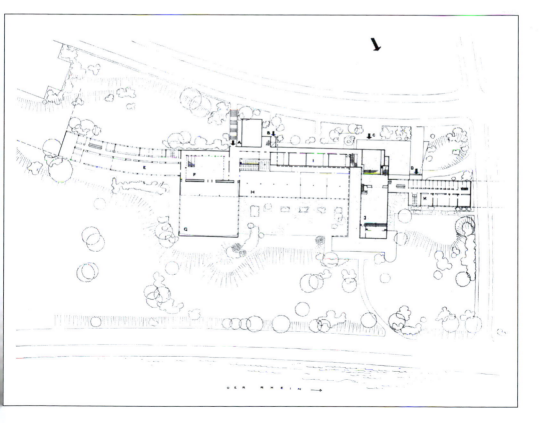

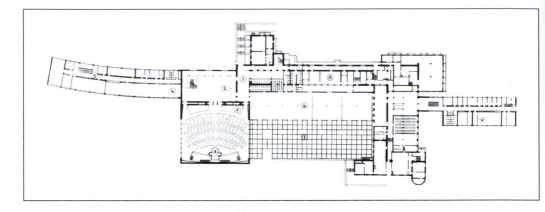

chamber, the green space serves this function for Schwippert's project. In this
way, Schwippert hoped to reinforce the connection between the people and
the land while diminishing the relative importance of parliament. In German,
earth is "*die Erde*," a mother principle not dissimilar from the female persona
the Earth assumes in other cosmogonies such as the Greek goddess Gaia.
She is the origin of life, nurturing, and healing, eminently different from
the nation, which is a masculine principle referred to as "the Fatherland." The
huge glass walls that face into the courtyard on one side and to the Rhine
garden on the other side make nature almost physically present inside the
building (Figure 5.10). As Schwippert writes, "Seven hundred men behind a
glazed wall, through which, beyond cheerful and colorful drapes, they perceive
the large terrace and the Rhine"[58] (Figure 5.11). The landscape is also a dominant presence around the building, from the pastoral Rhine walkway to the
suburban neighborhood surrounding the Bundeshaus. Because it is perceptible from so many spaces, from the lobby, the restaurant, the plenary
chamber, and many of the offices, nature becomes a part of the building and
part of the experience in it. In this way, Schwippert reaffirms the German connection to their land, especially to the Rhine, the mythical origin of the German
race. Seen from today's perspective and decades of progressive interest in the
relationship between building and landscape, Schwippert's approach seems
progressive. However, in the context of German history it is progressive and
reactionary at the same time; progressive when associated with the modern
movement, reactionary when compared to the Nazi use of the origin myth
in their "*Blut und Boden*" creed. "*Boden*" means "ground," and it was from
the ground that the superior German race supposedly sprang. Thus, this
aspect of Schwippert's argument would have appealed to a conservative
audience in the 1940s as much as, if not more than, to a progressive one.

Schwippert argued for transparency because he claimed that it was
an appropriate concept for the times. Transparent buildings are fragile like
"life, happiness and glass," he wrote. He designed large glass surfaces on

5.9
**Lower floor plan
showing the
plenary chamber.**
Schwippert Archiv,
Germanisches
Nationalmuseum,
Nuremberg.

5.11
**The plenary
chamber in 1952.**
Bundesbildstelle
Bonn.

5.10
**A view of the patio outside the restaurant addition, looking towards
the plenary chamber. Here, the glass appears to be opaque rather
than transparent.**
Schwippert Archiv, Germanisches Nationalmuseum, Nuremberg.

two façades of the plenary chamber to create physical transparency in the building envelope that would allow the proceedings to be observed from the outside. Not only do the glass surfaces extend from floor to ceiling but they are also highly articulated. The glazing units are set into the floor and ceiling at an angle making a wave-like form in plan, which was designed to improve the acoustics in the room.[59] In an unusual move, Schwippert placed bleachers outside the plenary chamber to encourage the public to sit and witness the parliament in session. This was important because the tribunes added to the sense of openness and accessibility Schwippert claimed for the building. Schwippert speaks in at least one interview about the parliament as a "House of Conversation," a phrase Behnisch also uses 50 years later.[60] The idea was to promote dialog between the general public seated outside and the MPs seated inside, a quality Schwippert took as part and parcel of a working democracy. In addition to the tribunes assembled outside the chamber, Schwippert outfitted the space with a loudspeaker system to make the proceedings audible from outside. In a famous photograph from the first day of parliament on September 7, 1949, a group of enthusiastic looking observers are shown seated and standing on the bleachers, waving their hands, and looking towards the open windows of the plenary chamber (Figure 5.12).[61] The bleachers did not remain for long, however, because they were a security concern. Access to the courtyard in front of the restaurant where they had been placed was soon restricted to parliamentarians and their guests. Visitors could only watch sessions from the interior balconies to which access was limited by both the small number of seats available and the vetting process. Furthermore, the architectural transparency was likewise limited. Only two of four walls were actually transparent glass; the other two were opaque. Even these two glass walls can hardly be called transparent in the sense of de-materialized because they were made of two layers of glass set in standard sized panes held by substantial frames so that the mullion system drew the eye. Long drapes were hung on the inside to keep the sun out, but effectively, they would keep curious viewers from looking in too. Even publicity photographs show them drawn shut – completely negating the transparent intent! Finally, the glass itself, like all glass, worked both as a see-through and as a reflective medium on the building's exterior. This too is evident in period photographs. In short, Schwippert's claims as to the building's physical transparency were greatly exaggerated.

In elevation, the older building appears subtly framed by the glazed surfaces of the new restaurant and the two new office wings (Figure 5.13). The elevations are, like the plans, rectangular forms oriented lengthwise parallel to the ground. Even at five stories, the buildings are lower than the surrounding trees, making them seem diminutive in scale. The repetitive banks of small punched windows reinforce the horizontal direction helping further

5.12
**People gathered
on the bleachers
outside the
plenary chamber
on the first day of
parliament,
September 7,
1949.**
Bundesbildstelle
Berlin.

establish the relationship between the Rhine and the building. The only compositional element that stands out is the volume holding the plenary chamber
because it, unlike its neighbors, is a large, blank, white stucco surface. On the
side of the public courtyard, Schwippert calls attention to the chamber by
glazing the entire 32-meter long façade, thereby rendering it visible because of
reflections on the glass but simultaneously making it completely see-through.
In this way, he signals the building's theme as the "house of openness,
an architecture of encounters and discussions."[62] Although the chamber's
presence is apparent on the Rhine elevation, there is no indication whatsoever
of it on the public street elevation, the south side of the building complex.
Thus Schwippert barely called attention to the parliamentary chamber.
Although its material contrasts with that of the adjacent façades, when viewed
from the north, the chamber is placed off to one side, and is smaller than
the central portion of the Bundeshaus complex. When seen in context, the
façade is so subtle that it can hardly be called monumental. Schwippert's
skilful and subtle handling of compositional forces on the façades underscores
the understated and anti-monumental quality. Even more importantly, the
manner in which he composed the north elevation renders the plenary
chamber, if not see-through, then transparent to view in the sense that it does
not attract attention. This is in keeping with the goal of making the seat of
parliament unassuming. The eye naturally moves right and left over this large
surface, resting on the more animated elevations of the two flanking wings
whose design makes them appear to hold more visual interest. But the kind of
transparency Schwippert describes in his writings is not apparent on these

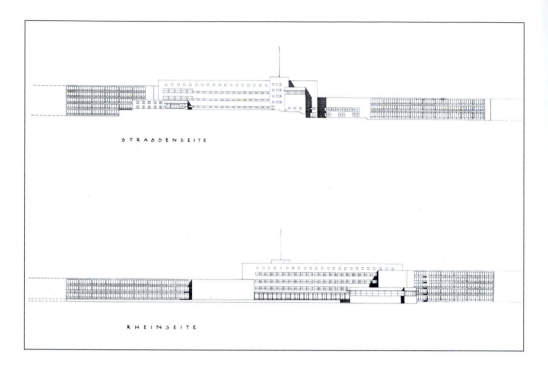

STRASSENSEITE

RHEINSEITE

elevations. When seen from afar, the windows appear to be black opaque surfaces rather than see-through ones, rendering the elevation impenetrable to view.

Schwippert made it clear that understatement, impermanence, anti-monumentality in addition to openness and transparency were intentional in his project and that these qualities worked together to the same ends.

> . . . this is a temporary house for the constitution of a new political life in Germany, I take temporary to be the correct approach so that this beginning has a light-filled house and a simple one, a contemporary house, and one that is open to the world.[63]

Schwippert expressed the tendency towards anti-monumentality in numerous ways in the design, not just in the material dissolution of the plenary chamber walls. As mentioned, the subtle and understated massing and façade development in no way resembled the historic model for a state building in Germany. Furthermore, Schwippert intentionally forsook the use of most devices associated with monumentality: a massive, single, solid building body, closed form, a colonnade, an over-scaled entrance, over-scaled architectonic elements like windows and doors, and symmetric treatment of formal elements. The main entry on the street side is so understated, inserted between the foyer for the plenary chamber, and the administrative wing, and marked

5.13
Elevation drawings for the Rhine Side and the Bonn Side of the Bundeshaus complex.
Schwippert Archiv, Germanisches Nationalmuseum, Nuremberg.

by a small, cantilevered concrete awning, that it is never included in press photographs documenting the building.

The lack of any ornament, symbolic sculpture, and allegorical decoration like that at the Reichstag was both as important as the anti-monumental character of the Bundeshaus and part of the esthetic that made the building seem so anti-monumental. The sculptural and ornamental programs at the Reichstag were carefully developed to communicate a series of messages to any visitor including the majesty of the Reich, the power of the state, and the qualities Germany was thought to embody at the time (see Chapter 7 for more detail). To these ends the building was decorated inside and out with statuary, in stark contrast to the unadorned plainness of Schwippert's building. In an article from the *Westdeutsche Zeitung* printed on September 7, 1949 and subtitled, "A Building without Pastiche and Allegory," the journalist writes that, "one can say that this is one of the few Parliaments that honestly tries to not hide itself behind patterns and allegories."[64] The author praises the lack of representational architecture that he, like Schwippert, takes for a sign of humanity in the building. The lack of ornamental program fits with Schwippert's desire for an abstract architecture, for in this atmosphere, the visitor must respond to the intangible qualities of space, spatial organization, and light.

In spite of Schwippert's claims for the architecture, contemporary critics did not remark on the transparency at the Bundeshaus, but many noted the lightness. *Bauen und Wohnen* (*Building and Living*) describes, "the objectivity, the practicality, and above all inner lightness that from the representatives of the Parliamentary Council themselves was adopted instead of the qualities of Wilhelmine Palace construction."[65] *Neue Bauwelt* cites the "light" and cheerful spaces that are everywhere in the project.[66] In a different article about the building, *Bauen und Wohnen* extols the "clear organization, lightness, simplicity, and rigor" as the "qualities notable in this building which, in the best sense, represent the new Germany."[67] It is interesting to consider the plenary chamber in the context of Schwippert's "mysterium trinitatis" where light represented the highest achievement and the ultimate goal of artistic production. By extension, a house of light must represent the ultimate in state architecture since according to this world-view there is nothing beyond the light. This too is an idealized view of the plenary chamber as a place where democratic illumination takes place, that is, illumination of the general public and mutual illumination of the representatives. Unfortunately, the general public has never had full enough access to the parliamentary sessions in order to become fully informed while parliamentarians attend with fixed points of view, so discussion rarely results in changed positions. The MPs use the debate as an opportunity to go on record supporting their point of view. More often than not, discussion results in some sort of a compromise between the two sides rather than one side illuminating the other.

Schwippert's focus on human scale and ordinary materials helps make the building understandable because it is familiar, comfortable, and not laden with hidden symbolism.

> The human feeling! The other rooms in the building, restaurant, foyer, and especially the offices and official corridors are concerned with it. The sound does not reverberate, is not hard and cold as in many offices for business and administration, and it is equally little swallowed up by dead means of representation. The rooms are especially designed for the human scale and a correct application of simple materials that are used for foyers, chief's rooms, sitting rooms, and meeting rooms.[68]

Schwippert designed common-looking, modern office furniture for the delegates' spaces as opposed to ornate, antique objects (Figure 5.14). He intentionally chose exactly the same furniture for every government employee, from secretaries to ministers to the President, in order to reinforce the egalitarian nature of democracy. Moreover, Schwippert's words echo the contemporary belief that Bonn was a temporary capital. Schwippert uses this fact to help justify the sparse furnishings and the egalitarian approach he used for appointing the various offices in the new building. Here again, there is nothing "representative," nothing elite, just sensible, everyday furnishings for the common man. Schwippert's approach suggests that the non-hierarchical way of furnishing the building represents the open, non-hierarchical nature of

5.14
A typical office with the furniture Schwippert chose.
Schwippert Archiv, Germanisches Nationalmuseum, Nuremberg.

5.15
View out to the courtyard from inside the plenary chamber. Seats for guests placed outside the glass façade are visible.
Schwippert Archiv, Germanisches Nationalmuseum, Nuremberg.

democratic society; Schwippert's design strategy is meant to be an analogy for democracy in its purest, ideal form.

Transparency is the dominant character in the spatial development of the building. The section of the plenary chamber is two-story; the second floor is a mezzanine, or visitor's gallery, intended for the press, political aides, and members of the public. Photographs of the gallery from 1949 show an unadorned, metal rail mounted atop the balcony edge with no other boundary between the viewer and the legislators (Figure 5.15). The illusion is of almost no real separation between balcony and floor, other than the sectional division. The glaring absence of security glass as a separating device illustrates the changes in security concerns over time – by 1989 security glass was mandated for the barriers between outside public space and interior space, between public galleries and plenary chamber. The access to the gallery in Schwippert's building is through the entry foyer, a double-height room surrounded by a circulation gallery (Figure 5.16). The gallery floor is an almost paper-thin concrete slab with white edges, supported by slender white columns, and enclosed with a filigree steel handrail. The handrail is fabricated of such thin members that it is almost immaterial. On a bright, sunny day, the gallery seems to float above the first floor. Photographs of the building from

131

1950 also show cane-backed chairs and hanging light fixtures made from open metalwork that continue the transparency theme in the furnishings.

     Schwippert was not permitted to realize one of his most radical proposals: to arrange the seats in the plenary chamber in a perfect circle, an arrangement Schwippert believed most representative of the egalitarian aspect of West German democracy because of the lack of hierarchy in a circular form (Figure 5.17). He also thought that a circular arrangement would promote discussion more than any other form, an idea that was appealing to Schwippert because of his desire to make the building a "house of conversation." Schwippert made a series of sketches for the chamber design in which he explored the arrangement with and without differentiated areas for ministers, the chancellor, and the president. In the most daring of all the proposals, Schwippert drew several rows of concentrically organized seats with no speaker's podium at all. In a letter from Adolf Arndt, dated January 18, 1963, Arndt explains Schwippert's initial intentions to create a completely egalitarian chamber in the spirit of the new West German government.[69] Arndt makes it perfectly clear why Schwippert's radical design was not realized; Konrad Andenauer found it too much a departure from the norm and was afraid that, for this reason, it would hamper the work of the new parliament. Seen in the

5.16
View of the entry lobby with its almost transparent handrails.
Schwippert Archiv, Germanisches Nationalmuseum, Nuremberg.

5.17
Sketch studies of the potential seating arrangements for the plenary chamber.
Schwippert Archiv, Architecture Museum, TU, Munich.

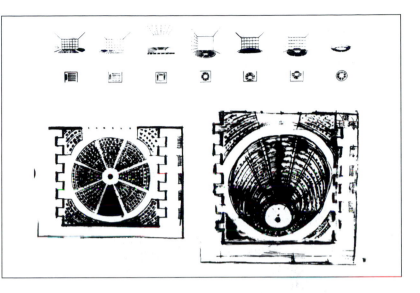

light of the disinformation and misinformation disseminated during the National Socialist period, Schwippert's goals are laudable, if naïve. The circular arrangement would not promote dialog any more than any other seating arrangement nor is it really without hierarchy, as Behnisch would discover years later. In the circular form importance is determined by proximity to the center. Finally, Schwippert's choice of analogy is strange in the context of German history. Conversation is not the same as action and political effectiveness, as the experience of Weimar showed. During the Weimar Republic, parliament was nicknamed "*Quasselbude*," which means "Hut for Babbling," because the parliamentarians seemed to talk endlessly without achieving anything. Hitler exploited parliamentary inaction and German disillusionment with the government by promising "an end to babbling."

Considering the German situation in 1949 – a newly-formed democracy whose first democratic effort had failed, whose future was uncertain, a country still partly occupied and governed by American, British, and French forces, a country that had caused two of the bloodiest international conflicts ever – the desire to be quietly anonymous may have influenced the drive towards transparency as a means to render Germany invisible. In a sense, the building is as stylistically transparent as it is physically in that it assumes the style of the pre-existing structure without imposing much of its own. While the building can be read as the invention of a new architectural type for a parliament, it can equally easily be interpreted as eschewing type altogether, as having no typological meaning and therefore as being as anonymous as possible. Ironically, the daring esthetic experiment perpetrated by Schwippert with the Bundeshaus, Europe's first "modern parliament building" contradicts Adenauer's "no experiments" dictum even while it supports it.

Who was Schwippert's intended audience when he described the project for *Neue Bauwelt* or wrote his manifesto "*Glück und Glas*"? Like it or not, the members of parliament had to accept the building as a fait accompli. Schwippert may have tried to ease the resentments of MPs who disliked progressive architecture, as well as appeal to those who still hoped to move the government to Frankfurt, who resented the decision for Bonn, and resented Adenauer's commissioning of the new building in the first place. A cartoon in *Westdeutsche Zeitung* on August 7, 1949 entitled "About the Capital City," depicts five men in all-white suits fighting with four dressed in black. On one side of the page is a pile of bricks under a banner that reads, "Bonn," while on the other side sits a second pile of bricks under the banner, "Frankfurt." One of the men in white is hitting one of those in black over the head with a large mallet. Underneath the image are the words of a popular song, "We are going to build a house, a house made of true love!"[70] Perhaps Schwippert hoped to convince the recalcitrant legislators to accept both Bonn and his building, at least for the time being. Quite possibly, too, Schwippert was writing for the future German politicians who would commission the next, perhaps permanent, seat of parliament or for the architects who would receive the commission for the next parliament building. Or, perhaps Schwippert was writing for his forward-thinking colleagues in the architectural profession? His unedited description of the building appeared in *Neue Bauwelt*, the organ of progressive architecture in Germany at the time but the article only appeared in 1951, some two years after the project was completed.[71] Articles in the contemporary non-architecture press appeared in a timely fashion and mention many of the qualities Schwippert wrote about. Although several discuss the outdoor viewing stalls, the articles do not single out transparency as a topic for discussion. The light-filled quality of the building and its very contemporary character seem to have made the greater impression.[72] Another article, already mentioned above, points to the lack of allegorical and symbolic program in the building.[73] Several other pieces quote Schwippert on the project referring to its humane design, lack of political and sentimental pathos, appropriateness for democratic government.[74] It is very unlikely that Schwippert's manifesto appeared anywhere but in the architecture press since only an audience in the know would have understood the references implicit in its title and its wording. Because of the nature of the publications that printed his essays, it is hard to imagine that they would have reached a political audience at all. It is also possible that he wrote in order to contribute to the contemporary debate over the correct architectural style for postwar West Germany.

Schwippert must have had an international audience in mind when he designed the Bundeshaus, perhaps composed of citizens of the occupying nations and members of the military governments, whose interest in West

German affairs was particularly acute in the immediate postwar years. After all, the British, American, and French press reviewed his building and, as already noted, were uniformly positive about its symbolic intentions and the constructed result. The *Architectural Review* featured the project in a four-page spread with quotes from the architect, drawings, photographs, and a description of the addition expressed in positive terms only.[75] As already discussed on page 107, the British *Picture Post* lauded Schwippert's achievement for its originality and, more importantly, for its ability to project an appropriate new image for German state architecture, one that is decidedly different from the architecture of the Third Reich. This new addition to an older building, then, is acceptable to the outside world because it severs ties to the immediate past, to the Third Reich, and houses the future hope for West German democracy. Although the *Picture Post* article does not refer to transparency by name, it features two photographs of the transparent walls in the plenary chamber – one view from within, and one from without. The caption underneath the latter reads, "What the men without see of the men within" suggesting the force and importance of the transparent division between public and state.[77]

Interestingly, the journalist writing for the *Picture Post* is a West German named Fenno Jacobs who focuses on the future of West German democracy and whether it is an attainable goal. The new Bundeshaus is only tangentially important to him. He uses the architecture as a backdrop for an analysis of the German question, or questions, as Jacobs poses it. The two German questions Fenno poses are: who are the constituencies in contemporary Germany and can the politicians solve the multiple problems facing the rest of the country?

> Behind you, the expellee camps and the rubbed-out cities; in front of you, the green lawns and the white walls of the Shangri-La Parliament House, Behind you, the heaviest agenda of the century; the great, sprawling agglomeration of economic, spiritual, and power problems-to-be-solved, that goes by the name of Germany. In front of you, the improvised political instrument called Bonn. . . .[78]

The building is a concrete symbol of change, of improvement, of democracy even, but it is only a symbol. Jacobs' tone of voice is even a bit sarcastic. His reference to the "Shangri-La Parliament House" suggests the implausibility and idealism embodied in the new parliament especially when it is considered in connection to recent German history. Jacobs uses his article, and the images of Schwippert's project, to illustrate the divisions in West Germany between "We the People" and the government, between the Allied Powers and the West Germans, between hopes for a successful democracy and the challenges that lie ahead. His point of view is even more interesting considering for whom he wrote, both in terms of who would read the article and who sponsored it. The journal was a British publication financed by the military government and intended as much for West German consumption as for British consumption back home. Thus Jacobs' article can be interpreted as a propaganda piece as much as a review and informational piece. Alternatively, because he was writing for a British publication outside West Germany, Jacobs had freedoms a journalist writing inside the country would not have had at the time.

Moreover, Jacobs' position vis-à-vis the architecture seems to have been common outside the architecture press. A review of the newspaper articles published from August 1949 through to the end of December of the same year revealed hundreds of articles filled with discussions of politics, of the form the new government might take, who was elected, and where the seat of government should be, but there is little discussion of the Bundeshaus as a piece of architecture. That is not to suggest that the building was not mentioned, but that it was usually mentioned as a small detail in the context of a much larger discussion rather than as the central subject of the article. Furthermore, the tone of articles in the popular West German press is optimistic, patently without the sarcasm evident in Jacobs' piece.

In the article for *Neue Bauwelt*, Schwippert asserts that the time will come when German democracy is mature, when it will be possible to build a more permanent structure for parliament. His building is intended as "the temporary house for the resumption of the new political life in Germany . . . we will build it (a permanent parliament) when politics once again achieve a noteworthy success."[79] Thus, the impermanent and transparent structure reflects the political situation in Germany in 1948 and 1949 – at least in Schwippert's eyes. By extension, if the building represents the political status quo, it also reflects the political identity of the new nation. Although he never uses either the phrase "political identity" or "national identity" in his writing, the concepts lie just below the surface of the text. They appear, briefly, here and there when Schwippert uses words like "representative" and "political," to describe aspects of the architecture. In a speech from 1968 Schwippert explained the architect's role as the "advocate of meaning," saying that he is neither engineer, painter, nor poet but that "he stands for the accommodation and population of the earth, stands there for the qualified reality of creative human existence, for the lost meaning to come."[80] If the architect's role is to reveal the underlying meaning of man's existence, in all its forms, through architecture, then this would include revealing his identity as a member of the state, as a political animal. Furthermore, Schwippert does explain the Bundeshaus as a place for the formation of a "new political life in Germany," which suggests that it will also serve as the locus for the formation of a new political identity. What else, if not a positive national image, would the Germans want to embody in their future building, the one they should design after their country's politics "again achieve a noteworthy success?" Transparency ideology certainly helped support the positive image many Germans wished to regain of their country in the aftermath of the National Socialist period, even if it was based on myth rather than substance.

Chapter 6

House of openness, architecture of encounter

> Should not there be a relationship between the public principle of democracy and the outer and inner transparency and accessibility of her buildings?
>
> Adolf Arndt.[1]

The promotion of transparency ideology and the use of transparent building techniques in parliamentary architecture reached their apotheosis in the architect Günter Behnisch's design for the Bonn Bundestag building (Figure 6.1). Whereas Hans Schwippert had used a modest amount of transparency to signal the desire for democracy, Behnisch seemed to use transparency in order to celebrate the successful establishment of a democratic system.[2] After all, Behnisch was able to look at the successes of 40 years of Modell Deutschland (Model Germany) with pride. And while Behnisch was fully conscious of Germany's totalitarian past, the fragility of democracy, and the many failures of the Federal Republic, he chose to focus the rhetoric supporting his building design on Germany's many postwar achievements and a positive view of political identity. In the hundreds of articles, essays, interviews, and other publications about the project, Behnisch promotes the new Bundeshaus as a showcase for pluralism in the Federal Republic, freedom of speech, participatory democracy and, above all, German democracy at work.[3] The press is surprisingly rife with praise for Behnisch's work and devoid of any critical voice, any questioning of his and the parliament's stated goals for the building. But as with the Schwippert project, the architecture of the Behnisch

6.1
**The newly
renovated
Bundeshaus
seen from the
Parliament Plaza.**
Behnisch & Partner.
Photographer:
Christian Kandzia.

Bundeshaus is only partially transparent despite the tremendous quantity of see-through glass used, the open forms, plans, and sections. Also like the Schwippert project, the Behnisch building represents a desire this time not for democracy per se but for an ideal democracy, for one with perfect transparency. More than anything, however, Behnisch's choices underscore the mythological nature of transparency ideology and raise the question: why transparency?

It is important to note two aspects of the Behnisch project that distinguish it from Hans Schwippert's Bundeshaus, and from the later Reichstag renovation undertaken by Norman Foster. The Behnisch project spanned 20 years, several competitions and design proposals, and bridged the period before and after unification. Yet in its analogical and political orientation, the project is fundamentally tied to the pre-unification period. This is true both because of the timing of the work on the project and because of Behnisch's age at the time the building opened. Behnisch is substantially younger than Schwippert. He was born in 1922, briefly served in the German army during the Second World War, and lived through the reconstruction period as a student in architecture school.[4] He witnessed the founding of the FRG as a young adult. By 1992, when the Bundeshaus was finally opened, Behnisch was 70 years old. He was therefore a member of the generation after Schwippert. He was old enough to feel the full force of guilt after 1945 and the burden of the history of the Third Reich, which keenly affected his approach to the problem. As to the project's timing, parliament agreed to raze the Schwippert plenary chamber and replace it with Behnisch's design in June 1987. Behnisch & Partner had completed the final design by June of 1989, some five months before the destruction of the Berlin Wall set unification in motion. While some modifications were made after June 1989, these were minor; the basic design and the underlying concepts remained untouched. In other words, the political events that began in November 1989 affected West Germany, and West German political identity, but had little or no impact on the Behnisch architectural project. For these reasons, the political situation in Germany around 1989 is taken as the salient moment for the Behnisch Bundeshaus.

As evidence of the new political transparency in West Germany, Behnisch cites the lengthy democratic process used to select a new design for the Bundeshaus, a process that included numerous open competitions, public forums, feasibility studies, and often heated debate.[5] "There was an extremely open process leading to the Bonn project. I deplore the way the Reichstag project has proceeded . . . For Bonn, there was public discussion of how to build for the state and what to build."[6] Sometimes the attempt to be as democratic as possible stymied both the progress and the ability to make a final decision. The first competition results were thrown out and the second competition ended in a four-way tie!

Behnisch's ideology seems to have come as much from his interests as from the parliament itself, whose members struggled with questions of the proper way to build in a democracy. As former president of the Bundestag Rita Süssmuth put it,

> It is fully legitimate when the state tries to show itself. It can do this in different ways through representatives, through national symbols, hymns, orders and decorations, through national holidays, through a special ceremony or through its architecture. It is self evident that a liberal democratic basic order is harder to make visible than a neat and tidy structured permanent order . . . Is it even possible to ask state buildings to consciously show the citizens' historical identity? It is certain, that this is in no way easy to do.[7]

Here Süssmuth underlines as natural the tendency for the state to want to proudly represent its power and political identity architecturally. According to Süssmuth, the function of the plenary chamber as the center, the heart of the parliament was clear, as was the importance of architecture to the state. "The parliament is the heart and the workshop of democracy. The plenary chamber is the living center of our free democratic state . . . architecture has the difficult task of showing in built form what is understood by the citizens."[8] She goes on to acknowledge that, "Architecture is the physiognomy of the nation. . . ."[9] Therefore, Behnisch's building must embody his notion of the nation in concert with that held by the parliament and the people. It is difficult to ascertain how the parliament and the German people see their nation, however. Exactly which people are "the people" and what members of parliament hold opinions representative of the group? In fact, there is no such thing as a single understanding of the nation. In the case of the Bundeshaus, a parliamentary committee wrote the brief for each competition and other committees worked on the building program as it developed over the years, defining the nation and the way it should be represented through the new architecture. In 1971, Minister Dirigent Dr Schiffer and Minister Rat Jacob presented their summary of "Self-representation in a democratic state in the constructed formation of the Capital City."[10] Schiffer and Jacob enumerate qualities they believe ought to be embodied in West German state architecture including: the dependence on citizens, political openness, diversity of opinion, decision-making through discussion, transparency of decision-making, and citizens' engagement, all of which are ideals.[11] In this essay, transparency is referred to with the German word *Durchschaubarkeit*. The members of these committees therefore asked for transparency in the building, a request that was already written into the first competition brief in 1970.[12] In other words, the winning design for the competitions had to work with transparency because transparency was one of the qualities the briefs demanded.

I

Completed in October of 1992, Behnisch's building combined many of Schwippert's ideas with Behnisch's own notions concerning the appropriate image for state architecture in post-Nazi Germany. Behnisch acknowledged both his debt to Schwippert and his desire to present a Germany other than that of the Nazi period,

> Notably the old Academy buildings are an example of the white architecture of the 1930s, that was considered undesirable during the Third Reich and was discriminated against . . . this rather clear, direct, see-through, apparently functional, ascetic, and in fact the

> poetic of the Academy buildings was adopted. But [these qualities]
> were developed further, made more layered, differentiated, trans-
> parent, and with less material.[13]

Although the project was completed 45 years after the war, both the architecture and the politics of the National Socialist regime were primary concerns for
Behnisch. "Everything we have done since 1945 has been a reaction to the
National Socialist regime."[14] For Behnisch, reacting to National Socialism
meant creating a building style that was the antithesis of what he viewed as
typical for state architecture of the time. From the qualities Behnisch promoted for his work, it is apparent that he viewed the neo-classical buildings
of Speer and Troost as the ones whose style should be avoided at all cost.
His words position him in the camp of pro-Neues Bauen architects of the
immediate postwar period.

Firstly, he saw the opportunity to build a more humanitarian architecture. In terms astonishingly similar to those used by Schwippert 45 years
before, Behnisch described his project,

> The German Bundestag must not wall itself in. More, it must
> produce the impression of openness. . . . The nature and method,
> in which this material glass is applied can make it clear that one
> takes the goals, desires, wishes, and ideals seriously that we today
> associate with the notion of democracy. . . . Not least of all is the
> outer wall, the outer skin, that serves the building and the institution
> as the boundary between the outer world, the state, the landscape
> and the society . . . the enclosure should be transparent so that
> people can see into and through the building and find it understand-
> able. No one should believe that dark powers operate there.[15]

In other words, Behnisch rejected what he claims was National Socialist
architecture by designing a building with glass and steel, modest in scale,
welcoming to the public and open to the landscape. But by 1989 many West
Germans did see "dark powers" lurking in their parliament, the architect's
intentions notwithstanding. By the late 1960s, "*Politikverdrossenheit*" (dis-
enchantment with politics) had set in because of disillusionment with the
silence of the war generation and because of scandals involving bribery,
dishonesty, and authoritarianism. As a consequence, reformers began
attempting to improve the transparency in parliament. By the late 1970s, skepticism had deepened as the weaknesses in the economic model started
to show. Frustration with economic stagnation led to the first successful
constructive vote of no confidence in parliament in 1982, the vote that
ousted Helmut Schmidt and brought Helmut Kohl to the chancellor's office.

Transparency might have represented an ideal, but certainly not the real situation. Behnisch's comments do point to the general acceptance of Schwippert's ideas in certain West German circles by the late 1980s – by some members of parliament and some architects working for the parliament. Surprisingly, these ideas had become common currency through the political discourse rather than the architectural one. Schwippert's writings were largely unknown, since Schwippert's most important piece, the "*Glück und Glas*" manifesto, seems to have been lost for the intervening 45 years. Behnisch, for instance, had read articles reviewing the Schwippert Bundeshaus as well as relevant political discourse, but claims to have never seen Schwippert's mani-festo.[16] On the other hand, Adolf Arndt's speeches had been published in numerous editions as books while "On Building in Democracy" was reprinted in *Bauwelt* where it reached a broad audience in the architecture profession. The architect Egon Eiermann wrote to Arndt on June 10, 1969 that "I care for your essay 'On Building in Democracy' almost like a Bible . . . and what hair-raising things have occurred and occur still and have occurred to me in this democracy!"[17] Eiermann's quip both affirms the influential aspect of Arndt's ideas, their status as close to holy, as well as the existence of not so ideal circumstances in the West German democracy.

While Behnisch's design, like Schwippert's, uses transparency as a key design element, the underlying intentions diverge. Like Schwippert, Behnisch accepts transparency as a metaphor for openness and accessibility in the political realm, and for ideal democracy; like Schwippert, Behnisch exploits the transparent material, glass, as an analogy for open and accessible democratic government. But in spite of the rhetoric delivered by various polit-icians and by the architect, transparency at the Behnisch Bundeshaus still represents a desired condition as it did in 1945 although no longer the desire for democracy per se, but for the unattainable, perfect, ideal democracy. Behnisch deviates from Schwippert in his intentional work with the reflective qualities of the glass. Reflections make glass surfaces appear solid even when they are see-through in a layering trick that suggests the illusory aspects of life and parliament – things are never what they seem to be: architectural analo-gies may not be what they seem to be either. It is particularly ironic that the building served as the house of parliament for such a short period, and that its function proved to be so delicate. For in its pristine aspect, with its appearance of fragility and delicacy, Behnisch's project reminds the viewer of imperma-nence and the uncertainties of time although even these are illusory. Here too the gap between the ideology promoting the project and the reality is palpable. The building's glazing is a very expensive product chosen to assure a lack of color but also for its strength. Security concerns demanded the architects use exceptionally thick glass that in many instances is also bulletproof! Although by choosing glass for the Bundeshaus Behnisch wanted to suggest the fragility of democracy, a memory of the ease with which the first German republic toppled in the 1930s; but for anyone in the know, the building is anything but fragile.

Unlike the Schwippert project which was designed and built in a mere nine months, and commissioned without a public competition, the Behnisch building took almost 20 years to design and build, and was the culmination of many competitions. The scope of the project changed several times, as much reflecting conflicting visions for Bonn, views on German separation, and aspirations for the West German parliament, as the vicissitudes of the German economy and politics. Parliamentarians endlessly debated the decision to build new versus provisionally, to build an entire complex of buildings near the old plenary chamber versus renovating the provisional quarters.[18] From 1948 until 1969, several ad hoc additions made to the Schwippert structure effectively destroyed the building's original layout and analogical message. The additions were made around the plenary chamber obstructing all the glass façades so that by the late 1960s the plenary chamber was buried inside an opaque box and the transparent chamber no longer existed. The tremendous economic expansion the FRG experienced during the 1950s and 1960s precipitated a corresponding expansion of the parliament so that by 1965 it had grown beyond the capacity of its first postwar quarters. In 1965, the parliament decided to commission a new building near the old complex to accommodate some of the overflow staff. Egon Eiermann designed the skyscraper soon nicknamed the "Langer Eugen" after then Bundestag President, Eugen Gerstenmaier (see Chapter 2). At the time the Eiermann building was being completed, the discussion turned to the plenary chamber. Because the chamber had been hastily built, much of its construction and technical systems were sloppy and inadequate. SPD representative Karl Mommer called the room "the most unsuitable of all plenary chambers that I have seen in all my travels around the world."[19] Politicians on both sides of the aisle agreed with Mommer that the old plenary chamber was woefully inadequate. Furthermore, since Willy Brandt's election to the Chancellorship in 1969, attitudes towards East Germany and towards unification were shifting. Brandt's policy of rapprochement with the East was largely based on the argument that at least for the foreseeable future Germany would remain separated into two states. Under these conditions, he felt it made more economic and political sense for West Germany to develop warm relations with its immediate neighbors to the East, than to perpetuate the tensions begun in the 1940s. Brandt's attitude towards foreign relations undoubtedly affected internal politics as well since in 1970 parliament officially decided to replace the provisional quarters with permanent ones. After much debate, the parliament agreed to hold a design competition for a new federal complex in Bonn near the Schwippert building but completely separate from it.

Between September 1972, when the first competition was released, and June 1987, the project went through a series of inconclusive competitions and design phases. Parliament commissioned several expert feasibility studies to look at what was needed in Bonn and how to integrate the new government buildings into the existing city fabric. But the work stalled again and again because of competing political agendas, differing visions of the scope of the work, and budgetary constraints.[20] The last controversy over the project erupted on June 3, 1987 when the Minister for City Planning, Living, and Transportation, North Rhine Westphalia, Christoph Zöpel, sent a letter to Bundestag President Philipp Jenninger in which he emphatically rejected razing the old plenary chamber, in favor of a conservation solution. Zöpel argued for the historic importance of the existing chamber and pointed out that according to West German law, a national monument could not be destroyed. Nevertheless, on June 5, 1987 the Bundestag voted to replace the existing plenary chamber with a new one. Only 41 representatives voted for conserving the old chamber. Next, the representatives voted 178 to 174 for the circular seating arrangement that Behnisch had proposed after Schwippert's sketches from the 1940s. Lastly, the majority approved the addition of rooms for the political parties, representatives, and utilities south of the new building.[21] These votes paved the way for Behnisch & Partner to revise their design proposal. Their last, and final, scheme was presented to the *Bundesbaukommission* and the Bundestag for approval in June 1989. Behnisch advocated a combination of constructing a new chamber that would accommodate the needs of a contemporary parliament while restoring the "architectonic principles of the original Schwippert solution."[22] In other words, he argued for a completely new structure that would embody many of the analogical and architectonic expressions Schwippert himself had utilized.

II

The project Behnisch & Partner presented for final approval was not only different from each of their previous designs in approach and scope, but it articulated a schema based on the radical use of transparency. Although Adolf Arndt's ideas certainly were influential, Behnisch himself cites Carlo Schmid, who was also a member of the Parliamentary Council and MP for the SPD in the early years of the Bundesrepublik, rather than Arndt, as a major source of inspiration, especially his essay entitled "*Demokratie – die Chance, den Staat zu vermenschlichen.*" ("Democracy – the chance to humanize the state.")[23] Behnisch's archival copy of Schmid's article has key passages marked in the margins along with some short comments on the text.[24] Moreover, Behnisch repeatedly quotes from the Schmid essay in order to explain the ways in which architecture and politics can interact, the aspects of politics, especially democracy, architecture can analogize and symbolize, and the responsibility of buildings to convey a moral message.[25]

In his essay, Schmid outlines the social and political structures that make an ideal modern democracy. Certain key concepts in Schmid's text clearly can be read as influences on Behnisch's interpretation of democracy. To begin with, Behnisch adopted the idea that democracy offers the opportunity to make the state more accessible and more humane. Behnisch quotes Schmid's phrase in several essays on the Bundestag project and in interviews.[26] But what exactly does this mean? Certainly, to humanize the state means to include the voices of as many citizens as possible in parliament, to make bureaucracy accessible and caring, to remove the pomp from parliament and replace it with the familiar and ordinary. The parliament, as the representative body in government, is the "voice of the people" and for this reason, the plenary chamber is key. Behnisch also interpreted the phrase to mean making the place for parliament less serious, more playful and whimsical. Schmid begins his text by defining the egalitarian foundations of democracy, namely that everyone, rich and poor, educated and illiterate, farmer and urbanite, worker and manager, should be equally represented. Beyond representation, pluralism in all areas of life lies at the heart of democracy. Citizens must be permitted to hold differing political opinions, religious affiliations, and so on. Article 4 of the Basic Law guarantees these rights while Article 5 protects free speech, in all its forms.[27] Moreover, in order to form a democracy, members of a democratic society have to share a sense of community identity, in spite of their differences. And, society must be free of undue government controls, a freedom that allows circumstance to shape all sorts of aspects of everyday life. Most important to Schmid, and important to Behnisch as well, is the role the free will of the individual plays in the formation of a democracy. Democratic nations are created when citizens freely express the desire to be a nation; democracy cannot be imposed by authoritarian will or governmental fiat.[28] (The irony here is that in 1945 democracy was imposed on West Germans – of course many desired a democratic state, but they were not given the choice, there was no discussion.) In Schmid's view, the democratic party system is only possible in a pluralistic society, for the one supports the other. In order for pluralism to thrive, parliament must be open and accessible, participatory as well as representative. The notions of plurality, openness, and accessibility are all central to Behnisch's building, as is the idea of individual participation in a larger community. Each one of these concepts is present in numerous instances, at multiple scales, as analogies throughout the Bundeshaus' architecture.

Behnisch articulates his views on the relationship between politics and architecture in several published essays. He writes that buildings themselves cannot be political although he emphatically states their ability to repre-sent and embody political ideas. In "*Bauen für die Demokratie*" Behnisch explains his views in some detail. "Agendas exist before architecture," he writes, "We architects help realize only those that already exist in the realm of ideas to become part of the material, visible, meaningful and experiential world."[29] In other words, architects do not set the analogical program for state architecture; others do. Reading further between the lines, Behnisch's quip implies that the architect might not even believe the analogical program he realizes. He emphasizes the analogical power of buildings – their ability to rep-resent political ideas or movements or institutions, citing Speer's projects for Hitler and the Palace of Versailles for Louis XIV as examples. Most importantly, Behnisch writes, "I would call architecture 'political' when it makes the influ-ential political moments stand out."[30] In other words, for Behnisch, political architecture is the manifestation of salient conditions in contemporary politics. In another essay, "*Ein Gang durch die Ausstellung*" ("A walk through the Exhibition"), completed in 1992 when the building was just being finished, Behnisch is even more upfront about his intentions.

> The city of Bonn was also informed that every place and every point of focus would have its own individuality. This emanates from the uniqueness of the "Organs of the Society" that have landed there, the uniqueness of the pre-existing situation and the conditional con-temporary statement of contemporary problems, that are reflected in the art and manner with which we handled these circum-stances.[31]

Finally, Behnisch is emphatic about architecture's ability to convey meaning to people, to embody an ideology – a hotly contested issue in contemporary architecture. He first declares that one by-product of working on a building is that the architect learns something new. But it is not just the architect who is influenced by his work, "In the same way that we are changed in and through architecture, so can we also influence others through our work. When we are open, interested, and sensitive, then we can help some people realize what otherwise remains suppressed."[32] In other words, buildings can express an ideology; they can convey a message. The Bundeshaus, then, according to Behnisch should be read in part as the architectural embodiment of the polit-ical climate, and political identity, in West Germany in 1989. But is it an accurate expression of these or an ideal one?

In his collection of materials from the various competitions, collo-quia, and essays on the Bundeshaus project, Behnisch has copies of an essay dated December 1972 by the historian Ingeborg Flagge on the theme of self-representation. Flagge emphasizes the metaphors and analogies that were already being requested of architects competing for the Government Quarter commission. These include: "openness, self-representation, transparency and openness in the decision-making process, pluralism of the modern society, separation of powers, and different values for different voices, impersonality . . ."[33] As with the Schmid essay, Behnisch marked this piece by underlining and flagging in the margin phrases and sentences he found important and by writing notes to himself about the content. Words he underlined include: "transparency" and "openness". Most importantly, Flagge writes about the connection between the pressure for increased transparency and the resultant loss of transparency: "Something has to be pointed out . . . Experience in the last years shows that the demand for greater transparency has become a rallying cry for many discussions. But associated with every conquest in this area there was, at the same time, a loss."[34] In other words, even in 1972 when the project was barely begun, people participating in the design process knew that the transparency was an ideal, but the use of the analogy persisted nevertheless.

III

The Bundeshaus is a transparent glass and steel structure situated on the banks of the Rhine River, placed exactly in the void created by the demolition of the Schwippert building. For the new building, Behnisch chose to work with a box within a box parti, a compositional strategy that differentiates his design from its predecessor. Both the outer and inner boxes are transparent, making the MPs in the plenary chamber visible from many positions in and around the building (Figures 6.2, 6.3, and 6.4). The parti does more than suggest openness and accessibility; it suggests mutual dependence and interaction, even participation. The double condition of containing can be read as an analogy for the relationship between the parliament and society at large, since one is always dependent on the other for its existence and its authority. Because the contained volume is offset, asymmetrically placed within the larger box, an irregular form set within an irregularly shaped rectangle, the parti also hints at the ordinariness and imperfection of the building. Next to the plenary area sits another, separate but connected building – a box outside the larger box. The adjacent structure houses the presidential offices. It is attached to the plenary building by the most tenuous of spaces, a thin bridge, which could signal the dependent and secondary status accorded the Presidential Building as well as its independence from the parliament.

The choice of transparent glass as primary building material for the Bundeshaus seems to be a natural consequence of Behnisch's stated goals for the new building – to construct a place for open parliament and to reinforce

6.2
**Plan of the entry
level of the
Bundeshaus. The
lack of defining
borders between
spaces is
apparent.**
Behnisch & Partner.

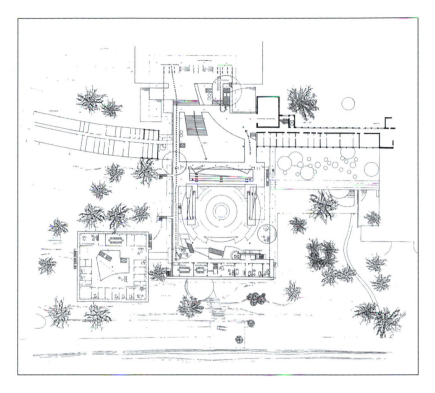

the connection between parliament, people, and the land. Although, as Ingeborg Flagge has pointed out, there is no single material that expresses transparency in architecture even if see-through glass seems to do so.[35] The use of transparency does follow Behnisch's promise to reinstate the spirit of the Schwippert building, if not the actual structure. While Schwippert intended a combination between physical presence and transparency to views, Behnisch expressly wished to dissolve the building envelope, to make the architecture as inauspicious and invisible as possible in order to focus attention on the workings of parliament.[36] The degree to which he wished to dematerialize the building is evident in an early sketch perspective study of the interior spatial relationships and views through the plenary chamber (Figure 6.5). The sketch gives the sense of a lack of substance throughout, a transparency so extreme that even the human figure becomes see-through inside this structure. Although certain elements are rendered opaque, many that would be are rendered transparent in the sketch. Stairs and platforms are suspended without any visible means of support to minimize their presence in the space as if they are necessary evils. In another sketch study for the interior of the plenary chamber, Behnisch makes the room appear transparent and lightweight on all sides, including the ceiling. The only exception is the solid backdrop on which the Federal Eagle is hung, a design conceit that serves to

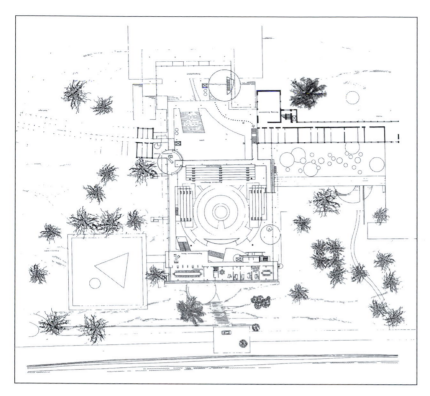

6.3
**Plan of the middle
level of the
Bundeshaus.**
Behnisch & Partner.

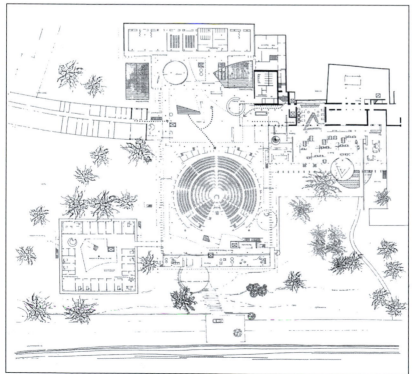

6.4
**Plan of the
lower level of
the Bundeshaus
showing the
plenary chamber.**
Behnisch & Partner.

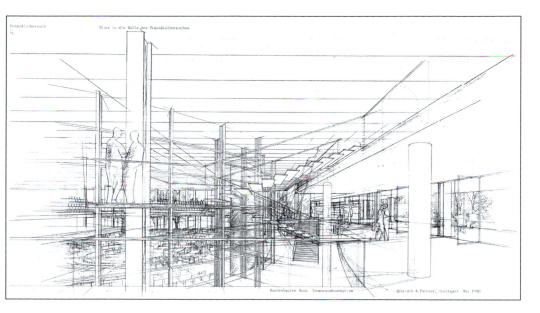

6.5

Sketch perspective study of transparency in the lobby areas surrounding the plenary chamber.

Behnisch & Partner.

6.6

Sketch perspective studying the placement of the Eagle and its effect on the plenary chamber.

Behnisch & Partner.

exaggerate the importance of the emblem beyond its actual size (Figure 6.6). As in Schwippert's studies, construction lines are allowed to overlap spaces and objects where they clearly do not belong, a drawing technique that heightens the appearance of transparent and dematerialized substance.

Although the Behnisch building is entirely clad in see-through glass, as opposed to the Schwippert building that was only partially enclosed with glass, the ability to actually see the plenary chamber varies. Transparency depends on the prevailing light conditions and on the viewer's position in and around the complex. At times, one or both volumes are reflective and therefore opaque to views. The architecture is so multi-layered that unless an observer presses his or her face up against the glass during the daylight hours, the actual chamber is impossible to discern from the outside. The different layers are often visually confusing because their transparent nature makes the relative depth of space difficult to perceive. Furthermore, most of the building perimeter is inaccessible to the general public. Visitors are only allowed to approach through the Parliament Plaza; a security fence and an entry checkpoint protect the Rhine side of the building while the watchful eyes of security guards protect the sides near the Plaza. When a visitor approaches any side, he is hailed by a guard and told that he is not permitted in the area. Thus, despite the extensive use of transparent glass, most of the Bundeshaus is not accessible to the general public at all, even for a peek inside. Transparency to view is not much more than a desire.

Behnisch claims to reject the symbols of the anti-democratic German past by constructing an anti-monumental, humanized Bundeshaus – to borrow from Carlo Schmid. Besides the transparency used throughout, Behnisch incorporated numerous unusual, anti-monumental and even playful gestures in the design. Although not transparent, these devices help bolster the general feeling of the building as an open and welcoming place that is free of undue and intimidating pomp. The choice of uncolored glass, undressed steel, natural wood, and exposed concrete as primary building materials underscores the modest aspirations for the building as do the relative scales of the building components, the playful aspects of the design, the spatial transparency, and the lack of axial symmetry.

The impression of modesty begins at the entry plaza to the building. In order to find the Bundeshaus, the visitor must know exactly where it is and how it is accessed beforehand since Görres Street is barely a two-lane road, and certainly not a monumental avenue. Furthermore, the Bundeshaus is not visible from either of the two roads leading to it, Heuss Allee and Adenauer Allee, or from Görres Street, but is fully obstructed by landscape elements and other structures. There is no ceremonial promenade leading to the parliament to give the visitor some hint at its presence. It is only discovered upon entering the Parliament Plaza, the public space that acts as mediator between urban context, such as it is, and the parliament building. The extent to which the entry sequence was made this way by design, or by necessity, is hard to determine. It was constrained by existing property lines along the road so that Behnisch could not change the approach or design a more generous plaza in front of the building. Behnisch certainly had the opportunity to construct some sort of urban sign for his building – a tower, for instance – to signal the presence of the Bundeshaus. But he did not. Instead, he opted for a highly unassuming placement, a decision that could be read as the desire to present West German democracy as unpretentious even as it is being celebrated.

At the Berlin Reichstag, one building precedent Behnisch was likely reacting against, entry is the culmination of a centralized, axial approach framed by monumental columns, topped by a classical pediment. The off-center relationship between the Parliament Plaza on the one hand, and the lobby and plenary chamber on the other, denies any notions of axial order. It is also an imperfect form; the southwest corner has been lopped off from a figure that was once a perfect square. The cut corner helps blend the Parliament Plaza into the landscape by dissolving the boundary between manmade space and natural landscape, the first suggestion of the importance Behnisch & Partner afforded the surroundings. In addition, the imperfection of the form introduces the theme of irregular forms used to signal the ordinary aspect of the building. Four steel columns asymmetrically placed in front of the building serve as an abstract reminder of the traditional entry portico although their very slender proportions bear no relationship whatsoever to the typical classical column. They are ordinary I-beams painted dark gray. The building is 10 meters (30 feet) high on the side facing the Parliament Plaza. When compared with the enormous front façade of the Reichstag that dwarfs the visitor, the entry to the Bundeshaus is understated. Above the two sets of doors sits a steel canopy that extends into the public space. Punctuated by square-shaped skylights, the canopy embraces both the visitor and the public plaza while framing the view of the sky above. At night, a series of randomly placed lights suspended from the canopy playfully illuminate the forecourt. Their seemingly haphazard arrangement signals another design theme present in the building: individuality and tolerance, since each light is allowed to exist in its own realm, outside a regulating system. From this position underneath the canopy, but outside the entry lobby, the plenary chamber, Rhine walkways, and the river are visible, immediately forming the visual connection between the landscape, the parliament, and the people.

Not only did Behnisch eliminate the ascent into the building typical of state architecture but, he had visitors descend into the lobby and plenary area from the entry hall, which he describes as a gesture of humility or humanity.[37]

It is a different scenario, following the downward slope on the way to the plenary chamber, conforming to the conditions imposed by the site – a different scenario to one where the plenary chamber is raised on a high plinth, and by that fact alone alienated from everyday reality.[38]

With the descent, visitors and representatives alike are brought closer to the Rhine and the surrounding landscape (Figures 6.7 and 6.8). In the middle of the grand stair, which is diagonally placed in the lobby space, lies an ochre colored rough and unrefined carpet. No smooth red honorific carpet here! The carpet is also set at an angle in relation to the stairs, a move that adds to the overall dynamism present in the space. At the bottom of the stairs, the carpet continues into the lower lobby thereby helping to fuse upper and lower rooms together and enhance the spatial layering. Although Behnisch argues that the anti-monumental effect of the entry promenade was intentional, it is just as likely that it was the easiest solution given the existing topography.

6.7
View of the grand staircase with the installation piece in the background.
Behnisch & Partner.
Photographer:
Christian Kandzia.

6.8
Closeup view of the grand staircase. The transparency to the outside is apparent in the background.
Behnisch & Partner.
Photographer:
Christian Kandzia.

Behnisch's original objective was to construct a large, green space for public meetings and demonstrations where the Parliament Plaza lies today, and have visitors from the general public and members of parliament share one entrance to the building.[39] The green space proposal was rejected early on and the common entrance had to be abandoned for security reasons. Visitors and MPs do enter through the same façade, albeit through separate doors, a vestige of the original egalitarian idea. But in both cases, security guards who sit in a booth that straddles the space between the entries attentively watch the doors. Before the parliament moved to Berlin, visitors from the general public had to present identification for a vetting process before they were permitted to enter the building even on days when the parliament was not in session.

It (the Plaza) was intended as an open, democratic area provided by parliament, and the entrance would have been the covered part of it. The necessary checkpoints would have been deep inside the hall. Ultimately, however, security considerations prevailed . . . Today, parliamentarians and visitors use separate entrances.[40]

Although separate, the entries are equal in everything but physical position, in the same way that public and MPs are supposed to be equal under German law. Unfortunately, even this is a myth since MPs are immune from prosecution while they serve and, as in the case of Helmut Kohl, even afterwards! Only the signage makes it apparent which door is for the public and which is for the MPs but the fact that the entries had to be separate underscores the idealistic nature of Behnisch's aspirations for the building and the tensions between the ideal and the real.

From the inside upper lobby, the visitor receives the impression of extraordinary material and spatial transparency.[41] The internal spaces in the building housing the plenary chamber are visible because of the incredible openness formed by glass enclosures, translucent screens, and sectional changes where there is no enclosure whatsoever (Figure 6.9). The impression is that the building is more like a set piece with infinite potential than an orchestrated work of architecture, which jibes with Behnisch's stated goals for the project: ". . . it is the localities that are prominent, both within and outside the walls. . . ."[42] Behnisch paints the picture of a place ready to receive action, not in a pre-programmed way, but in a spontaneous way. Behnisch was deeply affected by the Situationist movement in the 1960s and 1970s, especially by the Happenings, theatrical events whose course was not predetermined. The Happenings simply began and evolved naturally as an expression of pluralistic opinion, chance encounters, and unexpected influences.[43] For Behnisch, the Happenings reflected the pluralistic nature of democratic society. His open and fluid spaces were intended to analogize democratic society and to provide a forum for chance encounters and occurrences, and for the free exchange of ideas between MPs and members of the general public. Unfortunately, the chance encounters occur less often than Behnisch might have hoped partly because of the security separations between MPs and visitors and because of the limited access accorded the general public. The encounters between MPs and other officials that do occur do not necessarily promote the kind of open discussion Behnisch writes about; space cannot orchestrate human behavior. Further, in spite of Behnisch's claims for the architecture, the reality of consensus building in contemporary politics is that deals have to be made and these are usually made behind closed doors. Even in Behnisch's scheme, the few offices he provided for individuals are separate from one another and although they have transparent glass façades, they have translucent

6.9
Studies for the plenary chamber.
Behnisch & Partner.

Blick von Besuchern.....
in die Hall.

BUNDESTAG BONN
11.12.1984
Behnisch & Partner

screens that can be shut to keep out the prying view. Thus, the spatial arrangement remains more of an analogy for an ideal than a condition with real
consequences in daily events.

The open spaces did offer a good solution for a long, involved
design process whose programmatic brief was in constant flux. By providing
anonymous, unprogrammed spaces as much as possible, Behnisch could
present a building with the ability to metamorphose over time, to respond to
changing needs and conditions.

> A classic construction, from which nothing can be subtracted and
> nothing added would not have been adequate here. An open order
> had to be found instead, within which individual localities, areas,
> and objects could develop freely, in accordance with their own
> inherent laws. . . .[44]

Clearly, Behnisch saw monumental classical architecture with its formal
constraints as too inflexible spatially and constructively as well as programmatically to accommodate the new parliament building. More importantly,
Behnisch did not want to work in a way that would limit the potential of
any particular space. Similar to Louis Kahn's famous question, "what does the
building want to be?" Behnisch wished to provide a loose spatial structure in
which each space could evolve in its own way, independent of the architect's
desires. Here, he is according space the same freedom he accords every other
element in the building – freedom for individual interpretation.

The façades were conceived in this spirit of individuality and
transparency, more as permeable membranes than as barriers, to reiterate
the transparent relationship between public and parliament, parliament and
nature. Transparency to view naturally helps create the illusion of barrier-free
space, as does the fluid relationship between inside and outside space. For
example, the concrete ground plane is continuous from the Parliament Plaza
to the interior lobby space so the visitor merely passes through the façade
without stepping up or down or onto a different surface to enter the building.
Although functional and spatial boundaries clearly exist between the spaces,
those boundaries are virtually illegible in Behnisch's drawings. Instead, the
plans demonstrate spatial continuity, fluidity, and subtle layering. The building
perimeter is either rendered as a very light single line, or a dashed line, so that
it reads as part of the landscape rather than separate from it, a drawing technique similar to the one Mies van der Rohe used for his buildings beginning
with the Barcelona Pavilion. In Mies' work, this style of drawing was meant to
imply the boundless nature of universal space and architecture as a piece
of the larger continuum. In Behnisch's oeuvre, at least at the Bundeshaus,
this style of drawing has a similar effect. The drawing style is matched in the

building's seemingly fluid spatial overlaps. Wherever possible, Behnisch & Partner have eliminated interior partitions to help underline the transparent spatial divisions. Although there is a glass wall separating lobby and plenary chamber, the entry hall and lobby are separated in section only, situated in the same larger volume. A circular platform designated for exhibitions hovers over the entry hall and protrudes out into the outdoors. It too is separated in section only. A similarly shaped platform reserved for the press extends into the plenary chamber, the lobby, and the courtyard between the Presidential Building and South Wing. The spaces that are articulated by a full perimeter enclosure are the plenary chamber, security booth, individual offices, meeting rooms, restaurant and kitchen, and the Presidential Wing with its offices. Behnisch's presentation drawings make it difficult to read that the plenary chamber is actually separate from the space around it again, because the physical separation denies the notion of free access and denies the ideal condition.

The spectators' tribunes intrude into the air space belonging to the plenary chamber. Behnisch designed the forms for, and arranged the seating of, the tribunes to give them a distinct identity from the plenary chamber and to highlight their function as a place for observation rather than participation (Figure 6.10).

> The spectators' galleries on three sides of the chamber obey other formal concepts. Although they are in the chamber, they are not altogether a part of the events there. Nor, with their rows of seats and their parapet, do they belong formally. The spectators sit . . . in the aerial space of the chamber. But they are not involved in the proceedings: they merely watch.

This is a rare instance when Behnisch describes the architecture truthfully, without the ideal, although he does not acknowledge that the arrangement contradicts the "open house" goal of unrestrained access. Like so many other aspects of the building, this is reminiscent of Schwippert's chamber without being a copy of it. It places the press and the public as close as possible to the parliamentarians without actually being in their space and creates the illusion that they can speak out, and be heard, if they so desire. But this is no more than an illusion – the visitors would be asked to leave if they spoke during a session. As with the first Bundeshaus, the visitors are welcome to observe, but not to participate.

According to Behnisch, pluralism is the most important aspect of democracy therefore transparency is important to the extent that it fosters pluralism. Behnisch's architectural manifestation of pluralism is twofold: transparency to difference and to interpretation. His understanding of pluralism in

6.10
View of the tribunes on the interior of the plenary chamber.
Behnisch & Partner.
Photographer:
Christian Kandzia.

society is that the state is composed of the different people who reside there, the voters, from whom all political power is supposed to flow.[45] The people are all individuals who must mediate their differences in order to live together, the ideal concept of community proposed by Carlo Schmid. Pluralism also means the freedom to interpret events and architecture individually. Behnisch explains the significance of the individual in a democracy metaphorically by comparing the Bundeshaus' interior design to a game of "Mikado," or "pick-up-sticks," which is a game of chance and skill. In Mikado, each stick is a unique entity, much like each member of a democratic community, or each elected representative in a legislature.[46] The game begins by gathering all the sticks together and dropping them so that they scatter in a random order.

In a democracy, the accidental confluence of many individuals gives a town, state, and country their unique identity. Behnisch recreates the chance encounter between unique elements in numerous building details. In his handrails, especially the famous bird's nest, wooden members are skewed in a seemingly random fashion (Figure 6.11). The bird's nest resembles a giant pile of Mikado sticks whose elements were not placed using any rational ordering system, but allowed to fall where they may. Every meter of running length in the building, the handrail design changes, giving the impression of a congregation of handrails – again demonstrating the pluralistic notion of one community comprised of many different individuals. The concrete paving has randomly placed colored glass embedded in it. The skylights on the roof of the restaurant vary in size and are scattered over the roof, rather than arranged according to some regulating system. The variety of twentieth-century furnishings used throughout reflects a multitude of styles rather than a single style; there are just a couple of pieces from each designer including Frank Gehry, Zaha Hadid, and Mies van der Rohe (Figure 6.12). Significantly, the chairs are high art pieces esteemed for their unusual and individual character.

6.11
The Bird's Nest.
Behnisch & Partner
Photographer:
Christian Kandzia.

6.12
**Interior view
of the lobby
area near the
President's Wing.
A couple of pieces
of designer
furniture sit in
the space.**
Behnisch & Partner.
Photographer:
Christian Kandzia.

For one publication on the project, Behnisch & Partner composed a collage of many of the furniture pieces chosen for the Bundeshaus. It looks more like a catalog for a furniture store than the intentional selections for a single building.[47] Suspended between the entry and the lower lobby is the most dynamic screen of all, one composed of reflective metal, painted steel, and colored glass in an overlapping arrangement that seems to dance in space (Figure 6.13). Pieces of the screen extend simultaneously into the entry hall and lower lobby, acting as spatial unifiers. At the same time, the screen marks the border between the upper and lower spaces while it reinforces the notions of lightness, whimsy, and pluralism into the building.

Pluralism is also expressed by the separation and articulation of particular building elements throughout the project such as the building skin, which is not a ten-centimeter thick traditional curtain wall, but a multi-layered structure whose total thickness is about a meter, and whose boundaries are sometimes hard to discern.[48] The roof construction, when viewed from above, is likewise revealed as a series of layers (Figure 6.14). Large gray I-beams rest on smaller steel sleepers so that they seem to hover above the solid roofing. Even smaller steel beams rest on top of the I-beams and atop these are still

6.13
**Detail of the
installation piece
on the grand stair.**
Behnisch & Partner.
Photographer:
Christian Kandzia.

smaller members to which the glass panels are fastened, making the total construction over 40 centimeters deep (Figure 6.15). Portions of façades extend
out into space, asserting their independence from the building, like the
glass louvers on the Parliament Plaza that project one bay beyond the building
enclosure, steel beams supporting the roofs that overhang the building's
edges, and perforated linear metal elements adorning several façades that are
suspended between floors. The effect is three-fold: to heighten the impression of the architecture as a community of individual parts, to deepen the
illusion of limitless space, and to further the dissolution of traditional building
enclosure. These moves help articulate the connection between building construction and the surroundings, at the same time adding to the playful aspect
of the architecture.

6.14
**The roof
construction
viewed from
above. The layers
are visible at the
edges.**
Behnisch & Partner.
Photographer:
Christian Kandzia.

Every façade is subtly different, even when enclosing the same space, and even adjacent pieces of the same façade usually have subtle differences (Figure 6.16). At the junction between the volume housing the plenary chamber and the president's wing, the façade tilts to one side as if it is resting on the neighboring structure. The garden façade facing the restaurant courtyard sports three different façade treatments, all of which are partially integrated with exterior panels or screens collaged onto the outer layer of the façade. At the outermost corner, two balconies wrap the corner. Four of the next bays have banks of operable rectangular glass doors at the courtyard level, while the sizes of the glass panels on the last three bays is based on a square rather than a rectangle. Here and there, on both interior and exterior walls, hangs a perforated metal or wooden screen as a visual anomaly. In one part of the lobby, for example, large wooden screens hang in front of the handrails (Figure 6.17). The screens overlap the handrails and the expressed

6.15
Detail of the layers of roof construction.
Behnisch & Partner. Photographer: Christian Kandzia.

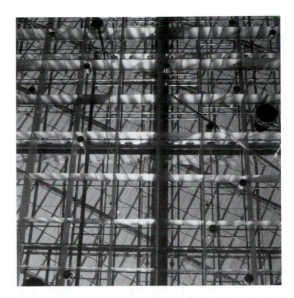

6.16
**Side elevation of
the Bundeshaus.**
Behnisch & Partner.
Photographer:
Christian Kandzia.

6.17
**Lobby view
showing some
of the wooden
lattice screens
used throughout
the building.**
Behnisch & Partner.
Photographer:
Christian Kandzia.

6.18
**View of the
restaurant interior.
Nicola da Maria's
frescoes are
visible on the
ceiling.**
Behnisch & Partner.
Photographer:
Christian Kandzia.

floor slab below, but do not align with the baluster rhythm behind. Behnisch uses these details to idealize the new German character as one that emanates from pluralism rather than singularity yet, together, forms a unified and coherent community. Even the pluralistic elements have a double meaning; they can either be read in a positive light as individual members working together to

6.19

Entry façade at dusk. The playful arrangement of the neon lights is apparent in this image.

Behnisch & Partner. Photographer: Christian Kandzia.

make the whole or in a negative light as individual members who cannot work together but whose presence signals dissonance and difference.

Color is used to enhance the building's light-hearted aspect. As described above, the large screen sculpture is rendered in pastel blues and pinks. Nicola de Maria's frescoes in the restaurant adorn the walls and ceiling and are painted with bright blues, reds, greens and yellows creating a fanciful atmosphere while the concrete in the restaurant area has colored glass and stone embedded in it (Figure 6.18). Here and there, without apparent reason, a wall is painted in bright Prussian blue or a vibrant green. Certain lighting elements, like the long, yellow fluorescent light suspended over the grand stair at an oblique angle, and the zigzag fluorescent light fixture in the restaurant, are whimsical additions to the building (Figure 6.19). The graphic use of lettering, points, and lines on the building surfaces as abstract decorative devices, designed by Baumann & Baumann, picks up on the fanciful esthetic present elsewhere and turns the necessity of using signage into design. It is important to ask the question to what extent the playfulness was truly specific to this project as Behnisch claims, and to what extent it is stylistic. Most of the buildings produced in his office at that time, the 1980s, use similar elements (the Diakonie Building in Stuttgart (1994) and the Albert Schweitzer School in Bad Rappenau (1991) are two examples). The argument that playfulness was anti-monumental and therefore appropriate for the Bundeshaus may have been no more than a convenient way to convince people to accept a style that Behnisch & Partner wanted to use regardless of its appropriateness to the program.

One of the most unusual decisions made by Baumann & Baumann, with Behnisch & Partner, was to incorporate written material on some of the transparent surfaces enclosing the building.

> Next to abstract graphic elements like points, lines, arrows typography is used as another element, as a meaningful and meaning-giving reference to the particular architectonic situation. Typography as a silent invitation to remain, to dawdle, to reflect, to think through, perhaps also to timid, light smiling to oneself.[49]

The text-covered glazing helps make the transparent surfaces tangible and visible, at the same time heightening the building envelope's see-through nature. Baumann & Baumann, together with Behnisch & Partner, chose texts reflecting either the purpose of the building or the mission of parliament, in order to integrate the text conceptually with the project. Many of the texts are therefore articles taken from the Basic Law, whose presence on the glass surfaces is supposed to remind the visitor of the essence of West German parliament. The articles are those most important to the overall building concept: Articles 1 through 16, which comprise the West German Bill of Rights, the Articles guaranteeing the voice of the people in parliament, freedom of speech, freedom of the press, freedom of dissent, and freedom of confession. The words remind the viewer of the building's purpose but because they are subtly written on transparent surfaces, they are unobtrusive. In fact, they are placed in areas where few members of the general public go and the words are difficult to make out in many light conditions. The visitor can easily overlook the text; see through it, in fact. Or, he or she can choose to discover the text and read into it the relationship between the Basic Law and parliament, between the Bill of Rights and the workings of parliament,

6.20
Detail of one poem on the transparent glass façade.
Behnisch & Partner.
Photographer:
Christian Kandzia.

between the public and the parliament and the architecture housing it. What neither Behnisch nor Baumann & Baumann acknowledge, however, is that only an educated viewer will recognize the source of the quotations and understand their larger meaning.

In addition to various Articles from the Basic Law, Baumann & Baumann chose poems by well-known German-speaking writers. Each poem treats a subject related to parliament, the polity, or democracy with subtle manipulations of spelling or placement of words that alter meaning and force the viewer to re-examine familiar notions (Figure 6.20).[50] Two examples are particularly relevant: Ernst Jandl's famous poem "*Lechts und Rinks,*" (literally, "reft and light"), and Eugen Gomringer's "*du blau du rot*" ("you blue you red"). The Jandl piece is a reversal of the first letters of Left and Right, the traditional designations of political orientation. The poem goes on to read, "some suggest that one cannot mix up left and right . . . " then, Jandl mixes them up anyway! The suggestion is that right and left are not so far from one another after all, therefore our differences are not as great as they may seem. In Gomringer's poem the words "you blue, you red, you yellow, you black" portray the multi-racial aspect of West Germany by the 1980s. Perhaps most interestingly, at the Bundeshaus, text is part of the architectural context rather than separate from, or imposed on it. Here is yet another play on words and their meanings since "context" is made by joining the prefix "con," which means "to join together," with "text" to form a word defined as "the circumstances in which a particular event occurs."[51] Text normally helps make the conceptual context for an architectural project, but it is not usual for the text to comprise the physical context as well. The poems operate in a manner similar to the building; they use play to make the audience comfortable then drive the very serious conceptual message home.

The plenary chamber is one space in which Behnisch was not mischievous but respected the gravity of the room's purpose (Figure 6.21). In keeping with its stature as the key space in the Bundeshaus, the chamber is situated at the very heart of the parliamentary building. Representatives' seats are arranged in a near perfect circle. Ministers and the chancellor sit within the circle side-by-side with other members rather than on a raised dais although their seats are separated from the rest. The perfect circle is meant to symbolize the equality accorded to all members whether of the majority or minority parties, and the community that exists in spite of political differences. But, as pointed out earlier, the non-hierarchical nature of the circle is itself something of a myth since proximity to the center is relative, making the seats closer to the center more important than those farther away. The circle is also thought to promote debate and discussion because members face each other from equal positions; Behnisch had the MPs speak from their seats rather than from a special podium to promote greater spontaneity in discussions.

6.21
View of the plenary chamber and the Eagle Wall.
Behnisch & Partner. Photographer: Christian Kandzia.

In actuality, however, the MPs did not like this way of presenting their opinions so it was soon scrapped in favor of the traditional presentation from a podium. Behnisch originally proposed to color the MPs' seats according to their party affiliations, but the parliament did not accept this proposal.[52] Instead, the chairs are all the same bright, Prussian blue.

Behnisch placed the plenary chamber at the center of the building composition not only to enhance its importance but to enhance its visibility from the different locations in the rest of the project.[53] It is true that from within the building many of the spaces are mutually visible but, as already noted, the general public does not amble through here. The circulation to the restaurant and the presidential wing passes next to the plenary chamber so that most official visitors to the complex will pass near and observe the chamber. Two outside courtyards also abut the room, making it visible from the adjacent outdoor space, but access to these too is restricted. Behnisch called the spatial effect the "open room" expressing the hope that by turning the public attention to the elected representatives as individuals, his building would epitomize the open democratic system in West Germany but the "open room" is not really very open.[54] Although passers-by promenading along the Rhine were supposed to be able to catch a glimpse of their representatives at work, this is no more successful in the Behnisch scheme than in the Schwippert one. Here, the actual distance from the building perimeter, across the intervening lawn, uphill to the promenade makes views into the plenary chamber quite difficult to find, if not impossible.

Integration of the building into the natural landscape was another important part of Behnisch's strategy to make the parliament unobtrusive while emphasizing the intricate connections between building and nature, between land, parliament, and people. "That was Parliament's wish – to meet on the banks of the Rhine, not simply in a hall that could be anywhere. They wanted to see the river, the Siebengebirge hills, the park-like landscape and the sky."[55] There are several ways in which the building is integrated into the site. The complex follows the natural slope of the site, cascading gently downwards from the Parliament Plaza towards the Rhine.[56] Nature is further incorporated into the building through gardens and courtyards that abut every façade, so that from every vantage point inside the parliamentary compound, natural life is visible. Three manmade pools of water are placed in the landscape, bringing the idea of the Rhine up to the very edges of the Bundeshaus. Most of the façades are made from floor-to-ceiling glass which helps give the illusion that the inside and outside are one. The walkways surrounding the buildings hover a few centimeters over the grass in the most delicate way. From a distance, this minimal step up virtually disappears so that the buildings seem to grow directly out of the earth. In the same way that floors project outward, roof extensions and balconies embrace the space around the complex. Several balconies are both exterior and interior spaces slicing through the transparent building envelope almost as if it did not exist. Projecting walls are yet another architectonic element Behnisch allows to penetrate from inside to outside. Just such a wall divides the public dining room from the private club and borders the restaurant patio. The extension of spaces and building elements from inside to outside traces back to early twentieth-century German modernism, to the Weimar era, and proposals like Mies van der Rohe's Brick Country House. In this way, Behnisch makes another connection, albeit in the subtlest of ways, to the Weimar democracy and the avant-garde German architecture of that period.

IV

Behnisch's use of transparency, unlike that of Schwippert and Foster, owes a debt to Baroque architecture as much as to its twentieth-century antecedents. Behnisch was intimately familiar with Baroque masterpieces like Versailles, an example he cites in "*Bauen in der Demokratie*" as exemplifying architecture with a firm political message.[57] Interestingly, the Palace of Versailles is more than the architectural embodiment of absolute monarchy. As Christian Norberg-Schultz points out, "Versailles is a true symbol of the absolute but 'open' system of seventeenth-century France."[58] Norberg-Schulz describes Versailles as a transparent building akin to a glass house because of its indeterminate structure, large openings, and fluid relationship to the landscape. Versailles' most illustrious space is the famous Hall of Mirrors designed by Charles le Brun and Jules Hardouin-Mansart in which 17 mirrored walls placed in false window casements face seventeen real windows to create an astonishing play of light, reflection, and spatial distortion. "The structure of the hall itself vanishes in the radiance of such shimmering surfaces and bursts of light; visitors described it as an architecture of emptiness."[59] The play of light and reflection at Versailles creates the illusion of endless space in the Hall of Mirrors and brings views of the outside into the interior by projecting them onto the "false windows."

Behnisch claims to have been as fascinated with the illusory and reflective quality of glass as much as its transparent quality, affording other interpretive dimensions to the Bundeshaus.[60] In many of the photographs of the building, the reflective characteristic of the façades is as apparent as its transparent aspect. The presence of reflections on the transparent surfaces acts like the textual pieces to materialize the otherwise invisible substance. Moreover, the reflections can be seen as yet another playful layer in an already intricately composed system of layers. Reflections appear and disappear in a largely unpredictable but always changing way making the building's exterior aspect an ephemeral moving picture. Furthermore, by projecting the image of an exterior object onto the façades, reflections conflate the barriers between interior and exterior space. In the Baroque period, mirrors were used on the interior in order to distort the sense of space, to create the illusion of bound-less space and to brighten rooms by reflecting light, whereas at the Bundeshaus, exterior surfaces usually act like mirrors, altering the building's outward, public manifestation.

In the end, despite the tremendous use of see-through glass, the architecture of the Behnisch Bundeshaus is only somewhat more transparent than that of the Schwippert building, since like its predecessor, architectural transparency is dependent on more than the material used to construct the building but also on light conditions and proximity to the structure. Likewise, political transparency was no more a reality in 1989 than in 1949 although the certainty of a democratic system existed. The most salient difference between the two eras is the degree to which the transparency ideology had taken root by Behnisch's time. Reading through the many competition briefs, expert reports, colloquia, and news articles, transparency is recommended and required, accepted but rarely questioned or criticized.[61] By 1989 the transparency myth had firmly taken hold.

Chapter 7

Coming to terms with the past

Transparency in Norman Foster's Reichstag

The epochal threshold, which simultaneously paves the way for a return to a happier status quo ante, awakens a dialectical expectation: on the one hand, entirely new problems demand entirely new answers; on the other, these answers are to be mined from the sealed treasure trove of a tradition with which we made, in 1945, an 'infamous' break.

Jürgen Habermas[1]

More than anything, Norman Foster's renovation of the Reichstag as the seat of the Bundestag casts doubt upon German transparency ideology and its near mystical association with democracy (Figure 7.1). Unlike the Behnisch building, whose glazed outer skin is as transparent as possible, the Reichstag is clad in solid stone. With the exception of the West Portal, whose large glass plates are obscured by the massive columns standing in front, transparent glass figures minimally on the Reichstag's exteriors. Even interior transparency is limited to parts of the circulation areas and the plenary chamber's enclosure. In fact, the competition brief seemed to recognize the challenges, if not utter impossibility, of trying to implement architectural transparency in the existing stone structure by prescribing a transparent plenary chamber rather than a transparent building. Nevertheless, transparency figured prominently in many of the competition design schemes, including the three

7.1
Aerial view of the renovated Reichstag.
Bundesbildstelle Berlin.
Photographer: Berndt Kühler.

runners-up for first prize, Santiago Calatrava's design with a new glass cupola, Pi de Bruijn's glass saucer-shaped plenary chamber situated next to the old Reichstag, and Foster's glass "umbrella." Since the initial competition, transparent ideology has been present in the debates about the renovation and in the literature about the project written by Foster and others. The *New York Times* announced the opening of the Reichstag in 1999 by writing,

> The new Germany, exquisitely sensitive to its past, informally welcomed back its Parliament to a refurbished Reichstag in Berlin. Topped with glass to symbolize the political transparency on which the country has based its postwar revival, the building was restored at a cost of $330 million by British architect Sir Norman Foster.[2]

The *Times* article seems to suggest the pervasiveness of the transparency myth not only because here it is used by the foreign press but because it is used in a case when there is almost no transparency at all. It is equally interesting to note that no one spoke of transparency when Paul Wallot completed the first glass dome for the building in 1897; at that time, the dome was described as a mark of modernity but not a signal for democracy and open government.[3] But 100 years later the new dome is spoken of almost exclusively in terms outlined by Foster and his design team as a "beacon," "lantern," and "symbol of transparency," whether the speaker is agreeing with Foster's claims, or refuting them. It is equally important to note that on the opening day, Chancellor Gerhard Schröder said it was the success of

"Bonn democracy" that "makes the Berlin Republic possible."[4] With this speech Schröder made certain no one would mistake unified Germany and its new capital for anything but a continuation of the FRG. The very act of making such an affirmation demonstrates history's presence looming over the project and the importance of debates over Berlin, the return to the Reichstag, German identity after unification, and old ideologies from the FRG to the newly united Germany. The use of transparency ideology after unification is only one way the FRG asserted its continuity after 1989. It is interesting to see how Foster's project addresses transparency as well as other issues related to continuity and history. On the one hand, the project cannot help but engage German architectural and political history because it is the renovation of a building whose history is long, rich, and layered and intimately tied to German politics and political identity. On the other hand, the way in which the Foster team approached the problem framed history in a particular manner: as a series of events that should be brought into the present and remembered simultaneously with current events, rather than forgotten or examined through the lens of historical distance. From postwar West German architectural history, Foster assumed the rhetoric of the transparency ideology without much of the architectonic logic. Foster does not adopt transparency as Hans Schwippert and Günter Behnisch had claimed to use it before, although he does make some similar assertions. At the Reichstag, transparency as an analogy for accessible, open, democratic parliament is weak, if not false. But in Foster's hands, transparency takes on another analogical meaning; the interventions into the nineteenth-century building are a means with which to confront the past and its relationship to identity, to reveal German history even as it is being made anew.[5]

I

The German parliament struggled with the questions of symbolism, national identity, and the appropriate form for state architecture after unification as it debated the decision to move the government from Bonn to Berlin, and to abandon the newly constructed Bundestag for a reconstructed Reichstag. Yet, the vote ultimately favored the force of one symbolic element over another by deciding to return to what some still considered the metaphoric heart of the German State and culture. The implication is that Berlin as a positive symbol of unity and German culture is stronger than the negative history some associate with the city; the memories of Wilhelmine despotism, the failings of the Weimar Republic, the transgressions of the Third Reich, the capitulation at the end of the Second World War, and 40 years of separation into two states. The relocation is also a rejection of the utopia that the garden city Bonn represents for the dystopia of the corrupt, schizophrenic Berlin whose cultural unification has, to date, remained an unrealized desire. Some Germans hoped that relocating the parliament in Berlin would help erase the memories and scars remaining from the 40-year physical and political split, since Berlin was the capital of the former unified German republic, the National Socialist government, Wilhelmine Germany, and the residence of the Prussian king. On the other hand, the choice of the monumental city of Berlin as capital raised fears about the emergence of a powerful and assertive Germany willing to exercise its newfound strength.[6] Placing the government seat right at the heart of the former East Germany makes the federal government closer to the East, presumably helping to solidify connections between the Federal apparatus and former East Germany as well as between Germany and its neighbors in Eastern Europe. Some alarmists even viewed the new position of the capital as the negation of the Westward orientation the FRG had cultivated since the end of the Second World War. Finally, abandoning Bonn forced the construction not only of new federal buildings but also of a new state identity for all of Germany, not just the East. This removed some of the sense that East Germany was absorbed into the Federal Republic without any substantive affect to the West.

Once the parliament decided to move the capital, the Bundestag debated how to occupy Berlin. Financial considerations largely dictated many of the choices – such as the decision to renovate and reuse Göring's old Aviation Ministry for the Ministry of Finance, and the Reichstag for the parliament. Reusing existing buildings, even with all the renovation costs, was cheaper than constructing anew. In a country so sensitive to symbol and to references to its past, the decisions concerning relocation were bound to cause controversy. Numerous articles appeared in the German press debating the symbolic import of the Reichstag. Some authors associated the building with the negative aspects of the German Sonderweg – with the aggressive, imperialist past.[7] Others pointed out that Hitler had never governed from the building while the first German parliament had made its home there and the first democratic German republic was declared from the Reichstag's balcony on November 9, 1918, and met in the building until the regime folded, making the building a symbol of German democracy. Still others argued that monumental stone architecture was forever tainted because of Albert Speer's use of such stone constructions to epitomize Hitler's Third Reich.[8] According to this view, neither the passage of time nor a new intervention could erase the negative historical associations embedded in the building. This is amusing given the future use Speer foresaw for the Reichstag in his master plan for Berlin; the building was to be converted into a cafeteria for the Great Hall. Still other Germans claimed that the building's symbolic meaning had been neutralized during the long years between the war and unification,

when the building lay largely unused, a neutral backdrop for Saturday after-
noon soccer games played by West Berlin youth and occasional political
demonstrations and rock concerts (Figure 7.2). In other words, the reading of
the symbolic import of the building was mixed. No matter what the point
of view, however, reconstructing and reusing the old Reichstag would certainly reconnect the present democracy both symbolically and physically to the
past. The question was, to what past? Inhabiting the Reichstag would force
the problems of German twentieth-century history to the forefront of parliamentarians' consciousness, making the past an everyday presence rather than
an occasional one.

The general discomfort Germans must have felt with the Reichstag
was already apparent in the open competition mounted in 1992 to explore possible ways of renovating the structure. Only 300 people requested the
competition brief, with a mere 80 submitting.[9] The low numbers are even
more astonishing when compared with the 600,000 plus registered architects
in the country who were all eligible to participate. Furthermore, there are
usually about 80 submissions for small, restricted, regional architectural competitions while open, national ones tend to attract hundreds of completed

7.2
**View of people
gathered in front
of the ruined
Reichstag on
September 9, 1948
when Ernst Reuter
made his famous
speech, "Shaut
auf dieser Stadt."
("Look at this
city.")**
Bundesbildstelle
Berlin.

proposals. The Jewish Museum competition of 1989, for example, had over 800 completed entries. The reluctance to confront the conundrum over the potential reading of the Reichstag was certainly one reason so few architects decided to enter, a reluctance that is understandable given the multiplicity of opinions about the building's historical significance. As Federal President Wolfgang Thierse points out in his introduction to *The* Reichstag: *The Parliament Building by Norman Foster*, "The Reichstag building was frequently referred to as a symbol. A symbol of what? Of the Wilhelmine era? Of the downfall of the Weimar Republic? Of the Hitler regime? Of the division and reunification of Germany?"[10] Any architect working on the design problem would have to develop a position relative to the building's history and meaning and would have to propose some symbolic schema for the new interventions. To do this necessitated some vision of German political identity after unification as well, a difficult task only three years after the event.

II

If Berlin is the city of ghosts, then the Reichstag is the building of ghosts since it is literally haunted by the past.[11] Any interpretation of the meaning of the Reichstag is wholly dependent on the reading of its history. The word Reichstag initially referred to the politically weak pan-Germanic parliament that began meeting in the seventeenth century. The name was next applied both to the all-German parliament convened to represent the individual states and principalities to the Prussian crown after unification in 1871, and to the building that was eventually constructed to house the legislative body. The first Reichstag was convened as a political concession Bismarck granted to the various kingdoms, principalities, and city-states comprising unified Germany. The body was only reluctantly accepted by the Prussian royal family who resented what they saw as an encroachment upon their power and hereditary right to rule. To some parliamentarians, the need for a special building was immediately apparent but it took over a decade to win the Kaiser's approval for the construction scheme, and over 20 years until the first German national parliament building was actually completed. Designed and built by the German architect, Paul Wallot, Germans read mixed symbolic intentions into the architecture from the start. The Kaiser clearly meant to use the building to celebrate German unity, military prowess, and cultural ascendancy while some members of the parliament intended the building to be a monument to nascent German democracy.[12]

In keeping with the grand aspirations for the building, Paul Wallot constructed an imposing stone structure, a rectangular body with towers in each corner, grandiose portico-covered entrances facing east and west, and

an impressive four-sided steel and glass dome. The building's style is difficult
to pinpoint since instead of working with one of the prevailing historic styles
in vogue at the end of the nineteenth century, Wallot borrowed elements
from many of them – the neo-Renaissance and neo-Baroque porticos and ped-
iments, square towers from the Renaissance revival, and medieval heraldic
devices used on the sculptural program. As many historians have pointed
out, the task of designing a seat for the newly unified Reich was not an easy
one. At the time, most architects worked with one historic style or another,
depending on the building type and function, each style having particular
though controversial symbolic associations. By eschewing a single style
and choosing to integrate elements from many styles, Wallot can be seen to
have created either an a-stylistic building, or a pan-stylistic one, depending on
the interpreter's perspective. In any case, Wallot used a consistent approach
throughout, adorning the interior and exterior with pictures, statuary, artworks,
and stained glass whose iconographic content was as varied as the historic
styles, and reflected the same themes as the building as a whole. Wallot
celebrated the imperial might by covering the Reichstag with crowns and
eagles. Other devices refer to German unification including coats of arms
and emblems that pointed to the federal nature of the German empire that
had joined the four largest German kingdoms, Prussia, Bavaria, Saxony, and
Württemberg, with several city-states, to form one nation. One pediment
features an eagle with a snake in its talons, a symbol meant to ward off
discord. The four corner towers signified the largest four German kingdoms.
Figures from German history such as Charlemagne and Maximilian I stood
alongside great cultural figures like Goethe and Heine, helping to reaffirm the
German Reich's claims to be the reinstatement of a pre-existing state whose
cultural antecedents were clear. The glass and steel dome erected atop the
Reichstag was meant to refer to other capital buildings around the world, to
signify democratic, or at least, parliamentary representative government.[13]
Wallot's original design called for a stone dome but because of design
changes during construction, the eventual structure could not support the
weight of stone so Wallot devised a new design out of the lighter materials
steel and glass. Calling this structure a dome is not strictly correct, however,
since its shape was not spherical at all but a series of arches extending from a
rectangular base, a form known as a polygonal cloister vault.

Almost from its completion, the Reichstag building was controversial. Parliamentarians were naturally delighted with their new home but the
architecture press of the day condemned the building for its confused mixture
of styles. Kaiser Wilhelm II publicly referred to it as "the epitome of bad taste"
and "the ape house."[14] The Kaiser probably took the installation of a dome
five meters higher than the one atop his city palace, the *Stadtschloss*, as a
personal affront. In the middle of the First World War, in 1916, the inscription

Dem Deutschen Volke (to the German people) was placed on the frieze above the west portico, the main entrance to the building, belatedly fulfilling Wallot's original intention. "The Kaiser disdained such egalitarian sentiments" but agreed to place it there in the thick of the First World War "as a patriotic gesture."[15] Thus, from the first, the building's meaning was layered and complex, nor was there any consensus as to whether the building was a success or not. It could be seen both as an architectural achievement of tremendous originality or a stylistic travesty, the epitome of imperial might or the symbol of nascent representative democracy.[16]

Faced with the imminent collapse of the German military towards the end of the First World War, and the Allies' refusal to negotiate a peace with the German military government, the Kaiser decided to abdicate and flee. He left a Berlin divided into two camps: those supporting the establishment of a republic under the Social Democrats and those supporting a Communist takeover under the Spartacus League. It was only when he heard that Karl Liebknecht and the Communists were preparing to march on the Imperial Palace to declare a Bolshevik republic that Philipp Scheidemann ascended to a first-floor balcony in the Reichstag and declared the formation of a demo- cratic republic. However, the new German parliament did not meet in the Reichstag until the unrest in Berlin died down, instead deciding to meet in Weimar, from which the regime took its name. From spring 1919 until Hitler's election to power in 1933, the Reichstag did function as the seat of parliament for the Weimar Republic. Some therefore associate the building with the first German democracy and democratic values, but because of the failures of the Weimar Republic many associate the Reichstag with failed democracy. For Stalin, and the Russian army, the Reichstag symbolized German aggres- sion and military might. It may also have symbolized Liebknecht's failed Bolshevik revolution for the Russians. The Russians therefore made the build- ing the target for bombs bearing the inscription "for the Reichstag" as well as the ultimate goal inside the city for their troops. On May 2, 1945, after the Soviet army entered Berlin, the photographer Yevgeny Shaldecz and several Soviet soldiers climbed onto the roof of the Reichstag, planted the Soviet flag with the hammer and sickle, and took the famous image showing the flag atop the burning building, with the Brandenburg Gate in the background.[17] On the same day, Russian soldiers covered the Reichstag with graffiti, messages ranging from the simple inscription of a soldier's name, to proclamations of victory, to expressions of downright anger and obscenity.[18] For the Russians, then, the taking of the Reichstag was synonymous with vanquishing Fascism; the Reichstag was seen as the symbol of the National Socialist state no matter how it was understood by the Germans and the other Allied Powers.

In point of fact, Hitler never governed from the Reichstag. He never even spoke in the building as a parliamentarian. The building was burned in

1933 soon after Hitler became Chancellor. The National Socialists used the fire as a pretext to declare a state emergency, suspend civil freedoms, and repress the Communist Party in the Enabling Act.[19] Although responsibility for the fire was pinned on a mentally disturbed Dutchman, Marinus van Lubbe, some historians attribute it to the National Socialists, since National Socialism certainly profited the most from the event.[20] The damage to the building apparently was not serious but Hitler decided to move the parliament to the Kroll Opera House rather than repair the Reichstag, and a paralyzed parliament, such as it was, continued to meet in the Opera House until the end of the war. In spite of the historic record, the Reichstag continued to symbolize National Socialism to many long after the war, into the 1990s when the renovation project began.[21]

III

Confrontation and coexistence with the past were, indeed, the most important concepts Foster cited for the renovation of the Reichstag. The Foster team had explored similar themes a year or so before in their suggestion for ways to deal with remnants of the Berlin Wall. For that project, they were going to preserve sections of the Wall in order to safeguard the historic record and its artifacts as reminders of the past. The design team argued that past and present must coexist in order for the lessons of history to remain accessible to future generations of Germans.[22] The notion is not unique to Foster. The carpet that sits in the atrium at the Ministry of Defense in Berlin, for example, is a woven version of an aerial photograph taken of the city in 1945. The image of ultimate destruction sits as a constant reminder to the Ministry of the tragedy of war. In his Reichstag competition entry, Foster proposed to make the connection between past and present evident by leaving the old structure of the Reichstag as a gutted shell, and by encasing it in glass, so that the building itself would become an artifact enshrined in a mammoth display case. For the competition scheme, the plenary chamber was a space enclosed by transparent glass, placed at the building's center, at the physical and symbolic heart of the structure. Old building and new interventions alike were to be covered by the massive transparent glass canopy (Figure 7.3). No viewer could fail to remark the irony involved in enshrining an object with so dubious a symbolic value.[23] Although some transparency was mandated by the competition brief, and strongly urged by one of Foster's first collaborators on the project, rather than a personal or ideological choice, the Foster team took the use of see-through glass construction far beyond the enclosure of the plenary chamber.[24] While transparency ideology dictated the association of see-through building with democracy, already in the first competition the transparency to history is far stronger than notions of accessibility and

openness. "To architecturally and politically acknowledge its presence (the old building's) – not to deny it – but to *transform* it as an integral part of a new composition," wrote Foster of his design, "the new total becomes a built response to the realities of Germany, as a modern European democracy."[25] Like Schwippert and Behnisch before him, Foster seems to be considering contemporary German political identity when he works out his design. But in his hands, transparency is not only supposed to connote the interaction between the Res Publica and the parliament, but between contemporary Germany and her past. Because Foster's architectural interventions occur in relationship to an older, solid stone structure, transparency is almost entirely internal and extremely circumscribed; there is no substantive visual contact with the outside and the landscape, except from the roof and cupola. However, the transparent construction presents an interesting juxtaposition between the "other," in the form of a contemporary esthetic using modern materials and constructive means, in direct confrontation with a building alternatively considered the symbol of Wilhelmine authoritarianism, botched Weimar democracy, and, however inaccurately, National Socialist oppression.[26]

The jury for the competition seems to have had as much trouble defining the appropriate architectural image for unified Germany as many

7.3
The Foster competition model.
Foster and Partners. Photographer: Tom Miller.

German architects. Rather than determine a clear winner, the jury declared a three-way tie. The choice of finalists, Norman Foster, Santiago Calatrava, and Pi de Bruijn, and their very different schemes, seems to reflect the general uncertainty about the correct path to take. De Bruijn proposed to modify the old building but to place a new plenary chamber adjacent to, but outside, the existing structure, creating a very obvious dialog between the historic building and the modern one. Foster's entry has already been described above. Calatrava's design was the most conservative in that it accepted the historic Reichstag as the basis for a new dome and some other internal and external architectonic additions. A second run-off competition was held for which the finalists were asked to re-work their proposals to accommodate more modest ambitions for the building dictated by concerns over the growing costs of uni-fication. The total square footage was reduced from 33,000 to between 9,000 and 12,000 square meters. Since the total size of the existing structure was 17,000 square meters, the proposed renovation would not utilize the total space available, leaving tremendous room for open spaces in plan and section. Finally, according to Foster, he and his team had a unique approach to the second phase of the competition in that they presented four loosely worked out options for reconstruction rather than just one more carefully developed one, as Calatrava and de Bruijn had. The clever strategy made the Foster team appear simultaneously more flexible and more thorough than the others. By July 1993 the various Bundestag committees had decided for Foster.

Foster differs from Schwippert and Behnisch, first and foremost, and perhaps most importantly, because he is not German. He is an outsider in every sense, by birth, citizenship, politics, and artistic training and interest. It can be argued that he therefore brings detached objectivity to the project, the view from afar, and the "other"'s point-of-view. Furthermore, Foster did not share many of the emotional issues Germans had for either the Reichstag or the Bundestag. The choice to have a non-German architect known for his international practice design the building most representative of the German nation could be read as the ultimate anti-national, pro-international, or pro-European, decision as well as a clear choice to adopt the "other." Of course, it is also fraught with problems. How is an outsider to discern and properly represent the post-unification German national identity in architectural terms? By his own admission, confirmed by project architect David Nelson, Foster grappled more with what he perceived to be the functional and programmatic requirements of the Reichstag rather than with questions of the appropriate architectural iconography for German democracy after unification, standing in direct contrast with Behnisch and his team who were very much involved in such questions.[27] In fact, Nelson claims that discussions of symbolism and meaning were very rare. The instances in which he remembers considering the potential meaning of their work in any focused way centered on the designs for the cupola and the federal eagle, two isolated pieces in the larger design. Nelson's assertions therefore call into question many claims made by the Foster team. Furthermore, in a country acutely aware of architecture and its meaning, the Foster approach could only arouse acerbic criticism. Some German journalists cynically pointed out that commissioning an architect known primarily for his commercial projects was inopportune because it made the image of capitalism and economic might the dominant one for the new German state.[28]

The Foster project differs too in that it was the redesign of an existing building, and one that had already been renovated once before. The constraints were therefore greater, as was the necessity to confront the various associations the Reichstag had in the minds of the German public. Arguably, one step in this process was Christo's wrapping of the building during two weeks in June and July 1995. After over 20 years of lobbying, an effort that began in the late 1960s, the artist Christo and his wife Jeanne-Claude finally succeeded in convincing the Bundestag to debate their proposal in February 1994. As former president Rita Süssmuth has pointed out, in the opinion of a majority of parliamentarians, the time felt right for the Christo project in spite of some public and political opposition, so parliament approved the proposal.[29] Christo and Jeanne-Claude chose shimmering silver polypropylene cloth for the wrapper, which they fastened with blue rope that crisscrossed the various building parts. The hundreds of photographs taken of the wrapped building show it as a pristine crystalline object, almost ghostlike in appearance. The silver material was not tautly stretched over the building, but rather permitted to drape itself over the tremendous mass in multitudes of delicate pleats. Foster called the wrapping "cathartic. It seemed to unburden the building of its more tragic associations and prepare it for the next phase of its career."[30] But in what way was this act cathartic? And for whom? After all, the Reichstag was unchanged by the installation. Although the perception of the building underwent a change in the eyes of some commentators in the popular press, the fact that the Reichstag's transformation was intended as purely symbolic meant that the event had virtually no effect on public opinion about the building, as numerous contemporary articles demonstrate. The wrapping and unwrapping did signal another potential reading of Foster's coming project and its relationship to history; the way interpretations of architecture are profoundly related to how people think and see the world, and the irrational force of associations. Christo and Jeanne-Claude referred to the project as a "memorial to democracy."[31] In which sense they intended this memorial is unclear, however, to the death of democracy or the rebirth, or the commemoration?

Foster repeatedly points to "lightness, transparency, permeability, and public access" as the concepts driving the Reichstag design. These four

concepts are intimately connected; transparency makes lightness and permeability possible while transparent materials and spatial arrangements are
analogies for public access and open government even if they only permit
visual, not physical, contact between visitors from the general public and
members of parliament. The four concepts seem strange claims, however,
given the architectural realities of both the pre-existing Reichstag building and
the renovated structure. Foster and his team certainly worked with some
transparency and lightness but these, as with permeability and public access,
are not only very limited, but far more limited here than they were in the
Behnisch Bundeshaus in Bonn. Furthermore, when interviewed, David Nelson
claimed that the office was highly pragmatic in its approach to the problem,
intentionally avoiding analogical solutions.[32] It is true that the four concepts are
deeply rooted in the German postwar parliamentary architectural tradition and
that Foster had been asked to work with them. But to what extent are they
really incorporated into the design? With his mantra Foster seems to accept
the German idea that "whoever builds transparently, builds democratically,"
but rather than try to use transparency in the way that Behnisch and
Schwippert claimed to have done, to reveal democracy at work, promote
public accessibility to MPs, and as an analogy for democracy, Foster ultimately
uses transparency to unmask the pre-existing historic architecture and thereby
focus attention on history itself.[33]

      In Foster's hands, the new architectonic elements act as backdrops
and frames for the historic architecture in a clever act of juxtaposition that
invites the viewer to consider the new building, and its meaning, vis-à-vis the
old. Thus, Foster's architectural interventions are similar to unification itself in
that they place two things face-to-face, in this case the German architectural
past and present, and by implication some aspects of German history and
contemporary viewers. As with other forms of transparency, however, the
architect can establish views but cannot guarantee that the viewer will do
more than observe what is set before him. That is, the architecture is not an
agent for action and participation. In this case, Foster can make aspects of the
historic record visible to the visitor at the Reichstag but he cannot force that
visitor to engage in thoughtful consideration of them. From the start, the
German parliament "meant" the renovation "to be a symbol of reunited
Germany."[34] By allowing the new interventions to subtly interact with the old,
Foster reminds the viewer that the old Reichstag was also intended as
a symbol of "united Germany." Immediately the question arises for the
thoughtful observer – what is the difference between the united Germany
of 1871, and the united Germany of 1989? And, what is the difference
between the Weimar democracy and the FRG? In Foster's hands the answer
to these questions seems to be a country that can live with the complexities
of its past, even as it moves into the future. But paradoxically, Foster's use of

7.4
Entry façade of the Reichstag.
Bundesbildstelle Berlin.
Photographer: Berndt Kühler.

the transparency ideology to defend his project also underscores another truth of mature German democracy – the tendency to create identity myths and to permit a degree of self-deception about the true state of democracy.

Foster uses many different architectural strategies to reveal the historic aspects of the Reichstag and to make the visitor aware of history. To begin with, he decided to preserve the building's outer shell intact while making the interior his work. (The building briefs largely dictated Foster's strategy although his team did have some freedom. It would have been possible, for instance, to restore the destroyed building fabric and ornamentation, a strategy Foster eschewed.) He decided to keep the outer walls more or less the way they were by the early 1990s rather than replace exterior ornament that had been removed after the war and during the 1960s renovation by the German architect Paul Baumgarten, what was effectively a decision to leave some marks of history in the form of absences on the contemporary building. The visitor approaches the building at the original entrance on the west side, with only two outwardly visible signs of change from before 1999: the glass façade inserted behind the portico, and the cupola atop the roof (Figure 7.4).

Preservation at the Reichstag took more than one form. For example, Foster was eager to preserve some of the scurrilous graffiti left by Russian troops in 1944, but preserved the scribbles in such a precious way as to diminish their power in the minds of many observers. The Russian inscriptions were uncovered during the restoration as the drywall from Baumgarten's renovation was removed. The inscriptions range from the names of soldiers to obscenities to phrases celebrating the Russian victory. "On the day of the victory over Fascism we send battle greetings to all members of our glorious Red Army"[35] or "They certainly paid for Leningrad!" and "Hello Moscow! Berlin's had it."[36] Foster argued for the preservation of the graffiti because it was part of the history of the building and the historical record (Figure 7.5). Saving the inscriptions, in his mind, would allow "the Reichstag to function as a living museum of German history."[37] Foster managed to convince the Building Committee to go along with his preservationist instincts. The writing was painstakingly preserved while the stone on which it appears was cleaned. The decision to retain the graffiti was controversial enough; the *New York Times* wrote, "Certainly there is something 'open,' if not plain masochistic,

7.5
**Inscriptions
preserved on one
of the staircases.**
Foster and Partners.
Photographer:
Nigel Young.

about Chancellor Gerhard Schröder going past Russian obscenities to reach his blue-doored parliamentary office. Schröder's father died in 1944 on his way back from the Russian front."[38] This confrontation was clearly the point for everywhere the past stares the visitor in the face. Not just the historic structure but the defacements made to it, the remains of all the events the building witnessed, anything that could be salvaged in the name of a "living museum" was saved.

Foster's approach to the project could be described as archeological in nature since the first stage involved removing the Baumgarten additions to the building, under which all sorts of historical artifacts were discovered, beyond the Soviet graffiti and stair remnants. Wherever he found marks left by some former event in the building, Foster worked to save them, arguing that these traces comprised the record of the building's history. Stone entryways and walls whose ornament had been torn off were carefully cleaned but left in disrepair, scarred testaments to the former condition of the building. In the east corridor, the rubble arches over the entryways resemble rough-hewn stone found in ancient Greek or Roman ruins. Above the doorways runs a crumbled stone frieze, a narrow band where some other construction had originally sat. The disfigured stonewalls where granite staircases had been ripped from their supports were left, visible behind the transparent glass handrails of the new staircases. Fragments of nineteenth-century moldings and mason's marks were left bare. Foster was careful to insert the new staircases into Wallot's stairwells so they are separated from the walls, clearly marking them as new insertions.

> I came to realize that the Reichstag's fabric bears the imprint of time and events more powerfully than any exhibition could convey. I was convinced that it should not be sanitized. Preserving these scars allows the building to become a living museum of German history.[39]

New additions are detailed to appear layered over the older fabric so that there seems to have been a peeling back of new to reveal the old. In the east corridor, for example, the stucco wall pieces protrude further than older, stone remnants, and are always slightly separated by a reveal. The stucco's color is also slightly different than the stone. The total effect is one of multiple material layers, a palimpsest of history. Looking down this corridor from original stone wall, to Russian graffiti, to war ruins, to new streamlined glass, steel, and stucco, the viewer is bombarded with historical references. What does this mean? How is one to understand the identity of the space? The viewer is left to his or her own conclusions.

Although Foster retained the exterior largely untouched in its solid, opaque state, he decided to render the interiors as open as possible within the

7.6

Section cut through the plenary chamber and the entry lobby. The spatial transparency is apparent in the flow of space between discrete areas.

Foster and Partners.

constraints dictated by working inside a pre-existing stone shell. He opted for a new interior spatial arrangement that conformed neither to the Wallot plans nor to the Baumgarten ones. Eliminating unnecessary partitions and floor plates opened the building in plan and in section (Figure 7.6). Floors removed include the third and fourth that had been inserted into the existing shell during the Baumgarten renovation.[40] Foster decided to take these two floors out because they closed off two large interior courtyards thereby blocking vertical access to light, air, and views. Furthermore, by reinstating the courtyards Foster was able to make the building somewhat more visually transparent on the north–south axis to match the openness in the east–west direction. He eliminated partitions in the circulation spaces and, where they were absolutely necessary for fire code or privacy reasons, used transparent glass so that views through the length of any particular corridor are unimpeded. Views into individual rooms, however, are blocked by opaque partitions; MPs did not want all of their interactions to be on display. Only a handful of rooms have transparent glass partitions between their interiors and the circulation space. Thus, the internal transparency was improved, but not made as extreme as it could have been or even as pervasive as it is in the Behnisch building. Today, the corridors are also typically open in section to floors above and below as well as to the courtyards so that the visitor has views through the building in multiple directions simultaneously. Plans to make the corridor floors out of transparent glass were not realized, however. One pleasant consequence of the remodeling is that natural light permeates to every space, if not directly, then at least indirectly.

> We have gouged through the building from top to bottom, opening
> it up – especially the chamber – to natural light and views.
> Members of Parliament on the floor of the chamber can now look
> up directly to see people on the ramps in the cupola . . . high above
> their heads.[41]

This claim is true but, unfortunately, the reverse is not true. The large mirrored
light-refracting device blocks views from the roof. The east corridor is typical
of the new arrangement. Rising through three levels, divisions between dis-
creet areas are made of transparent glass, as are all the handrails, so it is
possible to view the full length of the building horizontally, and the full height
vertically. In addition to opening the building spaces to one another, Foster
decided to open the shell wherever possible. This meant reinstalling windows
in all the original openings and, in some instances, breaking through the stone
shell to create new ones. For example, Foster decided to bring into use rooms
located behind the parapet of the four towers, on the third floor. These four
large rooms now accommodate the political factions, and a press lobby, with
service spaces. Because the spaces had never been used before, they had no
windows of any kind. Foster inserted glass clerestory windows and transparent top-lights to bring in natural light. The press lobby is adjacent to a glass
viewing gallery that looks into the plenary chamber below.

Foster claims that the new openness was designed to make views
to historic remnants simultaneously visible from many different vantage
points and was supposed to make the parliamentarians more accessible to
the visiting public. Although the Foster team did replace the original closed
layout with a somewhat more open plan, it is still a compartmentalized interior
with numerous small, autonomous rooms aligned along a corridor. Greater
accessibility was not realized at all. Even before September 11, 2001 and the
heightened security measures instituted afterwards, the security regulations
at the building severely restricted public access.[42] The general public was, and
still is, divided into two groups at the main entrance: those visiting the roof
deck only and those visiting the plenary chamber. Those who wish to visit the
plenary chamber must apply for permission weeks in advance. Security personnel vet them very carefully before granting permission to attend a session.
At the door, every visitor passes through a metal detector and places his or her
handbag and backpack through a detector in a secure zone between the
portico and the lobby. Once inside, the visitor is always accompanied by an
official guide and is always separated from the parliamentarians by some physical barrier. At minimum the separation is a see-through glass partition; at most
the separation is constituted of several contiguous spaces. Most parts of the
building are not accessible to the general public at all, either physically or visually. The one exception to security rules holds for guests of MPs. When an MP

brings ten or fewer guests to visit the Reichstag, they are not vetted. This rule was a concession to MPs who did not want to offend their supporters by the unpleasant vetting process.[43] The apparent spatial openness does create a condition in some parts of the building in which the visitor can see forward to spaces soon to be entered, and backwards to spaces already visited, thereby making his or her personal history in relation to the Reichstag legible, but in other respects the building is not at all permeable.

When comparing the Foster plans to those executed by Wallot, it is evident exactly how the Foster strategy played out (Figures 7.7–7.14). The exterior surfaces, and therefore the building's overall form, are virtually

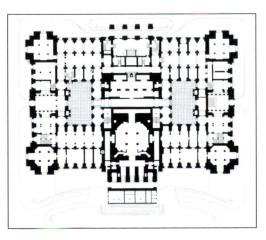

7.7

Plan at ground level of the Wallot design for the Reichstag.

Foster and Partners.

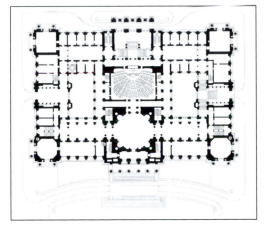

7.8

Plan of the plenary chamber from the Wallot design.

Foster and Partners.

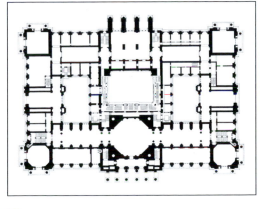

7.9

Plan of the intermediary floor from the Wallot design.

Foster and Partners.

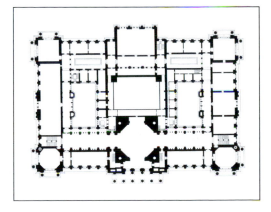

7.10

Plan of the second floor from the Wallot design.

Foster and Partners.

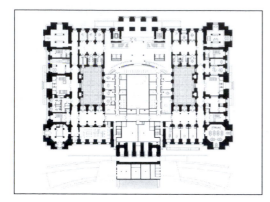

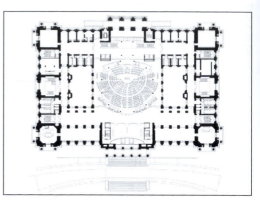

7.11
Ground floor plan of the Foster redesign of the Reichstag.
Foster and Partners.

7.12
Floor plan of the Foster redesign of the Reichstag showing the plenary chamber.
Foster and Partners.

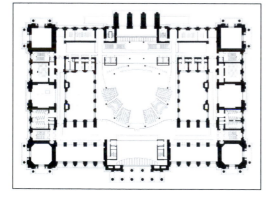

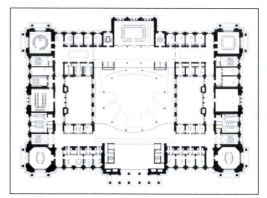

7.13
Floor plan of the first floor showing the tribunes in the Foster redesign of the Reichstag.
Foster and Partners.

7.14
Second floor plan of the Foster redesign of the Reichstag.
Foster and Partners.

identical in both versions. But the interior plans are quite different, especially in the central areas housing the plenary chamber and ceremonial spaces. In Wallot's plans the central spaces are self-contained and closed to one another while in Foster's drawings these same zones are largely visible to one another, reading as one continuous space rather than a series of individuated ones. The removal of interior partitions, both walls and floors, to allow increased visual connections and spatial flow was one way that Foster opened up the interior. (Figure 7.15). Another way was to make many of the partitions transparent glass so that even where physical barriers were necessary, they are neither vision- nor light-blocking objects. This is in keeping with his fundamental goal

7.15
View of multiple layers in the circulation space. The transparent glass partitions and handrails are evident.
Foster and Partners. Photographer: Nigel Young.

to increase lightness, by which Foster means both exposure to natural light, and the feeling of being without weight, for lightness directly contrasts the heaviness and darkness of the original building. The materials chosen, therefore, were transparent glass and light-reflecting stainless steel and aluminum to oppose the heaviness of the older stone structure. Wherever possible, the "lightness of the new stands in stark contrast to the heaviness of the old" and is a constant reminder of the presence of history.[44] Weightlessness is achieved not only through material means, but also through the suspension of almost transparent, floating bridge elements throughout the building, the introduction of natural light into unexpected places, the use of delicate metal members next to massive stone pieces, and the lightening of the stone's color caused by cleaning.

The connection between lightness and transparency is apparent in the team's thinking through the numerous perspective studies made of the project. One drawing shows the vista from the roof deck into one of the courtyards (Figure 7.16). A transparent glass elevator rises to the top floor. It is rendered with the fewest lines possible, heightening the sense of invisibility. Although some remnants of the stone façades of the original building are in

7.16
**Sketch
perspective
showing
transparency
through layers of
construction in
the courtyard.**
Foster and Partners.
Depot Conradi.

the sketch, most of the façades are glass, making the drawing appear more to represent a contemporary structure than the nineteenth century Reichstag. In another, more detailed, perspective the views into a courtyard space, probably the front entry, are sketched from a lower level (Figure 7.17). A huge transparent glass window frames the image through which the rest of the scene plays out. A series of transparent walkways were supposed to penetrate the courtyard just in front of the stone façade, making the contrast between new and old dramatically apparent, at the same time accentuating the potential weightlessness and lightness of the new. These were never realized, however. The closest realized moment is formed by a bridge bounded with see-through glass handrails that marks the transition between outer and inner lobbies.

The transparent glazing Foster used to replace the central portion of the west façade introduces the themes of light versus heavy, and transparency. The new see-through façade has the added advantage of making the plenary chamber, the most important honorific space in the building, immediately visible from the main entrance (Figure 7.18). The lightness of the new construction is rendered all the more weightless by its juxtaposition with the surrounding massive stone portico, the over-sized monumental columns, and the solidity of the flanking walls. In the daytime the façade is see-through while at night it lights up like a lamp. The contrast between old and new is striking because massive stones whose surfaces bear bas-reliefs of German coats of arms frame the quintessentially contemporary transparent glazed central portion of the entry.

7.18
View of the new transparent glass façade at the entry of the Reichstag.
Foster and Partners. Photographer: Nigel Young.

Like Behnisch, Foster situated the plenary chamber at the heart of the old building, so that it can be seen from the circulation spaces at every interior level around and above except directly overhead on the roof. Sketches executed during the design development phase show that Foster explored the encasement of the chamber in layers of transparent glass from early on in the project. The sketches also show the development of the open central section eventually realized in the building. A series of pulled away hand-drawn axonometric views make the desired relationship between roof deck, interiors, and plenary chamber evident. The plenary chamber acts as the transparent heart of the building, making visual connections possible in multiple directions although not in every one. The chamber is enclosed by transparent glass walls on the east and west sides. Windows looking into Wallot's restored courtyards so they admit light, but not views, frequently punctuate the more solid, stone walls on the north and south sides (Figure 7.19). The stone walls are also a constant reminder of the presence of the past, the only remnants of Wallot's structure still extant in the renovated plenary chamber. Looking east, through the

transparent glass partition supporting the German Eagle, the view is obstructed by opaque walls. Beyond the transparent wall to the west, however, the views are through layers of see-through construction and to the plaza in front of the west portico, and the massive stone columns framing the entry porch. Transparency in this building is always conditional, mediated by the opaque, the result of the constant juxtaposition of historic stone structure with the new interventions. As at the Bundeshaus in Bonn, the situation at the center of the building posits the chamber as the symbolic heart of parliament, and of the German state. Although there are no views to the iconic German landscape, or even to the surrounding city of Berlin from this chamber, visitors in adjacent spaces are visible. Because of its central position, the plenary chamber also acts as an orienting device (Figure 7.20). The chamber spans the area between the two large interior courtyards that Wallot had originally constructed and that Foster reinstated. All the other functional spaces are arranged around the chamber, pushed to the building's outer perimeter where they receive natural light. Choosing to place the chamber in a central position places the ghosts of German parliamentary history squarely in public memory – it is a reminder of the Bonn Bundeshaus and of Baumgarten's parliament (in Wallot's scheme the chamber was off-center), a subtle connection to the West German democratic

7.20
**View from the
lobby into the
plenary chamber
showing the many
transparent layers
of the
construction.**
Foster and Partners.
Photographer:
Nigel Young.

legacy and the roots of parliamentarian tradition in Wilhelmine Germany. Other historic traces present in the new chamber include the blue color of the seats, borrowed from the Bonn house, the particular type of seat, produced by the Vitra chair company, which is identical with those Behnisch had chosen, and the great Eagle. Against Foster's wishes, the Building Committee for the Reichstag demanded he use the same kind of chair for the chamber, and that they be blue. The parliamentarians evidently found the seats in the Bundeshaus tremendously comfortable and wanted the same ones in their new chamber.[45] After resisting, the Foster team capitulated but insisted on using a different shade of blue for the upholstery.

Foster himself was aware of the limited transparency he could achieve given the design problem at hand, making his claims at best contradictory, at worst intentionally deceptive. Foster used language reminiscent of Schwippert's and Behnisch's to defend his planning:

> In our rebuilding we wanted to banish any feeling that there were
> secret domains, or hives of bureaucracy. For security reasons, not

> every part of the Reichstag can be open to the public, but we have
> ensured that where possible it is transparent and its activities are
> on view. It is a building without secrets.[46]

When Foster refers to the Reichstag as a "building without secrets," he is
paraphrasing Hannes Meyer, Schwippert, and Behnisch, who used this phrase
to justify transparent glass construction for democratic institutions. But in
Foster's building, the lack of secrets more accurately communicates the building's relationship with history than with its own internal spatiality. There are far
too many incidences of opacity in the Reichstag to achieve the visual accessibility associated with open government buildings or the physical accessibility
desired by ideologues. Moreover, the "hives of beaurocracy" exist next door
to the Reichstag rather than inside it in the Paul Löbe House, Chancellor's
Ministry, and numerous other buildings. But the strategies for layering new
construction on top of historic fabric, preserving wherever possible traces of
the many stages in the Reichstag's history, and symbolically using new interventions to refer to other state architecture, form a transparency to history and
memory unique to the Reichstag.

IV

During the design process, Foster was forced to confront the debates over
German identity after unification. Some members of the German parliament
pressured Foster into abandoning his radical idea for the large glass canopy in
favor of a more modest reconstruction scheme that included rebuilding the
dome. According to several sources, Foster was told that he would have to
revise his scheme to include a dome if he wanted to win the commission.
Foster does not seem to have resisted the political pressure. When compared
with Behnisch who was notoriously stubborn about his design ideas, insulting
MPs along the way with his outbursts over the project, Foster capitulated
without much of a fuss. Predictably, the debate over the dome divided along
Left and Right political lines, with those on the Right favoring the historic
reconstruction of Wallot's dome, and those on the Left supporting Foster's
more contemporary design. Led by conservative CSU MP and Building
Commission member Oscar Schneider, members of the CDU/CSU coalition
supported reconstruction because they believed it would result in the most
appropriate symbol for a united Germany. After all, the first Reichstag symbolized the first unification of a German state, should not the reinstated Reichstag
symbolize the newly unified Republic? Would not a historic reconstruction
best demonstrate the return of German parliament to its first home by creating continuity with the historic cityscape? Furthermore, should not the new

Republic celebrate its antecedents by making clear the lineage from nascent parliamentary government under the Kaisers to the new Republic? The argument came to a head in a heated session of the Building Committee on April 28, 1994. The debate deadlocked along party lines, with the CDU/CSU members in favor of reconstruction and the FDP and SPD members against. A compromise was eventually brokered for a "modern dome."[47] The conservative members would get their dome, a reminder of the building's past, the liberal members would get their contemporary construction, a new image for united Germany.[48]

Although none of his previous schemes had included a dome, Foster agreed to explore the possibilities, abandoning the unique design proposal that won the first competition. Because at the core Foster was opposed to building a dome of any kind, he and his team looked at numerous ways of designing a dome that was not a dome – conical shaped, cylindrical, ovoid, flat-topped, and disc-like, as well as more traditional forms. In one well-known photograph there are some 30 different domes lined up together! From the start, Foster argued that any new dome design should "signal change," both the architectural changes that were taking place in the Reichstag and, symbolically, the political changes that unification was supposed to bring. By "signal change," Foster cleverly chose a turn of phrase that was bound to appeal to both sides of the dome argument – justifying the reinstatement of some sort of dome to those who were initially against any dome at all, and offering proponents of reinstatement a strong alternative to historic reconstruction of the Wallot dome. Foster's team explored four of the dome configurations in detail in a series of sketch studies, although the dome and cylinder variations seem to have been the two favored by the design team. The rationale for the round plan form of all four was the relationship between the cupola and the seating in the plenary chamber below. Foster's concern with transparency is everywhere apparent – in the pages of material treating the subject and in handwritten comments on the presentation drawings. On the sketch labeled, "Dome Option," someone wrote, "Heavy load-bearing trusses. 'Less light'!!! Too many columns . . . reduced transparency!"[49] (Figure 7.21). On the drawing labeled, "Glass Cylinder Option," the notes read, "Light tension net . . . light transparency!!! Less light columns . . . spatial transparency!"[50] (Figure 7.22). Both sketch perspectives show the view from the roof deck into the Reichstag, but the former truly seems denser, less see-through. In the first, the columns and trusswork are rendered as thick members. One side of each column is a dark thick line so that together the dark lines dominate the image, making it seem heavy, especially when compared with the second sketch. In this drawing, supporting structure is rendered as thin as possible. The tension net is drawn with one line only so that it is almost invisible. Whereas interior columns proliferate in the Dome Option design, in the Glass Cylinder Option

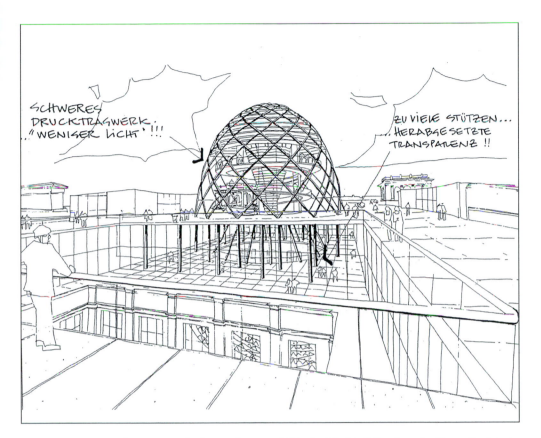

SCHWERES
DRUCKTRAGWERK...
"WENIGER LICHT"!!!

ZU VIELE STÜTZEN...
HERABGESETZTE
TRANSPARENZ !!

7.21

Sketch study of transparency in one version of the possible dome design.
Foster and Partners.
Depot Conradi.

there are only four columns visible just behind the façade. The effect is to make the Glass Cylinder Option appear to better fulfill the stated goals for visual transparency in the building. In the end, Foster presented two design possibilities to the Building Committee: the flat-topped, cylindrical "lighthouse," and the parabolic form (Figure 7.23). When asked by the Building Committee which design he preferred, Foster answered, "the lighthouse" because it was a contemporary interpretation of "dome" and would therefore best demonstrate the transformation of the Reichstag.[51] Nevertheless, the committee decided for the more traditional-looking parabolic form. Foster consistently argued for using the cupola to enhance other goals for the building renovation including improving its energy-efficiency, natural illumination, and ventilation. Both proposals already contained the mirrored, light-reflecting cone now such a prominent feature of the building, designed to help illuminate the plenary chamber. Later additions to the cupola include: the devices allowing for natural ventilation and blocking direct sunlight when necessary; and a built-in mechanical cleaning system for the dome itself.[52]

The completed dome embodies many of the functional and symbolic intentions Foster articulated. The completed structure has a diameter of 40 meters and a peak 23.5 meters high, making it tower over the neighboring

7.22
Sketch study of transparency in a second version of the possible dome design.
Foster and Partners. Depot Conradi.

7.23
Sketch studies of two different possible dome designs.
Foster and Partners. Depot Conradi.

buildings and rendering it visible throughout the city. The dome is made of 24 curved steel ribs arching into a steel tension ring at the top, supporting 17 horizontal steel rings. The outer skin is made from transparent glass pieces lapped over one another like fish scales so that it keeps the rain out, but is still open to air. Two ramps spiral up to a viewing platform, then down again, so the public can ascend for a spectacular view of Berlin (Figures 7.24 and 7.25). But there is no view of the parliament below. Thus, the dome may symbolize the building itself as a civic presence, but it is hard to argue, as Foster and others do, that it symbolizes transparent government when the thing itself is neither transparent to views into the parliament, nor transparent itself. The tremendous amounts of steel structure, coupled with the reflective qualities of the glass, make the cupola a solid, physical object most of the time. Photographs of the dome, whether taken during the daytime when portions of it are indeed somewhat see-through, or whether taken at night when the entirety emanates light, rarely exhibit transparency. The difference between this construction and the Wallot dome is that the first dome was a heavy, earthbound figure, was not positioned over the plenary chamber, and was not transparent to light. Around the Wallot dome's base was an ornate stone baluster, while crowning the glass and steel was a stone, temple-like piece. Foster's design is lightweight in comparison. Whereas Wallot's construction was purely ornamental, raised above an opaque glass ceiling, Foster's dome is situated so that it is on center with the chamber and allows natural light to filter into the room below. The new dome manages to respond to the Reichstag's history by recalling it, without imitating it.

Foster repeatedly describes the dome as a "lighthouse," "signal," "beacon," and "lantern," whose primary symbolic function is to proclaim the "Reichstag's transformation" on the Berlin skyline, communicating the themes of "lightness, transparency, and public access."[53] In other words, the dome is the sign in the public domain that the historic Reichstag building has been renewed and reoccupied. At night it literally becomes a beacon as it radiates light from its great height. Of course, it simultaneously signals the restoration of democratic government in Berlin, unification, and a new national identity. Treaties ending the war prohibited the use of the building as the federal seat of parliament; only unification could alter the taboo. In this sense, then, it proclaims an end to one phase of post-Second World War history and the beginning of a new one.

The new dome has assumed as many layers of meaning as the building on which it stands. Moreover, it has rapidly become a symbol, if not *the* symbol, of the new Berlin. It is already featured on numerous postcards available in souvenir shops all over town, on the cover of countless guidebooks, histories, and articles about Berlin, and is a major tourist destination in the city, mostly because of the incredible views across the historic center. That

7.24
Inside the cupola. Bundesbildstelle Berlin.

7.25
View up into the cupola.
Bundesbildstelle Berlin.
Photographer: Julia Fassbender.

is, tourists are attracted to the roof deck but not to the plenary chamber; they are interested in the vistas from above but not in the workings of German democracy. On a typical summer day, the queue extending from the front entrance is as many as 1,000 people long. Every history recounting Norman Foster's work at the Reichstag seems to feature an image of the dome. Reviews of the building renovation, articles celebrating the dedication and first parliamentary session held in the restored building, histories of German unification all seem attracted to this particular object. The dome has even been the subject of a couple of architectural "follies" in Berlin; Helmut Jahn quotes the light-refracting device at the BMW building in Potsdamer Platz and in a mall near Berlin Zoo where enormous inverted cones soar over the heads of shoppers and businessmen in newly-constructed public atria.

The decision to rebuild the dome was one of the most controversial aspects in the public debate over the renovation. Many found the dome the part of the Reichstag most representative of the authoritarian German past, associating domed capital buildings with expressions of power. Ironically, in its day, critics considered the Reichstag dome the one modern element, the one architectonic component representative of the New Order and a democratic future on an otherwise reactionary piece of architecture.[54] Further, domes top many state buildings in democratic capitals around the world. The American Capitol Building in Washington, DC, numerous American state capital buildings, the Australian parliament in Canberra, to name but a few, are all capped with domes. It is easy to argue that restoring the dome ties the German parliament building to an international architectural community by referring to those other precedents. Whichever point of view is taken, the dome certainly ties the Reichstag to a larger historical context and it is that aspect of its meaning that is most interesting to the question of the building's symbolic import. No matter what, the viewer will read some association into the structure – his or her memory will be engaged. It is perhaps here that democracy is most aptly represented in this, or any other building, because meaning cannot be assigned to architecture by its author, but is read into the construction by others. As with other art forms, one object can be interpreted in multiple ways, especially in a democratic society where single interpretations cannot be forced on the viewer.

The building has been vehemently criticized by some writers in the German press for its dubious symbolism and the confused sense of identity it conveys, another way of pointing to the multiplicity of interpretations. "Should this be the representational form of a representative democracy. . . . The new face of an old republic? It will be difficult for parliament in the Reichstag, for the picture that is portrayed here is one of caution and indecision."[55] The criticism also underscores a truism of artistic production; an author cannot assign meaning to a work of art; the interpreting audience reads meaning into the work. Moreover, meaning is consensual. An interpretation only gains currency to the extent that a group of people agrees to a particular reading of the work. Representation is a matter of discourse.[56] Although many of Foster's claims for his building do not hold up to close scrutiny as representations of real conditions, they do constitute a strong ideology, the ideology of transparency, and point to potent issues in contemporary Germany. After more than 50 years of democracy, Germans still struggle with both the concept of, and appropriate image for, their national identity. Rather than ease the question, unification seems to have intensified the debate, a fact supported by the recent controversy over the Reichstag renovation and its meaning. If the seat of parliament is read as the symbol for political and national identity, then the three projects discussed here demonstrate the evolution of that identity over 50 years from an immature democracy, fragile because of its newness, and because of the failure of democracy before, to a mature, established democracy able to confront and live with its past.

Chapter 8

Why transparency?

All of us, whether guilty or not, whether old or young, must accept the past. We are all affected by its consequences and liable for it. The young and old generations must help each other to understand why it is vital to keep alive the memories. It is not a case of coming to terms with the past. That is not possible. It cannot be subsequently modified or made not to have happened. However, anyone who closes his eyes to the past is blind to the present. Whoever refuses to remember the inhumanity is prone to new risks of infection.

Richard von Weizsäcker[1]

Weizsäcker uttered these words in May 1945 soon after German capitulation. Even though the National Socialist era had barely ended, Weizsäcker could already articulate the salient issues with which future generations would have to grapple: how to remember the past, how to share responsibility, and how to use memory to shape the future. Implicit in Weizsäcker's words is the admonition that the past, no matter how unpleasant, is part of German collective and individual identity. Indeed the intermingling of these very concerns, the past, memory, and identity, accounts for transparency ideology's emergence and duration after the war. In spite of the profound philosophical and esthetic orientations of Norman Foster, Günter Behnisch, and Hans Schwippert, transparency ideology was crucial to each project for the Bundestag, and ultimately helped make the architecture acceptable to a wide West German audience that included politicians, journalists, and lay people. There is no simple explanation for transparency's appeal to such a broad cross-section of constituencies in Germany but the coincidence of four factors related to the past, memory, and identity, might help. Briefly stated, these were: the association of sight with control in Western thinking, the workings of collective memory on the German psyche, the need for a way to represent democracy in state architecture, and the need for a means with which to identify with the newly established democratic form of government.

I

Transparency ideology may have persisted in postwar Germany because it offers a positive means Germans could use to identify with democracy. Identity formation is a function of the psyche. Although it is unusual to probe the psychological reasons people have for adopting an architectural style or ideology, in this case such a study offers some interesting insights. Identity formation and identity crisis were key issues in German history from 1871 onwards (and for a long time before as well). The first struggles were over a sense of national identity, how to form such a thing from a group of disparate local identities. Some of Bismarck's policies were directed at this problem. The constitution of a national parliament, discussed in Chapter 7, was largely a political maneuver designed to give the different parts of the empire a sense of belonging to the new union, that is, a sense of mutual identity. The Weimar Republic failed partly because of the inability of the democratic parties to work together to govern, and popular disillusionment with democracy. The wealthy and aristocratic classes were threatened by the Weimar government whose policies seemed to favor a redistribution of the wealth to equalize differences between the classes; the middle class lost financial ground because of the general decline of the 1930s; and the lower and working classes' support for the democracy was directly tied to the social benefits received from the regime. In other words, most Germans did not identify with the democratic regime. Conversely, the National Socialist party owed much of its initial success to its ability to make Germans identify with, and therefore support, its candidates and policies. The profound identity crisis many Germans suffered after 1945 is embodied in the Zero Hour proclamation already discussed in Chapter 3.

According to Georg Simmel in "The Metropolis and Spiritual Life," only a change in the objective world can produce a change in the subjective world of man, to his individual identity.[2] Simmel credited the increasingly dense living conditions modern man has created with concomitant rises in impersonal behavior, personal reserve, passivity, and detachment, characteristics he viewed as defense mechanisms developed to survive in the changed urban conditions. Although Simmel was concerned with urbanism rather than architecture, his thesis can be applied to architecture as well; changes in architectural conditions affect human beings. It is common knowledge that dark enclosed space tends to provoke melancholy, depression, and despair, therefore prisons have long been designed with dark, confined quarters in order to make the very occupation of the structure punishing. Conversely, being in a light-filled open space elicits a sense of well-being. The Dutch open-air schools were designed with this in mind typically using floor-to-ceiling transparent glass on the façades to bring in as much natural light as possible. Jan Duiker's Amsterdam School (1929) is one example of this type. Even more importantly, the inverse of Simmel's thesis is true – changes in human characteristics, activities, and ways of living result in new architectural types, forms, and styles. Examples abound: the cruciform-shaped floor plan of the church was invented to respond to the new needs of Christian worship; the protected but exterior long-span railroad shed was created to accommodate rail travel; the proscenium theater with raked stage and stacked public seating was developed to facilitate the presentation and viewing of stage productions. The transparent parliament building as a typological invention can be posited in a similar fashion; it responds to the new psychological needs of postwar German society for open, honest, and accessible government.

The political scientist, Murray Edelman, offers several plausible reasons why transparency ideology and transparent state architecture might appeal to the postwar German psyche. To begin with, he cites Bronislaw Malinowski, who identifies myth as the vehicle for accommodating "sociological strain."[3] Sociological strain includes all the negative pressures such as class and wealth inequalities that are endemic to any social structure. But sociological strain could come from unique historic events that exert pressure on the social makeup of a group. Thus, the collapse of three successive political systems, and the social upheaval caused by these events coupled with the loss of the Second World War, could account for the generation of myths of an open society and open, participatory democracy in Germany. Much more than myth, Edelman is concerned with political symbols and how they operate. In his view, the majority of people do not form their political opinions based on careful analysis of fact, but on an emotional response to symbol. In Edelman's work, symbol is a very broadly defined agent, compared with art historical definitions of the term, encompassing objects as well as words, places, and actions. The most potent symbols "condense into one symbolic event, sign or act of patriotic pride, anxieties, remembrances of past glories or humiliations, promises of future greatness . . ." writes Edelman.[4] He classifies political settings and the "drama of the state" as such symbols; in this view, parliamentary buildings are condensation symbols par excellence.

Edelman's work ties the settings for political action to mass perception of government and governmental policy. In his view, there is a reciprocal relationship between politics and the polity. Mass desires affect public policies that, in turn, affect mass desires. In Edelman's view, then, political settings abstract the collective political identity and simultaneously condition the public to a series of expectations. Edelman uses tribal totems and ritual dances to illustrate how settings influence the viewing group. The result "compels attention, emotional release, and compliance because it promises to end a source of deep and common anxiety if there is profound and shared faith in the symbol, with every individual an instrument of the common interest. . . ."[5] Transparency ideology does just this for many Germans. By virtue of its esthetic difference, transparency demands attention. Because transparent buildings present a new image of the state, radically different from historic state buildings, they encourage emotional release; the viewer will be relieved to see his parliament depicted differently from the negatively viewed historic models. Edelman goes on to assert that,

> Setting, one notices, fades in and out of attention in intriguing correspondence with: (1) the importance of impressing a large audience, as distinct from the need to convince an individual through logical demonstration; (2) the intention of legitimizing a series of future acts (whose content is still unknown) and thereby maximizing the chance of acquiescence in them and of compliance with the rules they embody; (3) the need to establish or reinforce a particular definition of the self in a public official.

A fourth category should be added to Edelman's list, namely the need to establish or reinforce a particular definition of the self in a citizen, since the citizen is also part of the political system. Following Edelman's logic, transparency ideology reinforces the German need to believe in his personal openness as well as the openness and accessibility of postwar government and society. Edelman's work is important because it affirms the connection between setting and political message, and between political symbolism and individual identity.

As discussed in Chapter 3, the Allied Powers focused many of their programs after the war on helping Germans learn about democracy, how democracy functions, and what the citizen's role is in a democracy. The overarching goal was to create a German citizenry that felt personally invested in democratic society and government, in other words, that identified with the new order. One result of these efforts is the strongly felt identification most Germans feel as a *Verfassungsstaat* (constitutional state) today. Perhaps more than any other measure, the surveys conducted by Elisabeth Noelle-Neumann and Renate Köcher for the Allensbach Institute register the changing attitudes of West Germans until 1989 and of all Germans since. The institute has been active since 1947. For each study, the institute questions thousands of Germans on every subject imaginable from history to politics to women's issues to immigration policy. It is, therefore, an excellent source for information on the general populace. When Noelle-Neumann and Köcher asked Germans in 1997 whether they felt, "that the democracy that we have in the Bundesrepublik is the best form for a state, or whether there is a better one?" 61 percent replied that democracy was the best form; 69 percent of respondents in West Germany and 23 percent in East Germany. Although the numbers are more pessimistic than they were six or seven years before, they still represent a solid majority. Perhaps more revealing are the number of qualities associated with transparency and the open society that survey respondents listed as most important to a successful democracy. These included: "that there is freedom of opinion and press, that everyone can freely express his political opinions (88 percent); that one can choose between many political parties (85 percent); that regular free and secret elections take place (82 percent); that a government can change without a power struggle (77 percent); that one can freely travel anywhere (73 percent); that there exist free courts that judge only according to the laws (74 percent); that everyone is free to practice their religion (73 percent); that the citizens can work together on many decisions of state (66 percent); and that much is done according to the wishes of the citizens (65 percent)."[6] According to these statistics, transparency is a constituent part of German identity in the late twentieth century.

II

Representation is to present anew an identity that exists and can be defined; political representation is to show again the political identity of the state. But does such a thing exist in any objective terms? Underlying the question of how to represent the state in architectural form, is the question what defines the state? What distinguishes one state from another and can that difference be shown in architecture? Is it the political identity of the state that should be presented, or some other identity? These questions were being posed from the very beginning of the Federal Republic and were shared, in one degree or another, with many nations as they rebuilt and built anew after the Second World War (see Chapter 3). Nor is West Germany unique in the esthetic means with which many of its state buildings were realized after 1945; contemporary architecture was used around the world from the United States and Canada to East Germany and Japan. The way in which West German state architecture differs from the rest is in the persistent use of the transparency ideology to justify esthetic choices. The notion that "transparency equals democracy," can be found to some degree in other cultures, especially since the advent of "open society" discourse in Western political philosophy in the 1960s, but nowhere is transparency ideology so strong and so pervasive as it

is in Germany. Although Woodrow Wilson advocated "open covenants . . .
openly arrived at" in his 14 points for the peace settlement after the First
World War, he was referring to public accessibility to the decision-making
process, not to the openness of League of Nations architecture. Transparency
ideology in architecture appeared first in West Germany, has enjoyed a lasting
following over more than 50 years, and has permeated more levels of society
there than anywhere else. Reasons cited for using contemporary glass and
steel architecture and Neues Bauen style designs elsewhere to represent the
state most often were: to show the modernity and forward-looking aspect of
a society, to connect a single state to world culture, and to reinforce the image
of technological prowess held by a country. Moreover, once the aftershock
of the Second World War gave way by the mid-1950s, the notion of modernity
became synonymous with progress in every realm: cultural, economic,
political, religious, and social. It was therefore easy to argue that "modern"
architecture was the most appropriate means with which to show the modernity of the state. Several examples should suffice to prove the point. In Canada,
for instance, there was a struggle between modern and traditional architecture similar to the one that played out in Germany immediately after the war.
By the 1950s, however, Canadian architects could brag that modernism had
triumphed. After 1945 the Canadian government planned and constructed
numerous schools, hospitals, and other government buildings, as well as
model communities, whose architecture, when it used the modern esthetic,
was meant to demonstrate how up-to-date Canada was at the time.[7] Integral
to this vision was the notion that the Canadian frontiers could be "conquered
and subdued by modern technology and industry . . . ," a concept embodied in
contemporary building design.[8] Equally important, the new architecture was
thought to reflect the latest principles of public administration, economic management, and technological advancement present in the country. The modern
state buildings constructed during this period exhibit the hallmarks of Neues
Bauen architecture: asymmetrical, Elementarist planning with steel or concrete frame construction, ample glass surfaces, white stucco, and flat roofs.
The Vancouver Customs House designed by CBK Van Norman between
1953 and 1955 typified the approach. The building was an asymmetrically
arranged series of flat-roofed volumes with exposed concrete surfaces
framing enormous façades of transparent glass. A surviving photograph of the
Customs House shows a mid-sized building reminiscent of the Dutch and
German projects of the 1920s and 1930s.

　　　　Like its neighbor to the north, the United States initiated several
building programs after the war that explicitly used contemporary architecture
to symbolize the state. The most ambitious was the embassy construction
program in the 1950s and 1960s. Ron Robin describes a series of attacks
launched at American embassies and libraries abroad in the 1950s and 1960s,

which he believes were responses to the image America was projecting through her new state architecture. According to Robin, the embassies built during this period were part of a State Department program whose buildings were meant to be "a reflection of the US role as a major world power."[9] Robin points to the American self-image after the war as a progressive, technologically advanced society, but also the ideological contrast between America and the Soviet Union where Social Realism prevailed, as the main reasons contemporary design was attractive for the embassy projects. The list of embassy architects is a Who's Who of contemporary design in America at the time and included Harrison and Abramovitz, Walter Gropius, Eero Saarinen, John Johansen, Jose Luis Sert, Edward Durrell Stone, and Harry Woese. Gropius explained his design for the embassy in Athens, Greece by quoting Goethe,

> "There is no past which we should long to resurrect,
> There is eternal newness only, reconstituting itself
> Out of the extended elements of the past,
> And true yearning should always be toward productive ends,
> Making something new, some better thing."[10]

Gropius is arguing against traditional architecture, against an imitation of the past, and for an expression of progress, especially the progressive political attitude of the US.[11]

The climate of optimism and belief in the possibilities of technology was everywhere in the 1950s. Christian Norberg-Schulz credits the surge in modernist public building in Norway with the new optimism. Norwegian architects debated the proper way to build after the war much as architects in Germany had, with the lines drawn between those advocating reconstruction of the historic city lined up against those supporting construction in the new way.[12] The situation in Denmark and Finland was like that in Norway. Many Scandinavians navigated a position between modern, traditional, and organic architecture; notable examples include Prtor Knutsen, Sverre Fehn, and Arne Korsmo in Norway, Eva and Nils Koppel, Kay Fisker, and Jorn Utzon in Denmark, and Alvar Aalto in Finland. Projects like Knut Knutsen's 1949 embassy building in Stockholm and Erling Visko's government building in Oslo designed and executed between 1940 and 1958 show the international Modern at work for the state in Norway. Arne Jacobsen's 1955 town hall at Rodovre is an excellent Danish example. The building is divided into two volumes for programmatic reasons; one contains the council chamber and committee rooms, the other contains offices. The two are connected by a narrow walkway. Most of the complex is clad in steel and transparent glass. Halidor Gunnlogsson and Jorn Nielsen's town hall in Tarnby, and their town hall in Frederica, are concrete frame buildings clad in see-through glass. According to Tobias Faber, Danish architects after the war were motivated by the desire to combine functional planning and rational design with some kind of absolute beauty. Architects were concerned with making buildings that were scientific and responded to contemporary ways of living.[13]

The one country where, not surprisingly, transparency ideology has been argued for in similar terms to West Germany is France. But it was not until the Mitterrand era during the 1980s that the ideology was adopted and made manifest in a series of projects called the *Grands Projets* commissioned to celebrate the two hundredth anniversary of the French Revolution. Mitterrand defended the projects on the grounds that they would provide open, democratic institutions for the French public. The glass and steel structures of the new Opera House, National Library, La Defense, and the Grand Pyramid at the Louvre are examples of the transparent monuments erected under Mitterrand. Writing about the *Grands Projets* in Paris, Annette Fierro points to the unabashed monumentality of the transparent French state architecture whose realization celebrates a return to classical sensibilities but not necessarily to democratic principles in spite of the rhetoric of openness.[14] François Mitterrand was even dubbed, "*Le Roi Mitterrand*" (King Mitterrand) in a not so subtle reference to the royal building programs of the past. Finally, although the *Grands Projets* exploit transparency partly in the interest of public accessibility and openness, they are the achievement of one man in one French administration but not of a collective group like the German parliament. More significantly, these projects are not government buildings like the seat of parliament but buildings for public use financed by the government, as in the cases of the Opera and National Library, and office buildings to accommodate branches of the state apparatus. None can be construed as the national symbol of French democracy. Thus, the use of transparency ideology by the French state cannot be compared with its realization at the German Bundeshaus and Reichstag.

Returning to the question of what constitutes political representation in architecture, it is important to underscore the fact that politics and architecture have been associated with one another since the beginning of time. The questions of what constitutes the representative power of architecture and how architecture can represent different types of regimes are as old as human society. Rulers and their governments have always used architecture as an analogical expression of the power of the state. The ornate great palaces like Versailles in France, the Escorial in Spain, and Buckingham Palace in England, were intended to project the royal majesty and power, and splendor of the state to the people. Similarly, the simple, open spaces of Greek forums bespoke the democratic orientation of that state, the power of the collective. The difficulty is that interpretation of state architecture is not absolute but relies on the effective communication of the architect's and commissioning body's intentions to the public. The public must, in turn, accept the given analogy. Whether acceptance occurs consciously or subconsciously is not important as long as there is consensus about meaning. Thus, the meaning of political architecture can change over time as the receiving public changes, as the political climate alters, and as the memory of original intentions is lost. In Germany, "transparency equals democracy" has dominated parliamentary architectural design because the idea was successfully communicated by politicians and architects and accepted by critics and many of the public and, most importantly, because it suited changing political attitudes, values, and expectations.

III

Collective memory is so strong in Germany that it may be the primary force behind transparency ideology. Collective memory, rather than historical memory, best explains the public reception of transparency, because it is the emotional and personal memory of the past that influences the choice of transparency, not the real, objective facts of history. As Maurice Halbwachs and others have shown, collective memory collates around historical reference points that have meaning to members of a specific group and conversely, these shared memories define the social identity of the group.[15] More often than not the events that spark collective memories are unusual and often traumatic. In the case of West and East Germany, collective memories of the failures of the Weimar Republic, the traumas experienced during the Third Reich, the schism into two states, and the abuses of East German Marxism/ Leninism are particularly strong even today, although the collective memories pertaining to these events have shifted in content and relative importance over time. Transparency ideology has lasted because of its ability to respond to and to complement the ascendancy of one set of collective memories over that of another. It is the coincidental confluence of these different collective memories around transparency that best explains its ascendancy in postwar West Germany over any other state.

It is important to make clear from the start how collective memory is distinct from historical memory. Whereas history is supposed to be an objective reconstruction of the past based on a presentation and analysis of the factual record, collective memory is subjective, emotional, and biased, and can be based on fact, myth, or bits of both at the same time. While history usually records change over long periods of time, collective memory recalls moments from history and uses them to influence the present. The historian, the writer of history, has no fixed position in space or time, that is, he or she is not a member of a specific, namable group. At least this is the ideal position the historian takes. In reality, association with particular groups also affects historians so that even "objective" histories are shaped by some larger world-view. This explains the need to constantly rewrite the same history, each time from a new point of view. The collective memory, in contrast, does not pretend to be objective; it always resides in social groups that can be identified temporally and spatially. The collective memory records "currents of thought and experience" because they are significant to the group.[16]

The aspects of the past retained in the collective memory are key to any interpretation or understanding of the transparency metaphor and analogy because they help suggest the reasons these appeared in German culture. "The group, living first and foremost for its own sake, aims to perpetuate the feelings and images forming the substance of its own thought"[17] (see Chapter 1). The collective memory brings the past into the present in a personal, particular, and subjective way. Most importantly, "collective memory plays a key role in the symbolic discourse of politics, in the legitimation of political structures and action, and in the justification of collective behavior."[18] The same can be said for collective memory and the legitimation of architectural structures and discourse as well as form, space, and style. This occurs because members of a group construct their collective memory around historical "reference points," historical events that have significance to the group, that are in turn embodied in architectural expression. Monuments are perhaps the clearest embodiments of single reference points because they are usually designed to commemorate one historic event whereas the incorporation of collective memory into buildings is a far more complex and often indirect process. Finally, the collective memory can preserve historical events in the public consciousness long after an event has occurred, and for members of the group who were not witnesses to the original event. In this way, moments from history can be preserved as an influence on contemporary politics and culture.

The political scientists Andrei Markovits and Simon Reich demonstrate the power of collective memory by pointing to the contemporary importance of the Battle of Kosovo-Polye in 1389 for Serbs; the destruction of the Second Temple in 70 CE for Jews; and William III's victory over the Catholic armies at the Battle of Boyne in 1690 for Irish Catholics and Protestants.[19] In each of these cases, it is not the actual event but its image as a particularized memory that continues to affect the group in question. While collective memory is often fixated on negative historical events, it can adopt any event of lasting or palpable significance. The key is the way in which the memory is used to affect the present.[20] Adolf Hitler was keenly aware of the power of collective memory so that he, and the National Socialists, manipulated memory in any number of ways. They used the popular myth of

Charlemagne's great Germanic empire to help justify the aggressive consolidation of German-speaking territories under National Socialist rule. The
National Socialists used memories of mythic German culture in Goethe's
time to reinforce notions of German cultural superiority in the twentieth
century.

Collective memory operates on at least five distinct groups inside
West Germany in the case of the three parliament buildings: the architects,
commissioning bodies, politicians in the Bundestag who were not a part of
the commissioning process, journalists writing about architecture, and the
public. Outside West Germany collective memories help make transparency
understandable, even attractive, to people living in the former occupying and
occupied countries who are still fearful of a resurgence of German military
and economic power, especially of a return to totalitarianism. Thus, although
Foster is British, he shares certain collective memories of Germany during
the Second World War, and afterwards, with other British, Europeans, and
West Germans. Evidence supporting the existence and force of collective
memories can be culled from mass survey data collected by agencies like
the Allensbach Institute and from individual group members through their
essays, correspondence, and articles.[21]

Although there are at least five different constituent groups
involved in the adoption of transparency as an analogy in West German
state architecture, the collective memories that held sway over these groups
fall into two general categories: those specific to architects and architectural
critics, and those shared by most West Germans. The latter category encompasses the first, while the first is discipline-specific. The single most significant event affecting German collective memory after 1945 was Hitler's regime
and all that went with it; the second most important source for collective
memory was the Weimar Republic, its ambitions, successes, and its failure.
The presence of history in one form or another is apparent in the continu-
ing German debate over the need for an "*Aufarbeitung der Geschichte*"
(working through, or reflecting on, history) or "*Vergangenheitsbewältigung*"
(overcoming of the past), a debate that is largely divided into two factions:
those who argue that the time has come to forget the past, and those who
argue that because of its heinous past, Germany must never forget. In the
1980s the debate roiled in the popular press in the guise of the Historikerstreit
(historians' argument) although the arguments were not limited to historians.
Beyond this specific debate, articles on the proper relationship to the past
appear weekly, if not more often, in the German press in newspapers of every
political persuasion and intellectual degree. The numerous monuments
dedicated to the memory of Nazi atrocities further attest to the force and
presence of memory. The recent competition for a memorial to the Holocaust
in Berlin won by the American architect Peter Eisenman is just such an

example. The competition sparked heated arguments over memory and how to remember. Christian Boltanski's installation on the side of a house on Sophien Street, where he painted the names of former residents deported in the 1940s across from the site of the Nazi deportation station is another example. In the political arena, the past helped shape the very political structure of the FRG. Much of the political structure was based on either a rejection of National Socialist government, or the correction of perceived weaknesses in the Weimar constitution and government. The preamble was included in order to reassure West Germany's allies of its peaceful intentions. The first section, which amounts to a Bill of Rights, was included to help safeguard West Germans from measures stripping citizens of their basic freedoms such as Hitler's Enabling Act. Article 67, the Constructive Vote of No Confidence, was legislated in order to prevent easy toppling of governments similar to that which occurred repeatedly during the Weimar era. These are just a few examples of clauses in the constitution that were instituted because of collective memory. In the arts, the famous "*Nullpunkt*" distinguishes 1945. The desire for a cultural rebirth was similar to the authoring of the Basic Law – it was as much a repudiation of the recent past as the first step towards constructing a new future. Thus, it can be argued that the eventual adoption and perpetuation of the transparency metaphor and analogy was part of the same impetus, a parallel drive towards the future and away from the past, a reaction to multiple collective memories.

Markovits and Reich use an analysis of the German collective memory as the basis for examining foreign policy in unified Germany. According to Markovits and Reich, collective memory defines aspects of political and national identity and therefore plays a central role in determining policy. The same can be argued for national symbols and nationally accepted metaphors and analogies since they too are tied to self-perception. State architecture, as former federal president Rita Süssmuth has pointed out, is as much an embodiment of national self-perception as symbols, hymns, and other ceremonial figures.[22] Süssmuth is not the only figure to point to this truth; architects and architectural historians writing about the postwar period as well as the building organs of the West German state have recognized the importance of architecture to national identity. A number of books have been devoted to the subject of state representation in West German architecture since the end of the Second World War including: *Bauten des Bundes* (*Building the Federation*), *Architektur in der Demokratie: 40 Jahre Nordrhein-Westfalen, Bauen und Stadtentwicklung von der Nachkriegszeit bis heute* (*Architecture in Democracy: 40 Years of Building in North Rhine Westphalia, Buildings and Urban Development from the postwar Period to Today*), *Parlamentsarchitektur: Zur Selbstdarstellung der Demokratie in ihren Bauwerken. Untersuchung am Beispiel des Bonner Bundeshauses* (*Parliamentary*

Architecture: Towards the Self-Representation of Democracy in her Built Works: An Investigation Using the Example of the Bonn Bundeshaus). The West German government sponsored the first two books; they are catalogs of built work more than critical evaluations of that oeuvre. In contrast, Heinrich Wefing's dissertation is analytical. Although these books do not present a definitive representational system for West German democratic architecture or a consensus as to what and how state buildings should carry meaning, their existence shows that there was an active concern with these issues.

Markovits and Reich identify key events in recent German history whose embodiment in the collective memory has had a continued influence on contemporary politics and culture. Of these, several have affected architectural design, although none so profoundly as the various memories of the Third Reich. The memory of: "Germans as victims of National Socialism" and "Germans as perpetrators of National Socialism" share importance with German amnesia, the desire to put the Third Reich in the past and keep it there. The memory of the Weimar Republic as the first democratic republic and as a failed experiment as opposed to the "Bundesrepublik as Germany's most successful democracy," are key to understanding postwar parliamentary architecture. The memory of German victimization by Hitler and the National Socialists, the memory of 1945 as "the liberation of Germany and Germans from National Socialism," and especially the notions that "Most Germans were not complicit" and that "Most Germans had no control over events during the Third Reich," are key to understanding transparency after the war. By the time the Foster project was underway, unification added the set of East German collective memories to those already extant and operating in the West. East German collective memories of the privations under the Communist state were mixed with distrust of West Germans, and new myths concerning the positive sense of community experienced in East Germany under the old regime. The collective memories operating on postwar architectural design are even more specific and can be summarized as follows: the architecture of the Weimar Republic was modern and progressive which was an apt representation of the young democracy; the architecture of the National Socialists and Third Reich was neo-classical, monumental, and intentionally intimidating; the architecture of the National Socialists was an effective political tool; the members of the Neues Bauen movement in Germany were ostracized by the Nazis and either run out of Germany or forced into internal exile during the years of the Third Reich; and transparent architecture reflects progressive ideas, open society, worth, and utopia. The evolution of these ideas has already been discussed in previous chapters. Without these memories, transparency would not have become an analogy for German democracy; without the changing dimensions of these collective memories, the meaning of transparency would not have altered over time.

The sheer number of questions devoted to history, Hitler, National Socialism, and the Third Reich in every Allensbach Institute yearbook since 1947 speaks to the presence these memories still enjoy in the contemporary German consciousness. While the contents of the questions reveal the historical issues alive in discourse, either directly or indirectly, the responses catalog demographic facts related to each issue. For example, one question included in the 1984–92 yearbook asked, "Is there something in our history that makes us different from other countries, I mean, something that one can truly call German?" The question reflects years of concern on the part of many West Germans about a Sonderweg (special way), a unique characteristic to being German and to German history that could account, in a negative fashion, for Hitler's ascension to power, the Third Reich, and the Holocaust as well as the fact that Germany started the two worst wars of human history. The majority of respondents in West Germany answered "yes," and named the Third Reich, National Socialism, and Hitler, suggesting the prevalence of this collective memory in their group, but East Germans list other events entirely. As the demographers point out, the East German responses are so radically different that they appear to be speaking of an entirely different country.[23]

In the 1997 yearbook, the section on history begins with the survey question, "Do you believe that people can learn from history, and especially from specific mistakes?" and "Do you believe that Germany has learned from the history of the first half of this century and therefore in the second half avoided many mistakes?"[24] These questions are only slightly veiled references to the National Socialist era and Germany's role in starting the First and Second World Wars. Interestingly, an overwhelming majority in East and West, roughly 70 percent, responded positively to both questions. Participants in surveys beginning in 1989 were shown a list of opinions and sayings and asked to rank them according to how strongly they agreed or disagreed. Among those sayings with which most people agreed were collective memories, "Through Hitler's appearances and his talent as a speaker most people were deceived about his true goals," "The defeat in World War II was a logical result of German megalomania," and "We should openly confront our National Socialist past even when it hurts."[25] In the 1991 survey the interviewers also asked whether people believed that contemporary Germans were too preoccupied with the Third Reich. Respondents split evenly, 40 percent answering "yes" and 42 percent answering "no," although when the question was phrased slightly differently to ask whether Germans were too preoccupied with the past, 53 percent answered "no" compared with only 28 percent who answered "yes."[26] To the question whether or not Germans had the opportunity to oppose Hitler during the Third Reich, the percentage of respondents answering "no" steadily declined over the years as the generation that was alive during the period died out. Thus, in 1969 63 percent said "no" while in 1991 only 55 percent said "no," and only 52 percent said "no" in 1995. When broken into age groups, it is the one over 60 that in 1991 and 1995 still answered overwhelmingly "no" to the question supporting the belief that those who were alive share the memory of being powerless in the face of National Socialism.[27]

One way collective memory helps legitimize the analogical paradigms devised by the individual architects for the Bundeshaus is by using what is popularly perceived as "National Socialist architecture" as the foil against which other formal, spatial, and stylistic alternatives are measured. Although many historians have disproved the veracity of the collective memory of National Socialist architecture as always being Neo-classical, monumental, overbearing in scale, and opaque, in the popular imagination this memory persists.[28] The acerbic debates over the move to Berlin generally, over the reuse of the Reichsbank for the Foreign Ministry, over Martin Gruber's and Helmut Kleine-Kraneburg's design of the new presidential office, an oval-shaped structure whose cladding was originally to be black stone, over Stefan Braunfels' federal office building, Axel Schultes' Kanzleramt, and the renovation of the Reichstag in particular, demonstrate how persistent this memory still is.[29] If this is not enough, the many references to the architecture of the Third Reich made by Schwippert, Behnisch, and Foster are further proof of the persistence of memory (see Chapters 6, 7, and 8).

Collective memory kept alive the prewar utopian belief in architecture's power to influence people and the way they live. Many members of Schwippert's generation believed in the impact architecture could have on politics – the Novembergruppe and Arbeitsrat für Kunst are examples of activist organizations for architects and artists with clearly stated political missions. It is not surprising to find the notion of architecture as a didactic tool coincident with such activism. Hitler and Speer referred to architecture as the "word in stone"; Adolf Arndt's writings and essays propose a similar intrinsic connection. Today, as Winfried Nerdinger suggests, we may hold a more skeptical view of the power architecture truly has and of its ties to political expression.[30] But this does not diminish the existence of Schwippert's, Behnisch's, and Foster's claims for their buildings; only the reception of those claims. Moreover, transparent glass was more than just the material of political utopia – it was for many architects of the Neues Bauen, the sign of progressive architecture and society, the material realization of a moral imperative to construct the contemporary environment using up-to-date technology. In a time when West Germany was trying so hard to change its image in the world, when the memories of both the Nazi era and the failed Weimar Republic were present inside and outside the country, an architecture that suggested progressive attitudes and modernity must have been appealing both to architects and to lay people. If not the utopian associations, then the connection between the importance of transparency to much Neues Bauen architecture and Weimar, the first and only democratic regime before the Federal Republic, must have made transparency appealing.

Schwippert's ties to Neues Bauen have already been described in detail but those of Behnisch and Foster have not. Behnisch accepted the logic behind the argument for transparent state architecture and a modern stylistic expression, although the ties between his work and Neues Bauen principles are far less obvious than with Schwippert, largely because Behnisch is more circumspect about the origins for his ideas than Schwippert was and because he comes from the next generation. Nevertheless, he does drop a few hints in his writings. In "Building for Democracy," Behnisch cites several figures from the Neues Bauen period as models: Wassily Kandinsky, Adolf Behne, and Max Bill.[31] He praises Mies and Eiermann. Moreover, while Behnisch never acknowledges the Neues Bauen legacy directly, many of the ideas he professes over the years and many of the esthetic values he embraces can be linked directly to the Neues Bauen. In an essay for the *Deutsche Bauzeitschrift* Behnisch explains why he hires so many recent graduates in terms that could have come from a 1920s manifesto, "Young architects bring the spirit of the age with them ... it is necessary to understand the times we are living in and take them into account."[32] Behnisch explains Situationist Architecture, the approach he developed for the Olympic Stadium and the projects that came afterwards, as design that responds to all the aspects of the situation as the architect finds them: program, functional requirements, site, contemporary expectations.[33] He repeatedly calls for open architecture, open plan, and attention to function. "Creating a form? Finding form? We believe in looking for form and, moreover, looking for the task. This approach allows us to view all elements individually. Individuality is first that of the task, its functions, parts and aspects, site and time...."[34] If the debt to Neues Bauen architecture is obscured in Behnisch's work, the belief in the myth of Zero Hour is not. Behnisch writes often about the dilemma facing architects who attempt to design for democracy, especially West German democracy, reiterating the need for distance from totalitarian forms of expression, and outlining an esthetic of openness and transparency.[35] Writing for the *Frankfurter Allegemeine Zeitung*, Michael Mönninger said of Behnisch's achievement, "Seldom has the myth of the reborn, innocent Germany been so convincingly realized as in this light presentation...."[36]

Although Behnisch was much more affected by memories of the Third Reich than the Weimar Republic, Foster, who renovated the building in which that Republic was declared, was confronted with memories of Weimar, the Third Reich, and to a lesser degree Wilhelmine Germany. For Foster, though, these memories had little to do with the esthetic and utopian aspects of Neues Bauen architecture and more to do with the multiple myths associated with the Reichstag building itself, although Foster considers himself deeply indebted to the first generation modernists.[37] Among the thousands of articles debating a return to the Reichstag were arguments in favor that reminded Germans of the Reichstag's positive historical associations. Philip Scheidemann declared the Weimar Republic from one of the Reichstag balconies in 1918, it was the first seat of parliament for a united Germany under the Kaisers, served as the parliament for the first democratic German regime, and was actually despised by the National Socialists who viewed it as a "talking shop for democracy" and abandoned the building for the neighboring Kroll Opera House.[38] Hanno Rauterberg, writer for *Die Zeit*, accused the foreign architects who participated in the Reichstag competition of misunderstanding German history and assigning the building false meaning because of Foster's largely negative interpretation of the building's historical significance.[39] Foster's view was likely affected by his personal history: he was a young boy in London during the blitzkrieg and, according to some, still harbors anger towards the Germans for the destruction they wrought during the Second World War.[40] One former associate even remembers Foster explaining his interest in the Reichstag competition as the desire to, "show the Germans we [the English] can do it better than they can" (design their national parliament). In the end, Foster confronted the various myths by accepting the Reichstag shell as he found it, by allowing the traces of German history to intermingle, and by not inventing a new representative system for his architecture.

Schwippert confronts the memory of Weimar as well. In the concluding argument of his manifesto, Schwippert justifies using glass because of its fragility, an analogy particularly appropriate to German democracy that had, after all, already failed once. The Weimar governments had fallen on average every eight months until the National Socialist takeover. No one could appreciate more than the Germans how fragile political structures could be.

> The illusion that life is everlasting and secure are also things of the past. Life, happiness, and glass: fragile things! Sudden or slow transitoriness – variations of the momentary. [. . .] How much stubborn resistance has been raised to such inconstancy and vicissitudes of life, of happiness, and of things: caves, castles, bunkers, and thick walls, closed and non-transparent, so as to feign permanency and conceal transience.[41]

By constructing a fragile building to house the parliament, Schwippert was creating a constant reminder to the legislators of how delicate the political balance was, how easily it could be destroyed. He contrasts his esthetic with the monumental state structures built by past rulers to reinforce the point.

"Poor Pharaohs," writes Schwippert, "What remains? Looted pyramids, that for thousands of years have crumbled and been wiped out; what, dictators, will remain from the borrowed splendor and strength of their thousand year delusions?"[42] Trying to construct for eternity is impossible. The obvious reference to Hitler and his constructions for the Thousand Year Reich posits National Socialist architecture as an example of a failed building program because the regime crumbled, many of the buildings were razed during the war, and the symbolism behind the projects was misguided. With this statement Schwippert is not only proposing transparent state architecture as the appropriate type because of what it is – transparent, open, accessible – but he is justifying his choice because of what it is not – solid, stone, monumental. Moreover, Schwippert uses the word "opaque" to describe these buildings he so dislikes, suggesting that transparency is an appropriate analogy for democracy because it is not opaque.

Behnisch is no less concerned with the National Socialist legacy in his project than Schwippert was, and is even more outspoken about the effect the memories of that era have had on postwar West Germany. "Our society and architecture are, in large measure, a reaction to the Third Reich."[43] Like Schwippert, it is the memory of the Third Reich that permeates many of Behnisch's pronouncements on what West German parliamentary architecture should be and how it should be designed. The Third Reich never seems to be far from his mind when Behnisch discusses the Bundeshaus. His interviews and essays abound with overt and oblique references to the period and to the architecture favored by Hitler. "No one should have the impression that dark powers work there," writes Behnisch echoing Schwippert's sentiments about the first Bundeshaus project. Behnisch cites as "Examples to clarify the notion 'political architecture' [include]: the plans from Hilter and Speer for Berlin or for the Reich's Party Parade Grounds in Nuremburg" in his essay explaining his views on democratic architecture and the proper representation of the state in built form.[44] Also like Schwippert, Behnisch reacts to his memories of the Third Reich by rejecting monumental, classical architecture as an appropriate style for state buildings and emphatically insists that his building must be, "open and see-through, visible, better understandable."[45] Politics and architecture are intimately connected in this vision, mutually supportive constructs.

As the quote from Behnisch demonstrates, much of the Schwippert, Behnisch, and Foster designs were considered in terms of vision – who would be able to observe whom, when, and from where. When Schwippert wrote, "Politics is a dark affair. Let's see that we shed some light upon it," he meant to illuminate the workings of government so that they could be *seen*.[46] Transparent walls and open sectional planning helped facilitate visual access; these were design conceits used by all three architects.

Placed in the context of memory, the attention to seeing responds to the memory of National Socialism and the German public's failure to resist, "We did not see what was happening in government, therefore we had no control." This belief has been twisted over the decades into another myth, "I can control what I can see." Accordingly, a transparent parliament building offers the promise of public control over government even if that promise is false.

IV

In Western philosophy, sight and visual perception have long been associated with knowing, understanding, and controlling in what David Michael Levin and Martin Jay, two scholars who write about vision, call our "ocularcentric" culture.[47] Levin traces the preoccupation with vision back to the pre-Socratic philosophers and forward to the beginning of the twentieth century. Not only do visual concepts dominate philosophy, but they dominate language as well. The phrase "I see," for instance, is synonymous with "I understand" because seeing is so closely tied to understanding and knowing in Western thought. Neither Jay nor Levin, nor the contributors to Levin's book, *Modernity and the Hegemony of Vision*, question the hegemony of vision before or even after the modern era, but posit a shifting model for the role of vision in modernity from a positive force to a negative one, in the public spectacle and the panoptic mechanism of control.[48] The philosophers Martin Heidegger, Michel Foucault, Guy Debord, and Jacques Derrida have all explored the power of vision but Foucault's analysis of the phenomenon in *Discipline and Punish* probably has the greatest consequences for architectural discourse, since Foucault treats architecture directly.[49] As an architectural idea, the panopticon building dates to Jeremy Bentham's eighteenth-century proposals described in Chapter 2. Bentham used the power of the gaze in an elaborate scheme to control the behavior of both viewing subject and viewed object. In his analysis of the genius behind Bentham's architectural invention, Foucault explains why it is so effective:

> . . . [The] panoptic institutions could be so light; there were no more bars, no more chains, no heavy locks; all that was needed was that the separations should be clear and the openings well arranged. The heaviness of the old "houses of security," with their fortress-like architecture, could be replaced by the simple, economic geometry of a "house of certainty". . . . He who is subjected to a field of visibility, and who knows it, assumes responsibility for the constraints of power, he makes them play spontaneously upon himself; he inscribes in himself the power relation in which he

    simultaneously plays both roles; he becomes the principle of his own subjection.[50]

Public responsibility, then, is forced on the person who is observed because being the object of surveillance makes people self-conscious and careful. Furthermore, the gaze endows people with power. (In French, the verb "to see" is conceptually and etymologically connected to knowing and controlling because "to see" is *voir*, "to know" is *savoir*, and "power" is *pouvoir*.) Foucault himself draws the parallel between Bentham's model and transparent architecture. "The seeing machine was once a sort of dark room into which individuals spied: it has become a transparent building in which the exercise of power may be supervised by society as a whole."[51] The transparent government building is a panopticon planned as the inverse of Bentham's prison where the observer was at the heart of the structure and the observed all around. At the Bundeshaus, the observer is either external to the architecture but watching from all sides, or inside the building but outside the plenary chamber and surrounding it. The situation is similar at the Reichstag where the observers are positioned on all sides of the transparent plenary chamber.

    The connection between sight and control in transparent structures has its genesis in Meyer's League of Nations project and in Schwippert's writings on the Bundeshaus. In the last passages of his manifesto, Schwippert suggests that transparency might serve multiple purposes: one benefit will be that the undesirable elements, the vermin, will have nowhere to hide. In other words, people will be able to see the vermin no matter where they are and, he implies, if they can be seen, they can be controlled. Herein lies the myth of control yet again – that which can be seen can be controlled. Schwippert used transparency at the Bundeshaus at least in part because it offered the illusion of control, control over the parliament and over government policy. After all, any discourse on transparency is one on vision too since transparency is a quality understood with the eyes. Again and again, when describing transparent buildings, architects and critics alike refer to seeing, sight, and vision either directly or by inference. The League of Nations building was to be see-through in the belief that politicians would not conduct backroom deal-making if they were being observed. The Barcelona Pavilion was to represent what Germans were, an open modern democracy, how they felt and how they *saw* their new democracy. Hans Schwippert's Bundeshaus was to be see-through in order to make the workings of government publicly visible in the hopes that a measure of public control over Parliament would result. Or, as German journalist Heinrich Wefing has observed, Schwippert, and Behnisch, and the parliamentarians who encouraged Foster's use of transparency, were part of the postwar West German consensus that cried, "*Nie Wieder*!" (Never again!): "Never again should state architecture intimidate, never again should the words out of stone threaten power and control."[52] Rather, the architecture should be designed to facilitate public control of state power, hence, transparency.

Behnisch, like Schwippert, acknowledges the importance of visual control at the Bundeshaus. In his interview with Jan Esche, "*Politik aus dem Glashaus*," Behnisch explains the building's transparency, saying "What happens inside must be public. One must not have the impression that secretive powers are at work. This might have something to do with being able to see inside the building."[53] Moreover, Behnisch describes his project in terms of seeing: ". . . the enclosure should be transparent so that people can *see* into and through the building and find it understandable. No one should believe that dark powers operate there."[54] For Behnisch, the connection between sight and knowledge is explicit – what can be seen, can be known and understood, not to mention controlled. Foster too uses the visual metaphor to justify transparency at the Reichstag. He even seems to share the belief that visual control is important – he describes the transparency between the press lobby and plenary chamber at the renovated Reichstag in terms remarkably similar to Hannes Meyer's defense of his League of Nations project, "At this level the lightness and transparency of the new interventions are most apparent: all the building's processes are on view – it has no secrets."[55] Foster refers to the transparency in his design repeatedly in the various texts published about it, consistently pairing the see-through aspect of the Reichstag interiors with vision, with the possibility of seeing multiple spaces and events taking place therein simultaneously.

The West German interest in visual control can be read in two diverging ways: as proof of German self-deception about the Nazi period or as proof of German rebirth after the war. In other words, the desire for visual control cannot be separated causally from the action of collective memory or identity formation. By expressing the desire for visual access and control, West Germans communicate the optimistic belief that they will be more involved in government, have a stronger personal connection to democracy and be better able to control it, if they can see what it is doing. The desire for visual access can also be read as an articulation of the need to correct the transgressions of the past by active public participation in government. Two postwar myths probably drove these desires: the belief that most Germans were not generally aware of what Hitler and the National Socialists were about; and the belief that those who were aware did not have the means or opportunity to defy them. Notions of limited culpability have been supported by the work of professional historians whose work has generally fallen into one of two methodological camps, the "structuralist" versus "intentionalist" explanations of the Holocaust. These were similar in their acceptance of the notion of relatively limited German involvement and culpability but differed in their methodological explanation for the Holocaust. The former attributes the

Holocaust to institutional, bureaucratic functions, to the machinery of the state, while the latter attributes it to Hitler's charismatic personality and the strong command structure held by the Nazis. In both cases, responsibility for any of the evil perpetrated during the Third Reich is limited in scope to a small group, excluding most Germans, and certainly most ordinary Germans. But there exists today ample evidence that most Germans did know a great deal more about what the National Socialists were doing than was generally admitted in the 1940s and 1950s when a cult of silence existed in West Germany. Sebastian Haffner's recently published autobiography of the prewar years, *Defying Hitler: A Memoir*, is an eyewitness account of Hitler's rise to power.[56] Haffner makes it abundantly clear that average Germans knew a great deal about the National Socialists, although his account supports the notion that resistance would have been difficult. Haffner attempts to explain why the average German citizen was stymied psychologically in any effort to resist while he hints at the practical reasons resistance would have been difficult. Another recent publication, Victor Klemperer's diaries that appeared in Germany in 1995, supports Haffner by showing how much ordinary people knew of the National Socialists. They chronicle the 12 years of the Third Reich and are unique in the way they mingle attention to everyday people and details with political commentary. Klemperer observes already in 1933, "I think it is quite immaterial whether Germany is a monarchy or a republic – but what I do not expect at all is that it will be rescued from the grip of its new government. I believe anyway that it can never wash off the ignominy of having fallen victim to it."[57] Also in 1995, the Hamburg Institute for Social Research opened an exhibition that explored the role of the German army in Nazi atrocities, "War of Extermination: The Crime of the Wehrmacht, 1941–1944." Christopher Browning's 1992 book *Ordinary Men: Hamburg Reserve Police Battalion 101* studied how "ordinary men" were transformed into murderers. Similarly, Daniel Jonah Goldhagen's *Hitler's Willing Executioners: Ordinary Germans and the Holocaust* is the work of a contemporary historian looking back who debunks the myth that only a handful of Germans participated in Nazi atrocities.

What came to be known as the Goldhagen Controversy supports many of the assumptions listed above. The debate erupted in Germany after publication of the English version of the book *Hitler's Willing Executioners*, but before the book's release in German, then continued after the German version was available. Goldhagen's questions were simple and straightforward: how did the Holocaust occur? And why did it occur in Germany? His answers were equally straightforward: the Holocaust occurred because ordinary Germans willingly participated in it; this was possible thanks to the "eliminationist anti-Semitism" Goldhagen thought was rife in prewar Germany. But it is not Goldhagen's theses that are interesting here but the book's reception in Germany and what that implies about the state of collective memories of the

Third Reich in the 1990s. Perhaps no critic put it more clearly or more elo-quently than Josef Joffe in his review of the controversy and the book that sparked it for the *New York Review of Books*,

> Subtly, indeed subconsciously, the "Barbaras syndrome" of Marlowe's Jew of Malta took hold of the official vocabulary: "But that was in another country." And so the crimes had been commit-ted not by Germans but "in the German name," by them, by "Hitler and his henchmen." The psychological mechanism was not one of transparent repression or projection, as in the Austrian or Japanese case. The function of these shibboleths was to sterilize the fester-ing past, to put a reassuring distance between the murderers and the masses, between Germany then and Germany now.[58]

In other words, Goldhagen's book arrived in a time when many Germans felt they could, or at least should, forget the past. Against this backdrop, Goldhagen's book seemed to make forgetting immoral.

The curator of the Hamburg Wehrmacht exhibition, Jan Reemstma, explained Goldhagen's reception in Germany in even more direct terms,

> It was not the apparent simplicity of Goldhagen's theses that led to their success over the more complex theories of the historians but his abandonment of any wish for denial . . . the fear of a study of the average man and the possibility of recognizing in him one's own grandfather, father, or uncle (or aunt or mother) has finally been replaced by the willingness to take the risk of such a recognition.[59]

More than one German commentator pointed to the timeliness of the book's appearance although Wolfgang Wippermann came right out and wrote,

> On the whole, the Goldhagen controversy . . . shows that the strug-gle for cultural hegemony in the present by mastery of the past continues, even if at the beginning of 1996 it still appeared as though the equalizers, relativizers, and deniers had already won. Goldhagen has written an important book at the right time.[60]

Earlier in the same essay, Wippermann tells the reader that, "Just as did the Historikerstreit, the Goldhagen controversy has much more to do with the present than with the past. Only when the past is fully 'mastered' can the Germans see themselves as a 'self confident nation' again." Even for Hans Mommsen, the distinguished historian who largely disparaged Goldhagen's book, it "teaches us that the emotional aftereffect of the German murder of the Jews still lingers after decades." For the German audience, it was clear that Goldhagen's book resonated because of its appeal to and challenge of collective memories. The book is also one instrument vision cannot control. If a book can so thoroughly rouse collective memories, although it is a tiny object whose meaning is tied to the opinions of one man, then state architecture by its very scale and import to the nation must stir as many, if not more, memories. By the 1990s the transparency metaphor and analogy enjoyed legitimacy based on 50 years of architectural history in the Federal Republic as much as any ties to collective memories and other factors. But without collective memories, it is unlikely that transparency would have taken such a firm hold on the West German imagination.

V

Today, transparency and democracy continue to be linked together even though they are ultimately not related. The notion, "transparency equals democracy" stubbornly refuses to disappear from either political or architectural discourse in Germany. Neither the failed experiments in radically transparent governance, nor the lack of a truly transparent society, or open and accessible parliament have dulled enthusiasm for the concept in the political realm. The calls for improved transparency in German government appear regularly in the popular press, on television, and in new books every year. Hans Herbert von Arnim's *Vom Schönen Schein der Demokratie: Politik ohne Vorantwortung – am Volk vorbei* (Democracy and its Beautiful Pretense – Politics without Responsibility – Bypassing the People) is one recent example. Similarly, neither the obvious inability of transparent buildings to improve access and openness, nor the inherent contradiction between the desired see-through characteristic of transparent glass and its performance as alternately transparent, reflective, and opaque, has quelled interest in transparent state buildings. Stefan Braunfels' new structure to house the parliamentary offices next to the Reichstag, and Axel Schultes' enormous transparent glass façades on the Chancellery in Berlin, exemplify the obsessive use of transparent glass no matter the general esthetic, scale, or overall appropriateness. Even unification, which brought the East German version of transparent state architecture squarely into view, had no palpable effect on transparency ideology. The apparent irony in the architect of the Palast der Republik (Palace of the Republic), Heinz Graffunder, using almost identical arguments to Schwippert, Behnisch, and Foster to support transparency in the service of a Communist state, does not seem to have caused a ripple. Graffunder declared his building a symbol of the new regime in the DDR, attributing the force of its symbolic message partly to its location on the site of the former Hohenzollern palace, and partly to its architectonic qualities. Graffunder extolled the building's lightness and accessibility, and "the clear openness of the Palace for all citizens [that] will be manifested through the optical transparency of the building mass and the plastic penetration of building elements."[61] Graffunder does not seem to have been deterred by transparency's service in the name of Western-style democracy in the Federal Republic. And, like his counterparts in the West, the larger questions of how to represent the state were looming large before him. Thus, he can argue that placing the new People's Palace on the site of the former Hohenzollern palace reminds East Germans of the triumph of socialism over monarchy. Graffunder is grappling with the selfsame questions of the representative power of architecture and the appropriate architectonic means with which to represent the state which concerned his Western counterparts. Strangely, he is drawn to transparency ideology for many of the same reasons that Schwippert, Behnisch, and Foster were drawn to it – because it seems to legitimate the goals of the state he serves! When juxtaposed with transparency ideology in the West, the irrationality behind associating transparency with any political creed and architectural manifestation thereof becomes apparent. Ultimately, transparency continues to be used because it legitimates certain political actions and architectural choices, not because it makes sense.

Former parliamentarian and architect Peter Conradi summed up the issues eloquently when he wrote,

> Often the question is put whether democratic architecture exists. Does dictatorship build differently from democracy? Occasionally it is attempted to imbue building materials and stylistic devices with higher meaning. Glass is more open and democratic than concrete, symmetry gives more the impression of repressive power, and freely formed buildings the impression of freedom. Such classifications are superficial. Public architecture must show more the attitudes and values of society. Not only the parliament, but also schools and hospitals, prisons and offices, city halls and museums should make known what is important to democratic building clients and their architects. The Bundestag engaged its architects to make freedom, openness, modesty, accessibility, and tolerance recognizable. The demand for openness and accountability for decisions, for the participation of the affected people and the users, is part of the democratic process. Building in democracy is more elaborate and time-consuming than building in a dictatorship.[62]

Without the special traumas of twentieth-century German history: Hitler's dictatorship, the Holocaust, and the Second World War, the impetus to develop alternatives to traditional state architecture would not have carried the force it has in West Germany. At the same time, without the aspiration to create an open, accessible, egalitarian society after the war, transparency would not have been adopted as the analogy for the new Germany. Transparency continues in German popular mythology because it appeals to collective memories and collective desires. As long as these persist in unified Germany, transparency will remain.

Appendix 1

Biography of
Hans Schwippert

Born in Remscheid, 1899
Died in Düsseldorf, 1973

1918	Soldier on the Western Front
1919	TH Hannover and TH Darmstadt
1920–23	TH Stuttgart (Dipl.-Ing.)
1924	Atelier Erich Mendelsohn, Berlin
1925	Contact with Mies van der Rohe
1927–28	Lecturer at the Aachen, School for Applied Arts, Introduction, Skyscraper Design Class
1930	Member of the Deutsche Werkbund
1935	Assistant to the Chair for Freehand Drawing Baukunst TH Aachen
1936–43	Adjunct Professor for Applied Studies at TH Aachen
1938–45	Participation in the setting up of Aachen's civil administration after the invasion by American troops
1945–46	Director of the Reconstruction Division of the Chief Committee for North Rhine Westphalia (later called the Reconstruction Ministry of NRW)
1946–66	Director of a building arts class at the *Kunstakademie* Düsseldorf
1946–62	and Professor, Chair for Applied Arts and Housing, TH Aachen
1952	A director of the Darmstadter Gesprächs: Man and Technology
1954	Highest decoration, German Red Cross
1947–63	Re-founding and Chair of the Deutsche Werkbund
since 1949	Founder and co-editor of the Werkbund publication, *Werk und Zeit*

since 1953	Co-founder and member of the "Rates für Formgebung"
since 1954	Administrator of the Cultural Circle of the Federal Association of German Industry
1955	Member of the Academy of Fine Arts, Berlin
1956–66	Director of the *Kunstakademie* in Düsseldorf
1957	Highest state award for building design, North Rhine Westphalia
1958	Officer of the Order of Leopold of Belgium
since 1958	Member of the European Foundation of Culture
1959	Highest decoration of the Federal Republic of Germany
since 1961	Member of the Academy of Sciences of North Rhine Westphalia
1961	Emeritus at Aachen
1962	Member of the Royal Society of Arts, London
1963–69	Chairman, Deutsche Werkbund, North West
1964–68	Member of the founding committee of the University of Dortmund
since 1971	Member of the German committee for cultural cooperation in Europe
since 1973	Founding member of the international design center, Berlin

Appendix 2

Biography of Günter Behnisch

Born in Dresden, 1922

1947–51	Technische Hochschule, Stuttgart
1951	Diploma
1951–52	Works with Professor Rolf Gutbrod
1952	Foundation of practice
1967	Professor of design, industrial architecture, and architectural design, and director of the department of construction at the Technische Hochschule, Darmstadt
1982	Member, Akademie der Künste, Berlin
1984	Doctorate at the University of Stuttgart
1987	Granted emeritus status
1989	Foundation of second office in Stuttgart Center
1991	Professor of the International Academy of Architecture, Sofia
1992	Honorary member of the Royal Incorporation of Architects, Scotland, Edinburgh
	Honorary member of the Bund Deutscher Architekten (BDA)
	Grande Medaille d'Or of the Academie d'Architecture, Paris
	Honorary Prize of the International Olympic Committee for Special Achievements in Sports and Architecture
1993	Hans Molfenter Award of the regional capital city of Stuttgart for outstanding artistic achievements
1994	Member of the International Academy of Architecture, Sofia

	Honorary medal of the Lithuanian Architectural Association, Vilnius
1995	Honorary member of the Royal Institute of British Architects, London
1996	Founding member of the Saxonian Academy of Arts, Dresden

Appendix 3

Biography of
Norman Foster

Born in Manchester, 1935

1961	Manchester University School of Architecture and City Planning
	Fellowship to Yale University
1963	Masters of Architecture degree from Yale University
1963	Team 4 with Richard Rogers
1967	Foster and Associates (later Foster and Partners)
	The practice now has offices worldwide with headquarters in London, England.
	It has won over 260 awards and citations for design excellence, and more than 55 competitions.
1983	RIBA Gold Medal of Excellence
1991	Gold Medal of the French Academy of Architecture
1994	American Institute of Architects Gold Medal
	Made an Officer of the Order of Arts and Letters, French Ministry of Culture
1999	Pritzker Architecture Prize Laureate
1990	Knighthood
1997	Order of Merit
1999	Life Peerage

Lord Foster of Thameside has lectured worldwide and taught in the United Kingdom and the United States.

He has been vice president of the Architectural Association in London, council member of the Royal College of Art, a member of the Board of Education, visiting examiner for RIBA, and a trustee of the Architectural Foundation of London.

"Happiness and Glass,"
Hans Schwippert

"How easily it breaks?" Only glass and happiness? The illusion that life is ever-lasting and secure are also things of the past. Life, happiness, and glass: fragile things! Sudden or slow transitoriness – variations of the momentary.

[. . .]

How much stubborn resistance has been raised to such inconstancy and vicissitudes of life, of happiness, and of things: caves, castles, bunkers, and thick walls, closed and non-transparent, so as to feign permanency and conceal transience. What vain efforts to deny fleetingness, to hush up with eternal structures, and to outwit with monuments.

Poor pharaohs, what remains? Looted pyramids, that for thousands of years have crumbled and been wiped out; what, dictators, will remain from the borrowed splendor and strength of their thousand-year delusions? Deceived petit bourgeois, where is the everlastingness of your granite grave-stone that the bomb struck? Are not, in the end, the great beauties of this world so great because they are fragile and transient?

Not to seek happiness at all, because it is fragile? Not to love flowers, because they wilt? Not to love day, because night follows? To shun joy, because it is coupled with pain? To reject life, because it abides in death? Not to contemplate beauty, because it passes away? To reject glass, because it shatters?

What exclusions, barrings, imprisonments and what ever-new abuse of accomplishments have occurred thus far to this very end. And hence-forth no more? A change is in the air. The protection of a thick wall no longer matters to us. As always, armor plating, enclosure, flight from progress is at our disposal. We, though, love the other side: openness, sensitivity, transparency, want light not darkness, want freedom not frightened caution.

This is new. This is remarkable. For, in actual fact, these "times" are not right! Is there a resignation here that, if worst comes to worst, would no longer help anyway? Or are we, in the face of the growing threat, genuinely doing away with illusions of security, cravings for eternity, dens of fear? Is a new spirit of life here simply saying yes to fragility? Not out of despair, but out of resistance? Are we beginning to realize that, while progress multiplies horrors, it fulfills dreams just as much and it turns fairy tales into reality?

Idle rationalization supposes that, merely because we have now arrived at steel beams and bars, ductile and pre-stressed concrete, crystalline mirror glass, these accomplishments will be put to use for better or for worse! Because our dream so desired it, we have won: [the freedom] to float on air, to hear distant voices, to see distant things, to construct filigree, to look through glass walls, to open doors without moving the hand.

Is wine bad, because drunkards are unpleasant? Keep away, you thin-blooded or mindless traditionalists, you mannish schoolmarms, fustily sniffing out the tried and tested without understanding, you apostles of blood and soil, confusing the homeland with reaction. You genre artists of strict and moderate convention. You jailers of all kinds and ranks. If glassy happiness is debased at present as immoderate, it is only your eternal negation and the evil of your questionable security that causes this revolt. Moderation will be found. Not because this will return everything to your dungeons and darkness, but rather because, out of the courageous willingness to "be on the road" to fragility, to openness, to transparency, to truth, there will emerge a different, a new strength, which is tougher and more viable than your massive walls, more beautiful than the deception of your ornamentation, more joyful than the deadly seriousness of your preservations, more lasting than the sentimental materialism of your embrasured houses.

But especially in regard to that lightness that large glass panes and transparent walls afford us and that you fear and that you admonish against, there is only one kind of living creature that cannot tolerate it at all: vermin. Thanks to your efforts, their eradication will be more difficult. Because we love fragility more, we shall understand more of it and shall also know better than you where feeling safe and secure is necessary. But we shall not confuse this with absolute security, and we shall soon learn how not to abuse fragility. And we shall not stop loving life, even though it dies, desiring happiness, even though it is fleeting, or building with glass, even though it breaks.

Notes

Preface

1 Vidler, 1992, pp. 217–27.

2 Korn, 1968.

3 Öchslin, 1997, p. 9. Öechslin recounts Rowe and Slutzky's motivations for writing the piece. The first three paragraphs of the essay "Transparency: Literal and Phenomenal" clearly outline Rowe and Slutzky's point of view, p. 22.

4 Ibid., p. 23.

5 Schorske, 1981, p. xxii.

6 Craig, 1991, p. 11.

1 Transparency ideology

1 Adolf Arndt, "*Das zeitgerechte Parlamentsgebaüde*," in *Bauwelt* 1964, Heft 9, p. 247.

2 Giedion 1962, p. 42. Giedion's observation is interesting for this discussion because it points to the importance of transparency in art history.

3 In this text, I will refer to the Federal Republic of Germany in a number of ways, by the full name, by the abbreviation FRG, and by the commonly used term "West Germany." Similarly, I will refer to the German Democratic Republic by its full name, by the abbreviation GDR and by the commonly used term "East Germany."

4 Bartetzko, 1992 and 1996, p. 120. Bartezko is only one of dozens of journalists and historians to work with this assumption by the 1980s. A very short list of journalists who accept the existence and importance of the adage includes Jan Esche (*Architektur & Wohnen*), Reinhart Wustlich (*Architektur*), and Hanno Rauterberg (*Die Zeit*); politicians include Peter Conradi (former SPD MP), Rita Süssmuth (former President), and Dietmar Kansy (CDU MP). This is not to say that all of these people agree with the expression but they acknowledge its importance.

5 Roger Cohen, "With Smoked Salmon and Beer, Berlin Greets Parliament," *New York Times*, April 20, 1999, Section A, p. 10, writes that the newly renovated Reichstag was, "topped with glass to symbolize the political transparency on which the country has based its postwar revival."

6 *Wettbewerbsprogramm Bundestag und Bundesrat*, 1970, calls for "making the working methods of the Bundestag and Bundesrat visible as well as the principle established by the Basic Law of the public being able to experience the plenary consultations" and *Realisierungswettbewerb Umbau Reichstagsgebäde zum Deutschen Bundestag*, Teil 3 Aufgabe, p. 68.

7 In the article, " '*Demokratie als Bauherr' Überlegungen zum Charakter der Berliner politischen Repräsentationsbauten*," in *Das Parlament, Beilage Aus Politik und Zeitgeschichte*, August 17/24, 2001, Karin Wilhelm underscores the role the presence of a divided Berlin and the memory of ruined postwar Berlin destroyed because of the National Socialist excesses, played in Arndt's formulations. Pp. 4–5.

8 Adolf Arndt, "*Bauen für die Demokratie*," in Flagge and Stock 1996, pp. 52–65.

9   Ibid. p. 59.

10 Schwippert 1952/53, p.1. Please note, there are no signature numbers for archival citations from the Schwippert collection because the material has not been cataloged. See Appendix 4 for the full text of "*Glück und Glas*" ("Happiness and Glass").

11 Schwippert, 1951.

12 Damus, 1988.

13 Numerous articles such as "*Politik aus dem Glashaus,*" by Jan Esche, or "*Die Tiefe der Transparenz,*" refer to transparency in the title and text, chapters in every monograph on the building discuss transparency, while several monographs have been published exploring the way to build in a democracy, including *Architektur und Demokratie* and Heinrich Wefing's well-researched thesis *Parliamentsarchitektur*.

14 *Wettbewerbsprogramm Bundestag und Bundesrat*, 1970.

15 Karpen, 1998.

16 The closest thing to a national parliament was the German National Assembly: 585 representatives from throughout the German Confederation, elected after the revolt of 1848, met in St Paul's Church in Frankfurt between May 18, 1848 and May 30, 1849 in order to attempt to design a unified German state and to write a constitution. Although the members succeeded in authoring a constitution, it was never adopted. The delegates could not agree on a model for Germany, nor did they possess the real political and military power necessary to achieve their goals. For more on Parliamentary Buildings in Germany see Durm, 1900.

17 Langewiesche, 1929a.

18 Damus, 1988, p. 24.

19 Ibid., pp. 11–13.

20 Ibid., p. 11.

21 Ibid., p. 12.

22 Cullen, 1999, pp. 65–71.

23 Michael Cullen's numerous books on the history of the Reichstag discuss the negative contemporary reception to the building on the part of architects who found its mix of stylistic elements tasteless, and the Kaiser, who never wanted the building in the first place.

24 Cited in Minor, 1994, p. 103.

25 Lakoff and Johnson, 1980. In their book, Lakoff and Johnson present a clear argument for their view that metaphor is the very root of all language.

26 Ibid., p. 22.

27 Ibid., p. 3.

28 Ibid., p.11.

29 Ibid., p.14–15.

30 Ibid., p. 25.

31 The quotes are examples of instances where the transparency metaphor appears. They are from four different articles in four different publications, three German, one English. The first citation is from an interview with Chancellor Gerhard Schröder published in *Die Zeit*, Nr. 6, 1999. The second phrase is the title of Peter Conradi's article from the September 1995 issue of *Der Architekt*. The third phrase comes from Peter Blundell Jones' "*Der Bundestag*" in the March 1992 issue of *The Architectural Review*, p. 24. The fourth phrase is part of Jan Esche's interview with Behnisch in *Architektur & Wohnen*, Nr. 5, 1992, pp. 120–6.

32 Lakoff and Johnson, 1980, pp. 26–7.

33 Esche, 1992, pp. 120–6.

34 Gentner, Holyoak, and Kokinov, 2001, p. 2.

35 Ibid., p. 200.

36 At the most basic level, *Transparenz* and transparency do share certain meanings. According to the English and German dictionaries, both words can describe the physical property of a material in relation to light and view as in "see-through" or "having the property of

transmitting light so as to render bodies lying beyond completely visible." They also can both describe the character attribute of a person as in "frank, open, and candid," or the factual condition "manifest, evident, obvious, apparent." Further, both indicate the quality "diaphaneity" in a substance. *Transparenz* is based on the Latin terms *trans,* which means through, and *parere,* which means to become evident, to show itself. According to the Duden book of German etymology, the word entered the German language at the beginning of the eighteenth century. *Durchsichtig* also entered the language at this time and means "that which one can see through" and that which "light lets through."

37 Putnam, 1988, p. 22. The text includes a lengthy discussion of the ways in which words have meaning and how mental representations relate to words.

38 Halbwachs, 1950.

39 Donald Preziosi provides a first-rate overview of the history of art historical method and the debates over representation in his book *The Art of Art History: A Critical Anthology,* 1998.

40 Ibid., p. 13.

41 See Bollerey, 2002, pp. 276–89, for a thoughtful examination of the issues at stake as the first-generation practitioners formulated their arguments and for a justification of the modern movement as a style.

42 See Tafuri, 1980.

43 Bollerey, 2002 p. 276. She cites Barr who, in 1932 in *The International Style,* wrote "that there exists today a modern style as original, as consistent, as logical, and as widely distributed as any in the past . . .," Hitchcock and Johnson, 1932, p. 30.

44 Goodman and Elgin, 1988, p. 33.

45 Vale, 1992, p. 6.

46 Tzonis and Lefaivre, 1988, p. 4.

47 The Ring of Ten is something of a misnomer, as far more than ten people attended meetings between 1926 and 1933. Founded by Hugo Häring, the membership list included many architects who are associated with the Neues Bauen, including Otto Bartning, Richard Döcker, Walter Gropius, and Ludwig Hilberseimer.

48 In his dictionary of terms for modern architecture (Forty, 2000), Adrian Forty discusses the rise of a new vocabulary for design during the twentieth century and demonstrates the importance concepts and terms from the 1920s continue to have today.

49 Instead of form, space, and style, the British architectural historian Adrian Forty points to form, space, and design as the triad of modern architecture, which is probably true for modern architecture taken as a whole, but style was very much in the forefront of architectural discourse in West Germany in the 1920s, 1930s, and 1940s. After the Second World War, style was at the center of a heated national debate. Forty, 2000, p. 149.

50 *"Aufruf zur elementaren Kunst"* in *De Stijl,* 1921, No. 10 reprinted in Passuth, 1985, p. 286.

51 Forty, 2000, p. 150.

52 Giedion, 1982, p. 442.

53 Cited in Behne, 1996, p. 146.

54 See Schwippert, 1940, for one of many essays in which he addresses this duality in architecture.

55 Hans Schwippert, letter to Hugo Kükelhaus, dated May 2, 1938 as cited in Dyroff and Tömena, 1984, p. 123.

56 Schwippert, 1953. This is only one of many examples of essays in which Schwippert uses the same terms to explain form.

57 Hans Schwippert. Notes dated Easter 1943. Schwippert Archiv, Germanisches Nationalmuseum, Nuremberg.

58 Hans Schwippert, *"Schule und Form: Zum Aufbau der gestalterischen Erziehung,"* speech given to the *Kunsthochschule und Werkkunstschule,* Düsseldorf, North Rhine Westphalia, February 1949. Schwippert Archiv, Germanisches Nationalmuseum, Nuremberg.

59 Cited in Gauzin-Müller, 1997, p. 19, from documentation of the design process for the German Bundesbank.

60 Behnisch, "*Bauen für die Demokratie*," in Flagge and Stock, 1996, p. 67.

61 Behnisch, 1996, p. 157.

62 Ibid.

63 Foster, 2000.

64 Foster, 2000, p. 23.

65 Forty, 2000, p. 256.

66 Gottfried Semper. *Der Stil in der technischen und Tektonischen Künsten, oder praktische Ästhetik. Ein Handbuch für Techniker, Künstler, und Kunstfreunde.* Bd. I. Frankfurt: 1860. Munich: 1878.

67 Forty, 2000, p. 266.

68 Giedion, 1982, p. 430.

69 Ibid., pp. 435–436.

70 Mies van der Rohe from "Working Theses" (May 1923).

71 Forty, 2000, p. 268.

72 Behne, 1996, pp. 103–17.

73 Lazlo Moholy-Nagy, "Modern Art and Architecture," reprinted in Passuth 1985, p. 340. This is the most extensive discourse on space Moholy-Nagy wrote, but by no means the first. Discussions of space and the need for a "space conception" in architectural design appear already in the early 1920s in, for example, "Man and his House."

74 Ibid., p. 340.

75 Ibid., p. 341.

76 Hans Schwippert, speech from 1951 at an occasion organized by Otto Bartning. Schwippert Archiv, Germanisches Nationalmuseum, Nuremberg.

77 Hans Schwippert. "On Steel and the Art of Building," speech at the meeting of the Steel Association, February 10, 1953. Schwippert Archiv, Germanisches Nationalmuseum, Nuremberg.

78 Hans Schwippert, speech from 1951 at an occasion organized by Otto Bartning. Schwippert Archiv, Germanisches Nationalmuseum, Nuremberg.

79 Behnisch, 1987, p. 7.

80 Foster, 2000, p. 76.

81 Ibid., p. 78.

82 Ibid., p. 131.

83 Tzonis and Lefaivre, 1988.

84 Behrendt, 2000, p. 126.

85 Behne, 1996, p. 120.

86 Behne, 1927, p. 103.

87 Ibid., p. 105.

88 Hilberseimer, 1928.

89 Gropius, 1925, p. 20.

90 Pulzer, 1995, p. 43.

2 Transparency in German architecture before and after the War

1 Framke, 2002, p. 17.

2 Botting, 1985, p. 80.

3 Wolf, 1985, p. 114.

4 Ibid., pp. 115–6.

5 Botting, 1985, p. 96.

6 Ibid., p. 96.

7 Schulze, 1998, pp. 286–7; Laqueur, 1993, pp. 3–11.

8 Botting, 1985, p. 95.

9 The Group of 47 was a large organization of writers and poets that counted among its members Günter Grass, Hans Magnus Enzensberger, Heinrich Böll, Paul Celan, Hubert Fichte, Peter Handke, Walter Jens, and Marcel Raich-Ranicki. Alfred Andersch and Walter Kolbenhoff founded the literary magazine *Der Ruf* in 1946 along with the Group of 47. The goal was to explain democracy to the German people and to help with democratic education in post-Third Reich Germany. The group desired a new beginning for society, politics, and language. They rejected the Weimar literature, as well as that of Exiles and Inner Exiles.

10 Schmidt, 1947.

11 Rowe and Slutzky, "Transparency: Literal and Phenomenal," in Rowe and Slutzky, 1997.

12 Giedion, 1982 and in Mertins, 1996.

13 Mertins, 1996, pp. 49–51.

14 Kohlmaier and von Sartory, 1981, p. 45.

15 See Starobinski, 1988.

16 This is not the place to provide a comprehensive overview of the development of German liberal political thought but some of the key texts include: *Wissenschaftslehre* by Fichte, *Critique of Pure Reason* by Kant, and *Elements of the Philosophy of Right* by Hegel.

17 Arndt, 1964, p. 242. See also Gosewinkel, 1991. Arndt was also an active member of the Deutsche Werkbund, eventually serving as its Director, beginning in 1965. He knew many architects and was familiar with the architectural debates of his day.

18 Arndt, "*Demokratie als Bauherr*," in Flagge and Stock, 1996, p. 53.

19 Ibid., p. 57.

20 Ibid., p. 59.

21 Markus, 1993, pp.41–94.

22 See Bollerey, 1977, for a thorough look at the utopian visions of Owen and Fourier.

23 See Bollerey, 1977, p. 20 and see also Bentham, 1983.

24 Cited in Markus, 1993, p. 123.

25 Bollerey, 1977, pp. 65–6.

26 Forty, 2000, pp. 286–9.

27 Junod, 1976.

28 See Kohlmaier and Von Sartory, 1981, for an extensive discussion of the history and evolution of nineteenth century glass and steel structures.

29 Ibid., pp.44–50 and 77–137.

30 Ibid.

31 See Lidtke, 1966, for a comprehensive discussion of the origins of German Socialism.

32 Point number 10 in *Glasarchitektur*, p. 44.

33 Sharp, 1972, *Glasarchitektur*, number 18, p. 46.

34 Sharp, 1972, *Glasarchitektur*, number 85, p. 66.

35 Sharp, 1972, *Glasarchitektur*, number 102, p. 70.

36 Translated by Dennis Sharp in his introduction to *Glasarchitektur*.

37 The second *Arbeitsrat* publication, *Ruf zum Bauen, (Call to Build)* was dedicated to "the spirit of Paul Scheerbart."

38 The Crystal Chain was begun by Bruno Taut in 1919. The letters have been published in English by Whyte, 1985.

39 Behne, 1977, p. 154, first published in *Fruhlicht*, Heft 1.

40 Whyte, 1982.

41 Taut, 1972, pp. 125–6.

42 Haag Bletter's article, 1981, traces the evolution of the crystal metaphor, pp. 20–43.

43 Sharp, 1972, *Glasarchitektur*, p. 74.

44 Hillegas, 1967, p. 4.

45 Moholy-Nagy, 1947, p. 72.

46 Ibid., p. 75.
47 Ibid., pp. 75–6.
48 Giedion, 1982, p. 76.
49 Moholy-Nagy, 1947, p. 80.
50 Ibid., p. 86.
51 Ibid.
52 His obsession with transparency was important but so was Moholy-Nagy's conviction that art and politics were inextricably connected – a belief shared by others in his circle like Walter Gropius, Bruno Taut, and Adolf Behne – all of whom were members of the politicized artists' groups Arbeitsrat für Kunst and Novembergruppe. "I believed that abstract art not only registers contemporary problems," wrote Moholy-Nagy, "but projects a desirable future order, unhampered by any secondary meaning, which the customary departure from nature usually involves because of its inevitable connotations. Abstract art, I thought, creates new types of spatial relationships, new inventions of forms, new visual laws – basic and simple – as the visual counterpart to a more purposeful, cooperative human society."
53 Schulze, 1929, pp. 101–10.
54 Section I is *Bauen mit Glas – Gestaltung und Funktion* (*Building with Glass – Form and Function*) whose sub-chapters are: *Das neue Wollen* (*The new Will*); *Der Gestaltswandel* (*The Formal Change*); and *Die Wandöffnung* (*The Wall Opening*). Section II is, *Glas als Baukörper* (*Glass as Building Body*); *Glas als Werkstoff* (*Glass as Work Material*); and *Warum Glas?* (*Why Glass?*).
55 Schulze, 1929, p. 9.
56 Ibid, p. 10.
57 Schulze, 1929, p. 11 and Korn, 1929, p. 29.
58 Schulze, 1929, pp. 12–13. In spite of Schulze's assertion, the AEG Building was not the first factory structure to use glass extensively. An earlier project dates from 1903 in Munich designed for the Steiff factory, the famous German toy company known for its stuffed toy animals.
59 Ibid., p. 15.
60 Ibid., pp. 18–19.
61 Ibid., p. 18.
62 Ibid., p. 22.
63 Ibid., p. 25.
64 Ibid., p. 91.
65 Ibid., p. 92.
66 Korn, 1929, p. 5.
67 Ibid.
68 Behne, 1996, p. 2.
69 In translation in Schnaidt, 1965.
70 From Lilly von Schnitzler, "*Die Weltausstellung Barcelona, 1929*," *Der Querschnitt 9*, (August 1929), p. 583, as cited in Schulze, 1985, p. 152.
71 Barbara Miller Lane, Gerhard Fehl, and Wolfgang Schäche are only three examples of historians who have debunked the myth that the National Socialists built exclusively in the neoclassical style.
72 Heinrich Wefing points to an almost identical set of buildings in his book but also discusses some other buildings including the Olympic Stadium designed by Günter Behnisch and Frei Otto. Although the stadium is important to the transparency discourse, because it was not a federal project, it is not included here.
73 Hoff in *Bauwelt*, 1958, p. 471.
74 Schirmer, 1984, p. 12.
75 Peters in *Baumeister*, 1958, p. 394.

76 Author's translation from Schneider in Wichmann, 1986, p. 35.

77 Hans Schwippert, speech from 1958. Schwippert Archiv, Germanisches Nationalmuseum, Nuremberg. Schwippert was a consultant for the Brussels pavilions so he may have had personal reasons for promoting the architecture, that went beyond sympathy for their artistic resolution.

78 Leuschner, 1980, p. 29.

79 Wichmann, 1986, p. 122.

80 As cited in Wefing, 1995, p. 96 from Shrieber, *Architektur*, p .3.

81 Leuschner, 1980, p. 30.

82 Ibid., p. 24.

83 "*Überblick*," in *Bauwelt*, Nr. 21, 1969, p. 732.

84 Leuschner, 1980, p. 179.

85 In German, *Glück ohne Glas – wie dumm ist Das?* From the Schwippert Archiv at the Germanisches Nationalmuseum, Nuremberg. For a detailed discussion of the essay see Chapter 5.

86 See Behnisch, 1996 and "Building for Democracy" in Gauzin-Miller, 1997.

87 See "*Spielerisches steht für Freiheit*," *Bonner Rundschau*, Nr. 254, Oct. 30, 1992, p. 3.

3 The quest for an open society

1 Cited in Kaes, 1989, p. 3.

2 Ismayr, 2001.

3 Ibid., p. 36.

4 Ibid., pp. 299–438.

5 See von Arnim, 2002. Von Arnim discusses the "fictive" aspect of West German participatory democracy.

6 Adenauer helped found the Christian Democratic Union (CDU), one of the conservative parties. Other important postwar parties include the Christian Social Union (CSU), the CDU's counterpart in southern Germany, the Social Democratic Party (SPD), the leftist party, the Free Democratic Party (FDP), a centrist party that alternates between alliances with the CDU and SPD, and the Communist party (KPD). In recent years the Green Party has also become a player.

7 Adenauer, 1966, p. 121.

8 Kommers, 1999, p. 96.

9 Clay, 1974, p. 563. In this letter to Baruch, Clay expresses his fear of a Red Army incursion into Germany and states this threat as the greatest one to European security. It is because of possible Soviet aggression that Clay wants to accelerate the political evolution, independence and consolidation of the parts of Germany not under Soviet control. In a letter to General Chamberlain, chief of Army Intelligence, dated March 5, 1948, Clay expresses his fears again.

10 Adenauer, 1966, p. 112.

11 Laufer and Münch, 1998, pp. 73–4.

12 Clay, 1974, pp. 475–8.

13 Von Arnim, 2002, p. 32 and Chapter 24, pp. 169–77. Von Arnim reminds his readers of Abbe Sieyes' famous saying, "What are the people? Everything! What have they to say? Nothing! What do they want? That they have something to say!"

14 *Information Bulletin*, April 20, 1948, p. 6.

15 Similarly, although the Allies mounted a concerted campaign to discredit the National Socialist government in part by publicizing the facts about the concentration camps in the press and by forcing Germans to visit the camps, many Germans were either reluctant or emotionally unable to absorb the horrible facts. In her new novel, *The Dark Room*, Rachel Seiffert dramatizes the different reactions to learning the truth.

16 Clay's "policy is to make fully and frankly known to press correspondents the facts of organ-
    ization, activities, problems, and results of work of the US Group Control Council in Germany."
    Clay, 1974, letter to Hildring, July 5, 1945, p. 49.
17 Clay, 1974, p. xxix.
18 Grace, 1949, pp. 3–5, 26.
19 LaFollette, 1949, p. 25.
20 Clay, 1974, p. 241.
21 "Authorized Anglo-American Text of the Basic Law," *Information Bulletin*, June 14, 1949,
    pp. 29–33.
22 Ibid., p. 29.
23 Wefing, 1995.
24 Laufer and Münch, 1998, p. 31.
25 Ibid., pp. 17–19.
26 Karpen, 1988, p. 306
27 An excellent summary of the organization of the German Federal Republic as well as an
    assessment of politics during the Adenauer era can be found in Stahl, 1963.
28 In his book *Adenauer: A Critical Biography*, Charles Wighton is extremely critical of Adenauer.
    Not only does Wighton accuse him of being an authoritarian, but he asserts that Adenauer
    expressed "open disregard and contempt for the normal practices of modern democracy."
    Wighton, 1963, p. 15.
29 Wighton's account is not objective in any way, Wighton was a journalist stationed in Germany
    during the 1940s and writes from his own observations. Therefore, his text has to be
    regarded with some skepticism. Nevertheless, he does provide a colorful picture of the first
    German Chancellor, and much of Wighton's book is substantiated by others.
30 Ibid., p. 53.
31 Adenauer, 1966, p. 33. Adenauer reproduces the letter from Barraclough in its entirety.
32 Ibid., pp. 30–1.
33 Heidenheimer, 1960, p. 82.
34 Birch, 1950, pp. 16–17.
35 Ibid.
36 Adenauer, 1966, p.79.
37 See the books on consensus building in the FRG by Ismayr.
38 Author's interview with Günter Behnisch on June 25, 2001.
39 "*Staatliche Repräsentation durch Bundesbauten*," *Vorwärts*, 12 August, 1973.
40 Ibid.
41 The government of Chancellor Gerhard Schröder recently "broke" the IG Metall Union for
    the first time in a move most analysts see as a major step towards achieving economic
    reforms in Germany. July 2003.
42 The literature devoted to the economic reconstruction of West Germany is as extensive as
    that devoted to the political reconstruction. Katzenstein, 1987, Markovits, 1982, and Arndt,
    1966 are three texts that present a balanced overview.
43 For a more thorough discussion of how these changes have affected West German politics
    and the polity, see Katzenstein, 1987.
44 Halfmann, 1999.
45 Noelle-Neumann and Köcher, 1997, p. 4.
46 From OMGUS, Report 105, March 27, 1948.
47 Noelle-Neumann and Köcher, 1993.
48 Germany, and France, have experienced high unemployment and stagnant economies for the
    last few years. Both countries have run deficits that exceeded the 3 percent of GNP allowed
    by the Union and both are now vocally advocating a change to this rule. July 2003.

49 Ismayr discusses these issues while other contemporary German writers like Hans Herbert von Arnim bemoan the lack of direct democracy in the German system.
50 Author's interview with Detlef Lenz in Berlin on July 17, 2003.
51 Author's interview with Detlef Lenz in Berlin on July 17, 2003.
52 See Schindler, 1999, volume 3, for a chronology of all the measures taken between 1949 and 1997 to improve communication between parliament and the German public.
53 Ibid., p. 3484.
54 Ibid., p. 3487.
55 Ismayr, 2001, p. 463.

4   Looking in the mirror: transparency after 1989

1 *Der Spiegel*, 46/1989, *"Jetzt Offenheit Beweisen!"*
2 Enzensberger, 1968, p. 90.
3 *Der Spiegel*, 46/1989, *"Jetzt Offenheit Beweisen!,"* pp. 32–7.
4 James, 1998, p. 4, Dieter-Klingemann and Hofferbert, 1994, Betz, 1997. The notion of the Wall in the Head was so important that the Allensbach Institute incorporated a question about the existence of this metaphysical separation in its post-unification surveys.
5 James, 1998, p.5.
6 Noelle-Neumann and Köcher, 1997, p. 577.
7 Niethammer, 1997, p. 136. In the same volume, Reinhard Kühnl also refers to "absorption" of the GDR by the FRG, p. 123. These are only two of numerous examples.
8 Kahn, 2000, p. xxii.
9 Niethammer, 1997, p. 135.
10 Melchior-Bonnet, 2001, p. 247.
11 Ibid., p. 250.
12 Nietzsche, 2002.
13 Karl E. Meyer, "The Horror Files," *New York Times*, April 12, 1992, p. 20.
14 Conversation with Joachim Lemann quoted in Stephen Kinzer, "Living and Living with Oneself," *New York Times*, May 3, 1992, p. 7.
15 Pulzer, 1992 p. 324. Many writers have pointed to the crisis of political identity after unification including Jarausch, 1997a and Merkl, 1993.
16 Böckenförde, 1995a.
17 Ralf Dahrendorf, "Citizens in Search of Meaning," in Dahrendorf, 1997, p. 26.
18 Schäuble, 1994, pp. 217–8.
19 Schönbaum and Pond, 1996, p. 55.
20 Noelle-Neumann and Köcher, 1997, p. 555.
21 Roger Cohen, "Germany's East and West: Still Hostile States of Mind," *New York Times*, October 25, 1999, p. 1.
22 Böckenförde, 1995b, p. B1.
23 *American Heritage Dictionary*, 1985, p. 831.
24 Gellner, 1997.
25 Buruma, 1998, p. 44.
26 Böckenförde, 1995b, p. B1. Schmitt, 1997, p. 45.
27 Buruma, 1998.
28 Smith, Paterson, and Padgett, 1992.
29 Noelle-Neumann and Köcher, 1997, p. 608.
30 Ibid., p. 611.
31 Ibid., p. 612.
32 Ibid., p. 605.
33 Ibid., p. 610.
34 Ibid., p. 612.

35 Jarausch, 1994, p. 142.
36 Padgett, 1992, pp. 187–207, for a discussion of the split economy in Germany after unification.
37 Ibid., pp. 200–5.
38 Fischer *et al.* 1999, p. 32.
39 Henryk M. Broder, "*Lebe Wohl, Alte Bundeskegelbahn,*" *Der Spiegel*, 52/1999, p. 78.
40 Ibid., p. 80.
41 Fischer *et al.*, 1999, p. 31.
42 Pulzer, 1992, p. 320.
43 Jarausch, 1997b.
44 Schwarz, 1990. Habermas, 1992.
45 Roger Cohen, "Searches for 'Normality,'" *New York Times*, November 29, 1998, p. 10. The dispute over normality spilled into the pages of *Der Spiegel* as well.
46 Schönbaum and Pond, 1996 p. 6.
47 Fischer *et al.*, 1999.
48 Herf, 1997, p. 7.
49 Ibid., p. 6.
50 Ibid., p. 33.
51 Henryk M. Broder, "*Lebe Wohl, Alte Bundeskegelbahn,*" *Der Spiegel*, 52/1999, p. 81.
52 Arnulf Baring, "*Unsere Schlöfrigkeit ist unbegreiflich,*" *Der Spiegel*, 45/1999, p. 56.
53 Herzog, 1997, pp. 6–7.
54 Ibid., pp. 11–18.
55 Ibid., p. 15.
56 Stephen Kinzer, "German Panel to Scrutinize East's Rule and Repression," *New York Times*, March 30, 1992, p.7.
57 Knabe, 1993, p. 8.
58 Matthias Matussek, "*Keine Opfer, keine Tüter,*" *Der Spiegel*, 10/1999, p. 124.
59 Wagner, 1999, p. BS2.
60 Barbel Bohley in Stephen Kinzer "One More Wall to Smash: Arrogance in the West," *New York Times*, August 12, 1992, p. 4.
61 Wagner, 1999, p. BS2.
62 Stephen Kinzer, "East Germans face their Accusers," *New York Times*, April 12, 1992, p. 24.
63 Ibid.
64 Ibid.
65 Ibid.
66 Ibid., Kinzer tells the story of Vera Wollenberger, whose file revealed that her husband had informed on her, and of artist Sascha Anderson, who had informed on his friends.
67 Stephen Kinzer, "Germans Anguish over Police Files," *New York Times*, p. 10.
68 Johannes Legner cited in Roger Cohen, "Germany's East is still Haunted by Big Brother," *New York Times*, November 29, 1999, p. 1.
69 From James and Stone, 1992, p. 233ff, cited in Jarausch and Gransow, 1994, pp. 128–31.
70 From T. Klau, "*Angst or dem bösen 'boche' geht in Frankreich wieder um,*" *Bonner Rundschau*, March 28, 1990, cited in Jarausch and Gransow, 1994, p. 132.
71 A. Riding, "On Germany, 'Not All is Joy,'" *New York Times*, 15 February, 1990.

5 A metaphor for the new Germany

1 Heuss, 1960, p. i.
2 Schwippert, *Neue Bauwelt*, Heft 17, 1951.
3 Birch, Lionel. "Where do they go from Bonn?' *Picture Post*, January 14, 1950, pp. 12–41.
4 According to August Hoff writing in Schwippert's sixty-fifth birthday *Festschrift*, in the Schwippert Archiv, Germanisches Nationalmuseum, Nuremberg.

Notes

5   Some of these sketches survive and are in the Schwippert Archiv at the Technical University, Munich.

6   From Mies van der Rohe's contribution to Hans Schwippert's *Festschrift* in the Schwippert Archiv, Germanisches Nationalmuseum, Nuremberg, dated July 22, 1964.

7   Numerous draft copies of speeches Schwippert made over the years that are in the Schwippert Archiv, Germanisches Nationalmuseum, Nurnberg refer to Mies and his architecture.

8   From a speech to the matriculating class at the Düsseldorf Kunstakademie, December 4, 1964, in the Schwippert Archiv, Germanisches Nationalmuseum, Nurnberg.

9   From Hans Schwippert, *"Zu Stahl u. Baukunst: Vortrag auf der Tagung des Stahlbau Verbandes,"* Koln, October 2, 1953, in the Schwippert Archiv, Germanisches Nationalmuseum, Nuremberg.

10 Hans Schwippert. *Schriften, Ostern 1943.* From the Schwippert Archiv, Germanisches Nationalmuseum, Nuremberg.

11 Hans Schwippert, *Neue Bauwelt*, Heft 17, 1951.

12 From a letter to Hugo Kükelhaus, dated May 2, 1938 as reprinted in Dyroff and Tömena, 1984a, pp. 123–5.

13 From the Schwippert Archiv, Germanisches Nationalmuseum, Nuremberg, Germany.

14 Ibid., p. 1.

15 Ibid., p. 2.

16 Ibid., p. 4.

17 Ibid., p. 2.

18 Terrell *et al.*, 1997, p. 124.

19 From *"Handwerk als Basis,"* Hans Schwippert, 1943, Schwippert Archiv, Germanisches Nationalmuseum, Nuremberg.

20 *"Glück und Glas"* was published in 1952/3 in *Wohn Form*, p. 3.

21 See Appendix 4 for the full text of Schwippert's essay.

22 As Director of the *Kunstakademie* in Düsseldorf, Schwippert delivered several public addresses annually. The drafts for these are in the Schwippert Archiv at the Germanisches Nationalmuseum, Nuremberg. Many of them return to transparency and glass construction as central ideas.

23 Schwippert, *Neue Bauwelt*, Heft 17, 1951.

24 Schwippert, 1952/3.

25 Ibid.

26 Ibid.

27 We know that there was not a public competition because of articles that appeared after the building was complete, complaining about how unfair the selection process for an architect had been.

28 *"Architekten-Vertrag,"* dated November 3, 1948 between North Rhine Westphalia, and Hans Schwippert, Schwippert Archiv, Germanisches Nationalmuseum, Nuremberg.

29 *"Vertragsentwurf: Architektenvertrag,"* dated August 26, 1949, Schwippert Archiv, Germanisches Nationalmuseum, Nuremberg.

30 Charlotte Werhahn. *Hans Schwippert (1899–1973): Architekt, Pädagoge und Vertreter der Werkbundidee in der Zeit des deutschen Wideraufbaus.* Dissertation at the Technical University Munich, June 25, 1987.

31 Ibid., By 1946, the department was renamed *Wiederaufbauministerium des Landes Nordrhein Westfalen.* Adenauer's acquaintance to Schwippert dates at least to 1945 when he tried to enlist Schwippert's help with the reconstruction of Cologne, a request recorded in a letter dated July 12, 1945.

32 From *"Schwippert als Baumeister"* by Josef Lehmbrock for what was going to be a book on Schwippert in 1981 with Econ. From the draft text in the Schwippert Archiv, Germanisches Nationalmuseum, Nuremberg.

33 *Architekten-Vertrag* dated November 18, 1949 in the Schwippert Archiv, Germanisches Nationalmuseum, Nuremberg. In an attachment, Schwippert asks Wandersleb to sign because the work has already begun on the project. In the note, Schwippert writes that, "he used verbal *Weisungen* from the Chancellor and *Anweisungen* from you [Wandersleb] in order to do the first work."

34 Although the picture has no credit, and the article does not mention Schwippert by name, the sketch survives in the Schwippert archival collection at the Technical University in Munich.

35 Two articles announced the reconstruction efforts in Bonn, "*Der Umbau der Päda in Bonn hat Begonnen!*" *Westdeutsche Rundschau*, February 24, 1949 and "*Die Päda ist im Umbau,*" *Kölnische Rundschau*, February 22, 1949.

36 In a letter from Wandersleb to Schwippert dated December 23, 1949 in the Schwippert Archiv, Germanisches Nationalmuseum, Nuremberg.

37 Both the articles in the *Westdeutsche Rundschau* and *Kölnische Rundschau* mention these plans.

38 Strodthoff, 1964, p. 5.

39 Lane, 1985, p. 124.

40 Ibid.

41 The letter, dated May 11, 1950 survives in the Schwippert Archiv, Germanisches Nationalmuseum, Nuremberg.

42 Meyer-Waldeck, 1950, p. 99.

43 Hans Schwippert quoted in "*Bonn erlebte seinen grossen Tag,*" *Die Welt*, Nr. 136, Sept, 8, 1949, p. 3.

44 Quoted in Wefing, 1995, pp. 114–15.

45 *Manifesto*, from the Schwippert Archiv, Germanisches Nationalmuseum, Nuremberg.

46 See Levin, 1993 and Jay, 1993 for two comprehensive surveys of vision in Western thought. Light figures prominently in the discussions.

47 "*Das Bonner Bundeshaus,*" *Neue Bauwelt*, Heft 17, 1951.

48 "*Das Bundeshaus in Bonn,*" *Westdeutsche Zeitung*, 2 Jahrgang, Nr. 109, September 7, 1949, p. 5.

49 Stark, 1983, is an excellent source for interpretations of the Basic Law that are accessible to the lay person.

50 Wefing, 1995, p. 118.

51 "*Das Bundeshaus in Bonn,*" *Westdeutsche Zeitung*, 2 Jahrgang, Nr. 109, September 7, 1949, p. 5.

52 Sketches from the Schwippert Archiv at the Technical University Architecture Museum, Munich.

53 Sketches from the Schwippert Archiv at the Technical University Architecture Museum, Munich.

54 Reproduced in Schwippert, 1982, p. 183. Other versions of this study are not so transparent.

55 The sketch is in the archives at the Technical University Architecture Museum of Munich.

56 Adrian Forty, Philippe Junod, and Bernard Tschumi, all discuss "transparency of meaning" in these terms.

57 "*Bundesrat u. Bundestag feierlich eröffnet,*" *Stuttgarter Zeitung*, 5 Jahr, Nr. 161, Sept. 8, 1949, p. 1.

58 Schwippert, *Neue Bauwelt*, Heft 17, 1951.

59 From a draft for the Neues Bauen article in the Schwippert Archiv, Germanisches Nationalmuseum, Nuremberg.

60 "*Bonn erlebte seinen grossen Tag,*" *Die Welt*, Nr. 136, Sept. 8, 1949, p. 3.

61 Many of the contemporary articles point to this unusual design decision. Two examples are: "*Bonn erwartet Parlamentseröffnung,*" in *Die Neue Zeitung*, a5 Jahr, Nr. 136, Sept. 7, 1949, p. 1 and "*Bundesrat u. Bundestag feierlich eröffnet,*" *Stuttgarter Zeitung*, 5 Jahr, Nr. 161, Sept. 8, 1949, p. 1.

62 Schwippert, *Neue Bauwelt*, Heft 17, 1951.

63 Ibid.

64 "*Das Bundeshaus in Bonn*," *General Anzeiger*, Nr. 100, Sept. 7, 1949, p. 5.

65 "*Das Bundeshaus in Bonn*," *Bauen und Wohnen*, Jahrgang 4, Heft 10, 1949, p. 466.

66 "*Das Bonner Bundeshaus*," *Neue Bauwelt*, Heft 17, 1951, pp. 65–72.

67 "*Bundesparlament in Bonn*," *Bauen u. Wohnen*, August 1949, p. 9.

68 Hans Schwippert. Draft of an explanatory article for the Bundeshaus project in the Schwippert Archiv in the Germanisches Nationalmuseum, Nuremberg.

69 Reprinted in Dyroff and Tümena, 1984, p. 65.

70 *Westdeutsche Zeitung*, September 8, 1949, page. 2.

71 *Neue Bauwelt* is the same as the magazine today titled *Bauwelt*. The title changed a few years after the war.

72 Typical examples include: "The Bundeshaus in Bonn" in the *Westdeutsche Zeitung* from September 7, 1949; the author ends by writing, "We look once more at the totality. In its lightness and openness [it is] a good piece of the Bonn cityscape."

73 "*Das Bundeshaus in Bonn*," *General Anzeiger*, Nr. 100, Sept. 7, 1949, p. 5.

74 "*Bonn erlebte seinen grossen Tag*," *De Welt*, Nr. 136, Sept. 8, 1949, p. 3; "*Bonn heute Bundessitz einst Residenz*," *General Anzeiger*, Nr. 108, Sept. 7, 1949, p. 7.

75 "Parliament Building at Bonn," *Architectural Review*, April 1950, p. 187.

76 Fenno Jacobs, "Where do they go from here?" *Picture Post*, January 14, 1950, pp. 14–15.

77 Ibid., p. 15.

78 Ibid., p. 13.

79 Schwippert, *Neue Bauwelt*, Heft 17, 1951.

80 Cited in Schwippert, 1982.

6 House of openness, architecture of encounter

1 Arndt, Adolf. "*Demokratie als Bauherr*," reprinted in Flagge and Stock, 1996, pp. 52–65.

2 Author's interview with Günter Behnisch in Stuttgart, Germany on June 25, 2001.

3 Ibid.

4 According to the biographical information in Gauzin-Müller, 1997, p. 298.

5 Author's interview with Günter Behnisch in Stuttgart, Germany on June 25, 2001.

6 Ibid.

7 Rita Süssmuth, "Speech," for the Colloquium "Democracy as Client," July 22, 1989 in Bonn, p. 4–5.

8 Ibid., p. 12.

9 Ibid., p. 21.

10 From the Behnisch Archiv at the *Südwestdeutsches Archiv für Architektur und Ingenieurbau (SAAI), Karlsruhe*. Uncataloged. The Behnisch gift is in boxes and file folders as it was donated but has not been cataloged as yet.

11 Ibid., p. 3.

12 Copy of the "*Auszug aus dem Wettbewerbs-Program*" from the Behnisch Archiv at the SAAI in Karlsruhe.

13 "*Spielerisches steht für Freiheit*," *Bonner Rundschau*, Nr. 254, October 30, 1992, p. 3.

14 Interview with the author, June 25, 2001 in Stuttgart.

15 Esche, 1992, p. 124.

16 In an interview with the author on June 25, 2001 in Stuttgart.

17 Letter from Eiermann to Arndt in the Arndt Archiv at the Friedrich Ebert Stiftung, Bonn, Germany.

18 Although there are countless articles in the German architectural press and the general press covering the various stages in the design process, Schindler, 2000, in the section titled *Parlamentsgebäude in Bonn und Berlin*, pp. 3270–3332, outlines the entire, complicated history in clear, concise, and broad terms.

19 Cited in *Baugeschichte*, p. 3293.

20 See the section titled, "*Parlamentsgebäude*," in Schindler, 2000, pp. 1286–1314, for a comprehensive but brief history of building for the West German government.

21 *Baugeschichte*, p. 3316.

22 Behnisch, 1987b, p. 86.

23 Not only does Behnisch cite Schmid in essays and interviews concerning the Bundestag, see Jan Esche's "*Politik aus dem Glashaus*" or Behnisch's own essay "*Bauen für die Demokratie*" as examples, but in an interview with the author, he gave a marked copy of Schmid's article as a gift!

24 Behnisch gave the author a copy during a visit to the Sillenbuch office in June, 2001.

25 Behnisch, "*Bauen für die Demokratie*," in Flagge, 1996, p. 70.

26 Esche, 1992, p. 120–6.

27 Article 4 reads, "Freedom of belief, conscience, and freedom of religion and ideological confession are inviolable." Article 5 reads, "Everyone has the right to express his opinion in words, writing, or images. . . ."

28 Schmid and Strätling, 1989, second page of Behnisch xerox.

29 Günter Behnisch, "*Bauen für die Demokratie*," in Flagge, 1996, p. 67.

30 Ibid., p. 68.

31 Behnisch, *Ein Gang durch die Ausstellung*, p. 79.

32 In Charles, 1996, p. 73.

33 Ingeborg Flagge, "*Zum Thema Selbstdarstellung*," from the Behnisch Archiv, SAAI, Karlsruhe.

34 Ibid., p. 2.

35 *Deutsche Bauzeitung*, September 1987, p. 86 and Ingeborg Flagge, "*Zum Thema Selbstdarstellung*," from the Behnisch Archiv, SAAI, Karlsruhe.

36 Interview with the author on June 25, 2001 in Stuttgart.

37 Peter Conradi cites the descent into the heart of the building as one of the crucial formal aspects of the design. Interview with the author on June 26, 2001 in Stuttgart.

38 Behnisch, 1996, p. 161.

39 See designs for the Green Plaza from 1975.

40 Günter Behnisch, "Entrance and Foyer," *Deutscher Bundestag: Neuer Plenarbereich*, p. 159.

41 Ibid.

42 Ibid., p. 157.

43 Behnisch discussed his interest in the Happenings and the Situationist movement with the author, in Stuttgart on June 25, 2001.

44 Behnisch, 1996, p. 167.

45 Esche, 1992, p. 124.

46 Behnisch & Partner, 1993, p. 87.

47 Behnisch & Partner, 1993, pp. 100–1.

48 Ibid., p. 90.

49 Baumann & Baumann, 1995, p. 101.

50 Poets include Ernst Jandl, Friedrich Achleitner, Kurt Marti, and Eugen Gomringer.

51 *The American Heritage Dictionary*, 1985, p. 316.

52 Author's interview with former MP Peter Conradi in Stuttgart on June 26, 2001.

53 Behnisch & Partner, 1993, pp. 75–99.

54 Ibid.

55 Charles, 1996, p. 155.

56 Behnisch & Partner, 1993, p. 78.

57 In Flagge and Stock, 1996, p. 67.

58 Norberg-Schultz, 1971, p. 299.

59 Melchior-Bonnet, 2001, p. 47.

60 Behnisch mentioned this interest in his interview with the author in Stuttgart on June 25, 2001 and at a lecture he gave at Pratt University in New York City.

61 The essay by Ingeborg Flagge from 1972 is one of the exceptions and even she seems to recommend transparency in spite of recognizing its mythological dimensions.

7 Coming to terms with the past: transparency in Norman Foster's Reichstag

1   Habermas, 1997, p. 167.

2   "Reichstag Reopens," *New York Times*, April 25, 1999, Late edition, Section 4, p. 2 and in Roger Cohen's article, "With Smoked Salmon and Beer, Berlin Greets Parliament," *New York Times*, April 20, 1999, Late Edition, Section A, p. 10.

3   Cullen, 1999, p. 118.

4   "Reichstag Reopens," *New York Times*, April 25, 1999, p. 2 and in Roger Cohen's article, "With Smoked Salmon and Beer, Berlin Greets Parliament," *New York Times*, April 20, 1999, Late Edition, Section A, p. 10.

5   Foster, 2000, p. 60.

6   The fears were raised by both foreign and German journalists including Dieter Bartetzko, "*Kein klärendes Wort,*" *Frankfurter Allgemeine Zeitung*, January 28, 1998, p.33; Roger Cohen writing for the *New York Times*, "With Smoked Salmon and Beer, Berlin Greets Parliament," April 20, 1999, Section A, p. 10; and Udo Bergdoll, "*Konsenssuche oder: Die Modelle der Töstungen; Was die Kompromissvorschläge im Hauptstadt-Streit wirklich bedeuten,*" *Südeutscher Zeitung*, June 11, 1991.

7   For examples see Bartetzko, 1998, p. 33 and Hanno Rauterberg, "*Der deutsche Kummerkasten,*" *Die Zeit*, Nr. 15, 1999.

8   Bartetzko, 1998, p. 33 and Frank, 1994 are two examples of many discussing the new Berlin projects and their meaning.

9   Foster, 2000, p. 57.

10 Schulz, 2000, p. 7.

11 Ladd, 1997, describes the many ways Berlin is a city of ghosts.

12 There are numerous comprehensive histories of the Reichstag. These include: Cullen, 1995, and Cullen, 1992, Schmädeke, 1994, and Wefing, 1999.

13 Cullen, 1995.

14 Discussed in Cullen, 1999.

15 Martin Pawley, "The Rise and Fall of the Reichstag," in Foster, 2000, p. 38.

16 Cullen, 1999, Cullen and Kieling, 1992, Wefing, 1999, Schmädeke, 1994.

17 Frank Pergande, "*Die sowjetischen Bomben trugen die Inschrift 'Zum Reichstag',*" *Frankfurter Allgemeine Zeitung*, April 19, 1999, p. 4.

18 Cited in Pergande, 1999, p. 4.

19 Burleigh, 2000, pp. 151–2.

20 Shirer, 1959, p. 192, is one example of many. Gerhard Hahn is currently finishing a book on the fire. According to his research, which centered largely on forensic evidence, Van Lubbe set the fire. But this does not take away from the political advantage the Nazis were able to gain by exploiting the event.

21 Hanno Rauterberg, "*Der deutsche Kummerkasten,*" *Die Zeit*, Nr. 15, 1999.

22 In two separate conversations Foster employees, Project Architect Mark Braun and Partner David Nelson, mentioned the competition as a precedent.

23 "Reichstag Unresolved," *Architectural Review*, April 1993, pp. 8–10.

24 See any of the numerous articles published on the competition or the books on the Foster Reichstag for images of the gigantic transparent glass roof that constituted the competition proposal.

25 "Reichstag Unresolved," *Architectural Review*, April 1993, pp. 8–10.

26 Foster, 2000, p. 36.
27 Ibid., pp. 8–9. Partner David Nelson confirmed what Foster has written in an interview with the author, April 2, 2002.
28 Hanno Rauterberg, "*Der deutsche Kummerkasten*," *Die Zeit*, Nr. 15, 1999.
29 Rita Süssmuth, "Foreword," in Foster, 2000, p. 8.
30 Cited in Schulz, 2000, p. 39.
31 Cited in Pawley, "The Rise and Fall of the Reichstag," in Foster, 2000, p. 57. Pawley does not give many details but quotes Christo in two places in the short description of the project.
32 Author's interview with David Nelson at Foster and Partners in London, April 2, 2002.
33 Cited in Wefing, "*Abschied vom Glashaus*," *Frankfurter Allgemeine Zeitung*, April 17, 1999, p. 1.
34 Werner Öchslin, "*Wie man Bedeutung vermeidet*," in *Bauwelt*, 1999, Helft 18/19, p. 1005.
35 Frank Pergande, "*Die sowjetischen Bomben trugen die Inschrift 'Zum Reichstag'*," *Frankfurter Allgemeine Zeitung*, April 19, 1999, p. 4.
36 Foster, 2000, p. 118.
37 Ibid., p. 116.
38 Roger Cohen, "Berlin Journal: The Reichstag Burns, This Time with Hope," *New York Times*, March 6, 1999, Section A, p. 4.
39 Foster, 2000, p. 77.
40 Ibid., p. 76.
41 Ibid., p. 78.
42 Author's interview with the Chief of Security at the Reichstag, Detlef Lenz on July 18, 2003 in Berlin.
43 Ibid.
44 Foster, 2000, p. 60.
45 Author's interview with Peter Conradi on August 26, 2001, in Stuttgart.
46 Foster, 2000, p. 86.
47 Author's interview with Peter Conradi on August 26, 2001, in Stuttgart.
48 Foster, 2000, p. 134.
49 In German the notes read, "*Schweres Drucktragwerk 'weniger Licht'!!! Zu viele Stützen . . . herabgeetzte Transparenz!*" From drawing set in the author's possession from the Depot Conradi.
50 In German, "*Leichtes zug netz . . . licht transparenz!!! Wenige leichte stützen . . . raum transparenz!*" From author's copies from Depot Conradi.
51 Author's interview with Peter Conradi, August 26, 2001 in Stuttgart.
52 Wise, 1966, pp. 130–1.
53 Foster, 2000. These terms are repeated throughout the book.
54 Cullen, 1999, p. 118.
55 Hanno Rauterberg, "*Der deutsche Kummerkasten*," *Die Zeit*, Nr. 15, 1999, p. 3.
56 Stepen Heath, "Narrative Space," *Screen*, 17:3, August 1976, p. 73.

8 Why transparency?

1 Weizsäcker, 1992.
2 Simmel, 1950.
3 Edelman, 1964, p. 18 from Malinowski, 1948, p. 93.
4 Edelman, 1964. p. 6.
5 Ibid., p. 98.
6 Noelle-Neuman and Köcher, 1997, pp. 657–8.
7 Wright, 1997, p. 254.
8 Ibid., p. 255.
9 Cited in Robin, 1992, from US Congress, Foreign Service Buildings Act Amendments, 1959, pp. 6, 11, 209.

10   Goethe quoted in Gropius, 1968, p. 71.

11   Walter Gropius quoted in "United States Embassy Office Building, Athens," *Architectural Record*, 122 (December 1957), p. 71.

12   Norberg-Schulz, 1986, pp. 87–109.

13   Faber, 1968, p. 12.

14   Fierro, 2003.

15   Halbwachs, 1950.

16   Ibid., Murray Edelman makes similar points in his work.

17   Halbwachs, 1950, pp. 85–6.

18   Markovits and Reich, 1997, p. 15.

19   Ibid., p. 16.

20   Ibid., p. 15.

21   Markovits and Reich use this method in their study of *The New German Predicament*.

22   See Rita Süssmuth's speech on the occasion of the Colloquium "Democracy as Client," pp. 3–7.

23   Noelle-Neuman and Köcher, 1997, p. 504–5.

24   Ibid., p. 503.

25   Noelle-Neuman and Köcher, 1993, p. 376.

26   Ibid., p. 380.

27   Ibid., p. 381.

28   See Lane, 1985 and Fehl and Harlander, 1986.

29   See the numerous articles in *Die Zeit, Frankfurter Allgemeine Zeitung, Süddeutsche Zeitung* that are cited in Chapter 7 for some examples.

30   Winfried Nerdinger, "*Politische Architektur: Betrachtungen zu einem problematischen Begriff*," in *Architektur und Demokratie*, pp. 10–32.

31   Behnisch, "*Bauen für die Demokratie*," in *Architektur und Demokratie*, pp. 66–75.

32   Cited in Gauzin-Mueller, 1997, p. 16.

33   Ibid., pp. 49–67.

34   Ibid., p. 121.

35   Günter Behnisch, "*Bauen in der Demokratie*," in Flagge and Stock, 1996, is only one of dozens of essays the architect wrote addressing these issues but it is the most thoughtful and comprehensive in its view.

36   Michael Mönninger, "*Wer im Glashaus sitzt*," *Frankfurter Allgemeine Zeitung*, 21 October, 1992, p. 33.

37   See Norman Foster, "The Economy of Architecture," in Henket and Heynen, 2002, pp. 26–37.

38   Helmut Engel, "The Marks of History," in Foster, 2000, p. 124. Cullen, "*Es geht um das Symbol*," in the FAZ, August 24, 1995, p. 32. Cullen refers to the many misunderstandings about the meaning of the Reichstag, "Many understand the Reichstag to stand for the Wilhelmine regime or for the Third Reich, although the cupola is not at all Wilhelmine, rather the most progressive thing about the building, and although Hitler did not govern from the Wallot building. . . ."

39   Hanno Rauterberg, "*Der deutsche Kummerkastern*," *Die Zeit*, Nr. 15, 1999.

40   Author's interviews with associates and employees of the firm.

41   Schwippert, 1952/3, p.1. See Appendix 4 for the full text.

42   Ibid., p. 2.

43   Author's interview with Behnisch on June 25, 2001 in Stuttgart.

44   Esche, 1992, p. 124, and Günter Behnisch, "*Bauen für die Demokratie*," in Flagge and Stock, 1996, p. 67.

45   Esche, 1992, p. 124.

46   As cited in "Parliament Building at Bonn," *Architectural Review*, April 1950, p. 187.

47   See Levin 1993, 1999 and Jay, 1993.

48 Jay, pp. 383–4.
49 Levin, 1993, p. 7.
50 Foucault, 1979, pp. 202–3.
51 Ibid., p. 207.
52 Heinrich Wefing, "*Abschied vom Glashaus*," FAZ, April 17, 1999, *Bilder und Zeiten*, p. 1.
53 Esche, 1992, p. 120.
54 Ibid., p. 124. This is only one of dozens of similar statements made by Behnisch and by German architecture critics writing about the building.
55 Foster, 2000, p. 135.
56 Haffner, 2000.
57 Klemperer, 1998, p. 8.
58 Josef Joffe, "The Killers were Ordinary Germans, ergo the Ordinary Germans were Killers: The Logic, the Language, and the Meaning of a Book that Conquered Germany," originally published in the *New York Review of Books*, November 28, 1996, reprinted in Shandley, 1998, p. 223.
59 Jan Philipp Reemtsma, "Turning Away from Denial," originally published in *Blätter für deutsche und internationale Politik* and reprinted in Shandley, 1998, p. 257.
60 Wolfgang Wippermann, "The Jewish Hanging Judge?" originally published in *Wessen Schuld* and reprinted in Shandley, 1998, p. 243.
61 Graffunder, 1977, p. 23.
62 Peter Conradi, "*Die Parlamentsbauten*," *Deutsche Bauzeitung*, August 1989, p. 24.

Bibliography

Periodicals cited

Architektur und Wohnen

Der Architekt

The Architectural Review

Architecture d'Aujourd'hui

Architektur und Wohn Form

Bau Rundschau

Bauen und Wohnen

Baumeister

Bauwelt

Die Bauzeitung

Deutsche Bauzeitschrift

Deutsche Bauzeitung

Information Bulletin, Office of Military Government, US (OMGUS)

Journal of Democracy

Journal of the Society of Architectural Historians

Die Kunst und das Schöne Heim

Neue Bauwelt

OMGUS Reports

Der Spiegel

Stern

Werk und Zeit (Published by the *Deutscher Werkbund*)

Newspapers cited

Allgemeine Zeitung, Mainz

Bonner Rundschau

Frankfurter Allgemeine Zeitung

General Anzeiger

Kölner Stadt-Anzeiger

Kölnischer Rundschau

Der Morgen

Die Neue Zeitung

The New York Times

Das Parlament

Das Parlament: Beilage Aus Politik und Zeitgeschichte

The Picture Post

Rhenischer Merkur

Stuttgarter Zeitung

Süddeutsche Zeitung

Der Tagesspiegel
Vorwärts
Die Welt
Die Welt am Sonntag
Westdeutsche Rundschau
Westdeutsche Zeitung
Die Woche
Die Zeit

Archives consulted

Stiftung Archiv der Akademie der Künste, Sammlung Baukunst, Berlin
Bauhaus Archiv, Museum für Gestaltung, Berlin
Behnisch Archiv, Südwestdeutsches Archiv für Architektur und Ingenieurbau, University of Karlsruhe
Behnisch Personal Archiv, Behnisch & Partner, Stuttgart
Bundesbildarchiv, Bonn and Berlin
Bundesarchiv, Deutscher Bundestag, Berlin and Bonn
Depot Conradi, in possession of Michael Cullen, Berlin
Presse Dokumentation, Deutscher Bundestag, Bonn and Berlin
National Library Collection, Berlin
Collection of the Technical University, Berlin
Collection of the Museum für Deutsche Geschichte, Berlin
Schwippert Archiv, Germanisches Nationalmuseum, Nuremberg
Schwippert Archiv, Technische Universität, Munich
Stadtarchiv, Bonn

Interviews conducted

Günter Behnisch
Christian Kandzia, Partner, Behnisch & Partner
David Nelson, Partner, Foster and Partners
Mark Braun, Project Architect, Reichstag
Michael Cullen, historian of the Reichstag
Dietmar Kansy, MP and member of the Building Commission of the Bundestag
Peter Conradi, former MP and member of the Building Commission of the Bundestag
Heinrich Wefing, journalist with Frankfurter Allgemeine Zeitung

Books consulted

Adenauer, Konrad. *Adenauer Memoirs: 1945–1953*. London: Weidenfeld & Nicholson, 1966.
Alter, Reinhard and Montheath, Peter (eds). *Rewriting the German Past*. New Jersey: Humanities Press, 1997.
American Heritage Dictionary. Boston: Houghton Mifflin, 1985.
Arndt, Adolf. *Das zeitgerechte Parlamentsgebäude. Bauwelt*, Heft 9, 1964.
Arndt, Adolf. *Politische Reden und Schriften*. Berlin: Dietz-Nachf, 1976.
Arndt, Adolf. *"Demokratie als Bauherr,"* reprinted in *Architektur und Demokratie*. Ingeborg Flagge and Wolfgang Jean Stock (eds). Stuttgart: Hatje, 1996.
Arndt, Hans-Joachim. *West Germany: Politics of Non-Planning*. Syracuse, NY: Syracuse University Press, 1966.
Bartetzko, Dieter. *"Ein Symbol der Republik,"* in *Architektur und Demokratie*. Ingeborg Flagge and Wolfgang Jean Stock (eds). Stuttgart: Hatje, 1996.
Bartetzko, Dieter. *"Macht und Monument," Frankfurter Allgemeine Zeitung*. January 28, 1998.
Baumann & Baumann. *Lechts und Rinks: Orientierungen zwischen Architektur und Parlament: Deutscher Bundestag Bonn*. Stuttgart: Hatje, 1995.

Bibliography

Behne, Adolf. *Neues Wohnen – Neues Bauen.* Leipzig: Hesse & Beder, 1927.

Behne, Adolf. *Glas Manifest*, (1920), cited in *Expressionismus*. Jost Hermand and Richard Hamann. Frankfurt am Main: Fischer Taschenbuch, 1977.

Behne, Adolf. *Der moderne Zweckbau* (*The Modern Functional Building*). Rosemarie Haag Bletter (intro.) Michael Robinson (trans.) Santa Monica, CA: Getty, 1996.

Behnisch, Günter. *Behnisch & Partner: Arbeiten aus den Jahren 1952–1987.* Stuttgart: Cantz, 1987a.

Behnisch, Günter *"Bonner Runde: Die Parlamentsbauten," Deutsche Bauzeitung.* September 1987b.

Behnisch, Günter. *"Bauen für die Demokratie,"* in *Architektur und Demokratie.* Ingeborg Flagge and Wolfgang Jean Stock (eds). Stuttgart: Hatje, 1996.

Behnisch, Günter. *"Ein Gang durch die Ausstellung"* ("A fascinating walk through the building") in *Deutscher Bundestag: Neuer Plenarbereich.* Heidelberg: Braus, 1996.

Behnisch & Partner (eds). *Plenarbereich des Deutschen Bundestages in Bonn: Zwischenbericht Mai 1991.* Stuttgart: Hans Lutz, 1991.

Behnisch & Partner (eds). *Ein Gang Durch die Ausstellung.* Stuttgart: Hatje, 1993.

Behrendt, Walter Curt. *The Victory of the New Building Style* (*Der Sieg des Neuen Baustils*). Harry Francis Mallgrave (trans.) Santa Monica, CA: Getty, 2000.

Bentham, Jeremy. *The Constitutional Code, Volume 1.* F. Rosen and J. H. Burns (eds). Oxford: Clarendon Press, 1983.

Berndt, Heide, Lorenz, Alfred, and Horn, Klaus. *Architektur als Ideologie.* Frankfurt: Suhrkamp, 1968.

Betz, Hans-Georg. "Perplexed Normalcy: German Identity after Unification," in *Rewriting the German Past.* Reinhard Alter and Peter Montheath (eds). New Jersey: Humanities Press, 1997.

Birch, Lionel. "The Outward and Visible Token of a Fresh Start," *Picture Post.* January 14, 1950.

Blake, Peter. *No Place Like Utopia: Modern Architecture and the Company We Kept.* New York: Knopf, 1993.

Böckenförde, Ernst-Wolfgang. *"Die Nation," Frankfurter Allgemeine Zeitung.* September 30, 1995a.

Böckenförde, Ernst-Wolfgang. *"Über ein Phänomen, das selbst die Merkmale bestimmt, die es bestimmen," Frankfurter Allgemeine Zeitung.* September 30, 1995b.

Bollerey, Franziska. *Architekturkonzeption der utopischen Sozialisten: Alternative Planung und Architektur für den gesellschaftlichen Prozess.* Munich: Heinz Moos, 1977.

Bollerey, Franziska. "Innovation or 'Nothing New under the Sun'," in *Back from Utopia: The Challenge of the Modern Movement.* Hubert-Jan Henket and Hilde Heynen (eds). Rotterdam: 010, 2002.

Botting, Douglas. *In the Ruins of the Reich.* London: George Allen & Unwin, 1985.

Brady, John S., Crawford, Beverly, and Williarty, Sara Elise (eds). *The Postwar Transformation of Germany.* Ann Arbor: University of Michigan, 1999.

Burden, Hamilton T. *The Nuremburg Party Rallies: 1923–33.* New York: Praeger, 1967.

Burleigh, Michael. *The Third Reich: A History.* New York: Hill and Wang, 2000.

Buruma, Ian *"Ohne Nation gibt es keine Freiheit," Frankfurter Allgemeine Zeitung.* May 25, 1998.

Charles, Martin (ed.) *Deutscher Bundestag: Neuer Plenarbereich: Acht Fotografen sehen den neuen Plenarbereich des Deutschen Bundestags in Bonn.* Heidelberg: Edition Braus, 1996.

Clay, Lucius D. *The Papers of General Lucius D. Clay: Germany 1945–1949.* Jean Edward Smith (ed.). Bloomington, IN: Indiana University Press, 1974.

Craig, Gordon A. *Germany, 1866–1945.* New York: Oxford University Press, 1978.

Craig, Gordon A. *The Germans.* New York: Putnam, 1982.

Craig, Gordon A. *The Germans* (revised edn). New York: Meridian, 1991.

Cullen, Michael S. *Der Deutsche Reichstag: Geschichte eines Monumentes.* Berlin: Frolich & Kaufmann, 1992.

Cullen, Michael S. *Der Reichstag: Denkmal, Symbol, Geschichte*. Berlin: be bra, 1995.

Cullen, Michael S. *Der Reichstag: Parlament, Denkmal, Symbol*. Berlin: be bra, 1999.

Cullen, Michael S. and Uwe Kieling. *Der Deutsche Reichstag. Geschichte eines Parlaments*. Berlin: Argon, 1992.

Dahrendorf, Ralf. *Society and Democracy in Germany*. Garden City, NY: Doubleday, 1967.

Dahrendorf, Ralf. *After 1989: Morals, Revolution, and Civil Society*. New York: St. Martins, 1997.

Damus, Martin. *Das Rathaus: Architektur und Sozialgeschichte von der Gründerzeit zur Postmoderne*. Berlin: Gebr. Mann, 1988.

Debord, Guy. *The Society of the Spectacle*. Detroit: Black & Red, 1983.

Dieter-Klingemann, Hans and Hofferbert, Richard. "Germany: A New 'Wall in the Mind'?" *Journal of Democracy* 5 (January 1994).

Documents on Democracy in the Federal Republic of Germany. Bonn: Press and Information Office of the Federal Government, 1994.

Duden Etymologie: Herkunfstwörterbuch der deutschen Sprache. Mannheim: Bibliographisches Institut, 1963.

Durm, Josef (ed.) *Handbuch der Architektur: Entwerfen, Anlage und Einrichtung der Gebäude*. Ed. Vierter Teil, 7 Halb-Band: *Gebäude für Verwaltung, Rechtspflege und Gesetzgebung; Militärbauten*, 2 Heft: *Parlamentsgebäude und Ständhäuser*. Stuttgart: Arnold Bergsträsser, 1900.

Durth, Werner. *Deutsche Architekten: Biographische Verflechtungen 1900–1970*. Braunschweig: Deutscher Taschenbuch, 1992.

Dyroff, Dr Hans-Dieter and Tömena, Paul (eds). *Hans Schwippert*. Cologne: Walter König, 1984a.

Dyroff, Dr Hans-Dieter and Tömena, Paul (eds). *Hans Schwippert: Architektur und Denkmalpflege*. Düsseldorf: Heinrich Winterscheidt, 1984b.

Edelman, Murray. *The Symbolic Uses of Politics*. Urbana: University of Illinois, 1964.

Ehmke, Horst, Schmid, Carlo, and Scharoun, Hans. *Festschrift für Adolf Arndt: zum 65 Geburtstag*. Frankfurt: Europaische Verlagsanstalt, 1969.

Enzensberger, Hans Magnus. *Poems for People who don't Read Poems*. Michael Hamburger, Jerome Rothenberg, and Hans Magnus Enzensberger (trans). New York: Atheneum, 1968.

Esche, Jan. "*Politik aus dem Glashaus*," *Architektur und Wohnen*. Nr. 5, 1992

Faber, Tobias. *New Danish Architecture*. New York: Praeger, 1968.

Fehl, Gerhard and Harlander, Tilman. *Hitlers sozialer Wohnungsbau, 1940–1945: Wohnungspolitik, Baugestaltung und Siedlungsplanung: Aufsätze und Rechtsgrundlage zur Wohnungspolitik, Baugestaltung und Siedlungsplanung aus der Zeitschrift "Der Soziale Wohnungsbau in Deutschland."* Hamburg: Christians, 1986.

Fierro, Annette. *The Glass State: The Technology of the Spectacle, Paris 1981–1998*. Cambridge, MA: MIT Press, 2003.

Fischer, Suzanne, Leick, Roman, Leinemann, Jürgen, *et al.* "*Planetarische Visionen*," *Der Spiegel*, 45 1999.

Flagge, Ingeborg and Stock, Wolfgang Jean (eds). *Architektur und Demokratie: Bauen für die Politik von der amerikanischen Revolution bis zur Gegenwart*. Stuttgart: Hatje, 1996.

Forty, Adrian. *Words and Buildings: A Vocabulary of Modern Architecture*. London: Thames and Hudson, 2000.

Foster, Norman. *Rebuilding the Reichstag*. New York: Overlook, 2000.

Foucault, Michel. *Discipline and Punish*. Alan Sheridan (trans.) New York: Vintage, 1979.

Framke, Gisela (ed.) *Das Neue Dortmund: Planen, Bauen, Wohnen in den fünfzigen Jahren*. Exhibit at the Museum für Kunst und Kulturgeschichte, Dortmund. 15 September–8 December 2002. Dortmund: Museum für Kunst und Kulturgeschichte, 2002.

Frank, Robert. "*Baulektionen von Staatswegen. Gemischte Gefühle nach und vor den grossen Berliner Wettbewerben des Bundes*," *Süddeutscher Zeitung*. December 15, 1994, Feuilleton.

Bibliography

Gauzin-Miller, Dominique. *Behnisch & Partners: 50 Years of Architecture*. New York: Academy Editions, 1997.

Gay, Peter. *Weimar Culture: The Outsider as Insider*. New York: Harper & Row, 1968.

Gellner, Ernest. *Nationalism*. New York: NYU Press, 1997.

Gentner, Dedre, Holyoak, Keith J., and Kokinov, Boicho N. (eds). *The Analogical Mind*. Cambridge, MA: MIT Press, 2001.

Giedion, Sigfried. *The Eternal Present: The Beginnings of Art*. Kingsport, TN: Pantheon, 1962.

Giedion, Sigfried. *Space, Time and Architecture: The Growth of a New Tradition*. Cambridge, MA: Harvard University Press, 1982.

Gieter, Alois, Meyer, Franz Sales, and Beinlich, Joachim. (eds) *Planen und Bauen im Neuen Deutschland*. Cologne: Westdeutsche Verlag, 1960.

Glazer, Nathan and Lilla, Mark (eds). *The Public Face of Architecture: Civic Culture and Public Spaces*. New York: Free Press, 1987.

Goldhagen, Daniel Jonah. *Hitler's Willing Executioners: Ordinary Germans and the Holocaust*. New York: Knopf, 1996.

Goodman, Nelson and Elgin, Catherine. *Reconceptions in Philosophy*. Indianapolis: Hackett, 1988

Gosewinkel, Dieter. *Adolf Arndt: Die Wiederbegründung der Rechtsstaats aus dem Geist der Sozialdemokratie (1945–1961)*. Bonn: J.H.W. Dietz, 1991.

Gössner, Rolf. "Big Brother" *Der moderne Überwachungsstaat in der Informationsgesellschaft*. Hamburg: Konkret Literatur, 2001.

Grace, Dr Alonzo G. "Democratizing Textbooks: Efforts to Erase Nationalism," *Information Bulletin*. April 19, 1949.

Graffunder, Heinz, Beerbaum, Martin, and Murza, Gerhard. *Der Palast der Republik*. Leipzig: Seemann, 1977.

Gropius, Walter. *Die Neue Architektur und Das Bauhaus* (*The New Architecture and the Bauhaus*). Morton Shand (trans.) London: Faber and Faber, 1925.

Gropius, Walter. *Apollo in the Democracy: The Cultural Obligation of the Architect*. New York: McGraw-Hill, 1968.

Haag Bletter, Rosemarie. "The Interpretation of the Glass Dream: Expressionist Architecture and the History of the Crystal Metaphor," *Journal of the Society of Architectural Historians*, 1981.

Habermas, Jürgen "*Wir sind wieder 'normal' geworden*," *Die Zeit*. December 18, 1992.

Habermas, Jürgen. "1989 in the Shadow of 1945," *A Berlin Republic: Writings on Germany*. Steven Rendall (trans.) Lincoln: University of Nebraska, 1997.

Haffner, Sebastian. *Defying Hitler: A Memoir*. Oliver Pretzel (trans.). New York: Farrar Strauss & Giroux, 2000.

Halbwachs, Maurice. *The Collective Memory*. Francis J. Ditter, Jr. and Vida Yazdi Ditter (trans.). New York: Harper & Row, 1950.

Halfmann, Jost. "Two Discourses of Citizenship in Germany: The Differences between Public Debate and Administrative Practice" in *The Postwar Transformation of Germany*. John S. Brady, Beverly Crawford, and Sarah Elise Wiliarty (eds). Ann Arbor: The University of Michigan Press, 1999.

Heidenheimer, Arnold J. *Adenauer and The CDU*. The Hague: M. Nijhoff, 1960.

Henket, Hubert-Jan and Heynen, Hilde (eds). *Back from Utopia: Challenge of the Modern Movement*. Rotterdam: 010, 2002.

Herf, Jeffrey. *Divided Memory*. Cambridge, MA: Harvard, 1997.

Herzog, Roman. "Speech at Bergen-Belsen on Yom Ha Shoah," April 27, 1995 in *Lessons from the Past, Visions for the Future*. Baltimore: Johns Hopkins, 1997.

Heuss, Theodor. "Introduction," *Planen und Bauen im neuen Deutschland*. Köln: Westdeutscher V, 1960.

Hilberseimer, Ludwig. *Internationale Neue Baukunst: im Auftrag des deutschen Werkbundes*. Stuttgart: Julius Hoffman, 1928.

Hillegas, Mark R. *The Future as Nightmare: H.G. Wells and the Anti-Utopians.* Carbondale: Southern Illinois Press, 1967.

Hitchcock, Henry R. and Johnson, Philip. *The International Style.* New York: W.W. Norton & Company, 1932.

Iden, Peter and Mössinger, Ingrid (eds). *Deutscher Bundestag Bonn: Neubau des Plenar- und Präsidialbereiches.* Bonn: 1993.

Ismayr, Wolfgang. *Der Deutsche Bundestag: 2er Auflage.* Opladen: Leske & Budrich, 2001.

James, Harold and Stone, Marla. *When the Wall Came Down: Reactions to German Unification.* New York: Routledge, 1992.

James, Peter. "The New Germany Eight Years on," in *Modern Germany: Politics, Society and Culture.* London: Routledge, 1998.

Jarausch, Konrad. *The Rush to German Unity.* New York: Oxford, 1994.

Jarausch, Konrad. *After Unity: Reconfiguring German Identities.* Providence, RI: Berghahn, 1997a.

Jarausch, Konrad. "Normalization or Renationalization? Reinterpreting the German Past," in *Rewriting the German Past.* Peter Monteath and Reinhard Alter (eds). Atlantic Highlands, NJ: Humanities Press, 1997b.

Jarausch, Konrad H. and Gransow, Volker (eds). *Uniting Germany: Documents and Debates, 1944–1993.* Providence, RI: Berghahn, 1994.

Jay, Martin. *Downcast Eyes: The Denigration of Vision in Twentieth-Century French Thought.* Berkeley, University of California, 1993.

Junod, Philippe. *Transparence et Opacité: essai dur les fondements theoriques de l'art moderne: pour une nouvelle lecture de Konrad Fiedler.* Lausanne: Editions L'Age d'homme, 1976.

Kaes, Anton. *From Hitler to Heimat: The Return of History as Film.* Cambridge, MA: Harvard University Press, 1989.

Kahn, Charlotte. *Ten Years of German Unification: One State, Two Peoples.* Westport, CT: Praeger, 2000.

Karpen, Ulrich (ed.) *The Constitution of the Federal Republic of Germany: Essays on the Basic Rights and Principles of the Basic Law with a Translation of the Basic Law.* Baden-Baden: Nomos, 1988,

Katzenstein, Peter. *Policy and Politics in West Germany: The Growth of a Semisovereign State.* Philadelphia: Temple, 1987.

King-Hall, Stephen and Ullmann, Richard K. *German Parliaments: A Study of the Development of Representative Institutions in Germany.* New Southgate: Chiswick Press, 1954.

Klemperer, Victor. *I will Bear Witness: A Diary of the Nazi Years – 1933–1941.* Martin Chalmers (trans.). New York: Random House, 1998.

Knabe, Hubertus. "*Die geheimen Lager des Staatssicherheitsdienstes,*" *Frankfurter Allgemeine Zeitung.* January 21, 1993.

Knopp, Gisbert and Schumacher, Angela. *Das Bundeshaus in Bonn: Geschichte, Baugeschichte, Architektur.* Bonn: Bonner Geschichtsblätter, 1984.

Kohlmaier, Georg and Von Sartory, Barna. *Houses of Glass: A Nineteenth Century Building Type.* Cambridge, MA: MIT Press, 1981.

Kommers, Donald P. "Building Democracy: Judicial Review and the German *Rechtsstaat,*" in *The Postwar Transformation of Germany.* John S. Brady, Beverly Crawford, and Sarah Elise Wiliarty (eds). Ann Arbor: The University of Michigan Press, 1999.

Korn, Arthur. *Glas im Bau und als Gebrauchsgegenstand.* Berlin: Ernst Pollak, 1929.

Korn, Arthur. *Glass in Modern Architecture of the Bauhaus Period.* Dennis Sharp (trans.). New York: George Braziller, 1968.

Ladd, Brian. *The Ghosts of Berlin: Confronting German History in the Urban Landscape.* Chicago: University of Chicago, 1997.

LaFollette, Charles M. "Democracy and the Occupation," *Information Bulletin.* January 25, 1949.

Lakoff, George and Johnson, Mark. *Metaphors We Live By.* Chicago: University of Chicago, 1980.

Lane, Barbara Miller. *Architecture and Politics in Germany, 1918–1945*. Cambridge, MA: Harvard University Press, 1985.

Langewiesche, Karl Robert. *Bürgerbauten aus vier Jahrhunderten Deutscher Vergangenheit*. Leipzig: Fischer & Wittig, 1929a.

Langewiesche, Karl Robert. *Wohnbauten und Siedlungen aus deutscher Gegenwart*. Leipzig: Julius Klinkhardt, 1929b.

Laqueur, Walter. *Weimar: A Cultural History, 1918–1933*. New York: Putnam, 1974.

Laqueur, Walter, *Europe in Our Time: A History 1945–1992*. New York: Putnam, 1993.

Laufer, Heinz and Münch, Ursula. *Das föderative System der Bundesrepublik Deutschland*. Opladen: Leske & Budrich, 1998.

Leuschner, Wolfgang (ed.) *Bauten des Bundes, 1965–1980*. Karlsruhe: Müller, 1980.

Levin, David Michael. *Modernity and the Hegemony of Vision*. Berkeley: University of California, 1993.

Levin, David Michael. *The Philosopher's Gaze: Modernity in the Shadows of the Enlightenment*. Berkeley: University of California, 1999.

Lidtke, Vernon L. *The Outlawed Party: Social Democracy in Germany, 1878–1890*. Princeton: Princeton University Press, 1966.

Malinowski, Bronislaw. *Magic, Science, and Religion and Other Essays*. New York: Doubleday, 1948.

Markovits, Andrei and Reich, Simon. *The German Predicament: Memory and Power in the New Europe*. Ithaca, NY: Cornell University Press, 1997.

Markovits, Andrei (ed.) *The Political Economy of West Germany*. New York: Praeger, 1982.

Markus, Thomas A. *Buildings and Power: Freedom and Control in the Origin of Modern Building Types*. London: Routledge, 1993.

Melchior-Bonnet, Sabine. *The Mirror*. Katherine H. Jewett (trans.). London: Routledge, 2001.

Merkl, Peter. *German Unification in a European Context*. University Park, PA: Penn State University Press, 1993.

Merkl, Peter H. (ed.) *The Federal Republic of Germany at Fifty: The End of a Century of Turmoil*. New York: NYU Press, 1999.

Mertins, Detlef. *Transparencies Yet to Come: Sigfried Giedion and the Prehistory of Architectural Modernity*. Dissertation at Princeton University, June 1996.

Meyer-Waldeck, Wera. "*Bundesparlament in Bonn,*" *Architektur und Wohn Form*. Heft 5, 58 Jahr, 1950.

Minor, Vernon Hyde. *Art History's Art History*. New York: Harry N. Abrams, 1994.

Moholy-Nagy, Lazlo. *The New Vision and Abstract of an Artist*. New York: George Wittenborn, 1947.

Nerdinger, Winfried. "*Modernisierung, Bauhaus, Nationalsozialismus,*" *Bauhaus Moderne im Nationalsozialismus*. Prestel, Munich, 1993.

Niethammer, Lutz. "The German Sonderweg after Unification," in *Rewriting the German Past*. Reinhard Alter and Peter Monteath (eds). New Jersey: Humanities Press, 1997.

Nietzsche, Friedrich. *Beyond Good and Evil: Prelude to a Philosophy of the Future*. Judith Norman (trans.). Cambridge: Cambridge University Press, 2002.

Noelle-Neumann, Elisabeth and Köcher, Renate (eds). *Allensbacher Jahrbuch der Demoskopie, 1984–1992*. Munich: Verlag für Demoskopie, 1993.

Noelle-Neumann, Elisabeth and Köcher, Renate (eds). *Allensbacher Jahrbuch der Demoskopie, 1993–1996*. Munich: Verlag für Demoskopie, 1997.

Norberg-Schultz, Christian. *Baroque Architecture*. New York: Harry N. Abrams, 1971.

Norberg-Schulz, Christian. *Modern Norwegian Architecture*. Oslo: Norwegian University Press, 1986.

Öchslin, Werner. "Transparency: The Search for a Reliable Design Method in Accordance with the Principles of Modern Architecture," *Transparency*. Birkhauser: Basel, 1997.

Padgett, Stephen. "The New German Economy," in *Developments in German Politics*. Gordon Smith, William E. Paterson, and Stephen Padgett (eds). Durham, NC: Duke University Press, 1992.

Passuth, Krisztina. *Moholy-Nagy*. New York: Thames and Hudson, 1985.

Pergande, Frank, "*Die sowjetischen Bomben trugen die Inschrift "Zum Reichstag*," "*Frankfurter Allgemeine Zeitung*. April 19, 1999.

Platz, Gustav Adolf. *Die Baukunst der neuesten Zeit*. Berlin: Propylaen, 1950, 2nd edition. First published in 1930.

Preziosi, Donald. *The Art of Art History: A Critical Anthology*. Oxford: Oxford University Press, 1998.

Pulzer, Peter. "Political Ideology," in *Developments in German Politics*. Gordon Smith, William E. Paterson, and Stephen Padgett (eds). Durham, NC: Duke University Press, 1992.

Pulzer, Peter. *German Politics: 1945–1995*. Oxford: Oxford University Press, 1995.

Putnam, Hilary. *Representation and Reality*. Cambridge, MA: MIT Press, 1988.

Realisierungswettbewerb Umbau Reichstagsgebäude zum Deutschen Bundestag, Teil 3, Aufgabe. 1993.

Robin, Ron. *Enclaves of America: The Rhetoric of American Political Architecture Abroad, 1900–1965*. Princeton: Princeton University Press, 1992.

Rogogg, Irit (ed.) *The Divided Heritage: Themes and Problems in German Modernism*. Cambridge: Cambridge University Press, 1991.

Rowe, Colin and Slutzky, Robert. *Transparency*. Bernard Hoesli (ed). Boston: Birkhauser, 1997.

Sagebiel, Ernst. "*Festliche Räume der Luftfahrt*," *Die Kunst im dritten Reich*. II:1. January, 1938.

Schäuble, Wolfgang. *Der Zukunft zugewandt*. Berlin: Siedler, 1994.

Scheffler, Karl. *Moderne Baukunst*. Leipzig: Julius Zeitler, 1908.

Schindler, Peter. *Datenbuch zur Geschichte des Deutschen Bundestages 1949 bis 1999: Gesamtausgabe in drei Bände*. Baden-Baden: Nomos, 1999.

Schirmer, Wulf. *Egon Eiermann: Bauten und Projekte 1904–1970*. Stuttgart: DVA, 1984.

Schmädeke, Jürgen. *Der Deutsche Reichstag: Geschichte und Gegenwart eines Bauwerks*. Munich: Erweitete Ausgabe, 1994.

Schmid, Carlo and Strätling, Erich. "*Demokratie – die Chance, den Staat zu vermenschlichen.*" *Der Parlamentarische Rat 1948–1949: mit der "Parlamentarischen Elegie" von Carlo Schmid*. Pfullingen: Neske, 1989.

Schmidt, Matthias. *Albert Speer: The End of a Myth*. New York: St. Martins, 1984.

Schmidt, Walther. "*Auf der Trümmerfeld der Bauformen*," *Bauen und Wohnen*. Jahrgang 2, Heft 6, June 1947.

Schmitt, Uwe. "*Stand ort Deutschland?*" *Frankfurter Allgemeine Zeitung*. December 2, 1997.

Schnaidt, Claude. *Hannes Meyer: Bauten, Projekte und Schriften*. Switzerland: A. Niggli, 1965.

Schoenbaum, David and Pond, Elizabeth. *The German Question and Other German Questions*. New York: St. Martins, 1996.

Schönberger, Angela. *Die neue Reichskanzlei von Albert Speer: zum Zusammenhang von Nationalsozialisticher Ideologie und Architektur*. Berlin: Mann, 1981.

Schorske, Carl E. *Fin-de-Siecle Vienna: Politics and Culture*. New York: Random House, 1981.

Schulz, Bernhard (ed.) *The Reichstag: The Parliament Building by Norman Foster*. Peter Green (trans.). Munich: Prestel, 2000.

Schulze, Franz. *Mies van der Rohe: A Critical Biography*. Chicago: University of Chicago, 1985.

Schulze, Hagen. *A Short History of Germany*. Deborah Lucas Schneider (trans.). Cambridge, MA: Harvard University Press, 1998.

Schulze, Konrad Werner. *Glas in der Architektur der Gegenwart*. Stuttgart: Dr Zaugg, 1929.

Schwarz, Hans-Peter. "*Das Ende der Identitätsneurose*," *Rhenischer Merkur*. September 7, 1990.

Schwippert, Hans. "*Werk des Sprechens*," Archives of the Germanisches Nationalmuseum, Nuremberg, 1940.

Bibliography

Schwippert, Hans. "*Das Bonner Bundeshaus,*" *Neue Bauwelt*. Heft 17, 1951.

Schwippert, Hans. *Glück und Glas*. In *Wohn Form*. From the Schwippert Archiv at the Germanisches Nationalmuseum, Nuremberg, 1952–3.

Schwippert, Hans. "*Zu Stahl und Baukunst: Vortrag auf der Tagung des Stahlbau Verbandes,*" Cologne. Schwippert Archiv, Germanisches Nationalmuseum, Nuremberg, February 10, 1953.

Schwippert, Hans. *Denken, Lehren, Bauen*. Düsseldorf: Econ, 1982.

Scott, Pamela. *Temple of Liberty: Building the Capitol for a New Nation*. Oxford: Oxford University Press, 1995.

Shandley, Robert R. (ed.) *Unwilling Germans? The Goldhagen Debate*. Minneapolis: University of Minnesota Press, 1998.

Sharp, Dennis (ed.) *Glass Architecture*. Shirley Palmer and James Palmer (trans.). New York: Praeger, 1972.

Shirer, William. *The Rise and Fall of the Third Reich*. New York: Simon & Schuster, 1959.

Simmel, Georg. *Metropolis and Spiritual Life: The Sociology of Georg Simmel*. Glencoe, IL: The Free Press, 1950.

Simon, Alfred (ed.) *Bauen in Deutschland: 1945–1962*. Essen: Vulkan, 1963.

Smith, Gordon, Paterson, William E., and Padgett, Stephen (eds). *Developments in German Politics*. Durham, NC: Duke University Press, 1992.

Smith, Jean Edward (ed.) *The Papers of General Lucius D. Clay, 1945–1949*. Bloomington: Indiana University, 1974.

Stahl, Walter (ed.) *The Politics of Postwar Germany*. New York: Praeger, 1963.

Stark, Christian (ed.) *Main Principles of the German Basic Law*. Baden-Baden: Nomos, 1983.

Starobinski, Jean. *Jean-Jacques Rousseau: Transparency and Obstruction*. Arthur Goldhammer (trans.). Chicago: University of Chicago, 1988.

Stern, Fritz. *The Politics of Cultural Despair: A Study in the Rise of the Germanic Ideology*. Berkeley: University of California Press, 1961.

Strodthoff. Werner. "*Dilettanten im Palais,*" *Kölner Stadt-Anzeiger*, 1964.

Tafuri, Manfredo. *Theories and History of Architecture* (Teorie e storia dell'architettura) Giorgio Verrecchia (trans.). New York: Harper & Row, 1980.

Taut, Bruno. *Die Stadtkrone*. Jena: E. Diedrichs, 1919.

Taut, Bruno. *Die Auflösung der Städte; oder Die Erde eine gute Wohnung; oder auch: Der Weg zur Alpinen Architektur; in 30 Zeichnungen*. Hagen: Erschienen im Folkwang Verlag, 1920.

Taut, Bruno. *Alpine Architektur*. Shirley Palmer (trans.). New York: Praeger, 1972.

Taylor, Robert. *The Word in Stone: The Role of Architecture in the National Socialist Ideology*. Berkeley: University of California Press, 1974.

Terrell, Peter, Schnorr, Veronika, Morris, Wendy V.A. *et al.* (eds). *Collins German English, English German Dictionary*. Third Edition. Stuttgart: Ernst Klett Verlag, 1997.

Tzonis, Alexander and Liane Lefaivre. *Classical Architecture: The Poetics of Order*. Cambridge, MA: MIT Press, 1988.

Vale, Lawrence J. *Architecture, Power, and National Identity*. New Haven: Yale University Press, 1992.

Vidler, Anthony. *The Architectural Uncanny: Essays in the Modern Unhomely*. Cambridge, MA: MIT Press, 1992.

Von Arnim, Hans Herbert. *Vom Schönen Schein der Demokratie: Politik ohne Verantwortung am Volk vorbei*. Munich: Knaur, 2002.

Wagner, Gerald. "*Das Unrecht eines Rechtsstaates,*" *Frankfurter Allgemeine Zeitung*. November 22, 1999.

Wätzoldt, Stephan and Haas, Verena (eds). *Tendenzen der Zwanziger Jahre: 15 Europäische Kunstausstellung unter den Auspizen des Europarates: in der Neuen Nationalgalerie, der Akademie der Künste und der Grossen Orangerie des Schlosses Charlottenburg zu Berlin, vom 14. August bis zum 16. Oktober 1977*. Berlin: D. Reimer, 1977.

Wefing, Hans. *Parlamentsarchitektur: Zur Selbstdarstellung der Demokratie in ihren Bauwerken. Eine Untersuchung am Beispiel des Bonner Bundeshauses*. Dissertation. Berlin: Duncker & Humblot, 1995.

Wefing, Heinrich. *"Dem Deutschen Volke." Der Bundestag im Berliner Reichstagsgebäude*. Bonn: Bouvier, 1999.

Weizsaecker, Richard. *Speeches for our Time*. David Clay Lange (intro.). Washington, DC: Johns Hopkins, 1992.

Werhahn, Charlotte. *Hans Schwippert (1899–1973) Architekt, Paedogoge und Vertreter der Wekbundidee in der Zeit des deutschen Wideraufbaus*. Dissertation at the TU Munich, June 25, 1987.

Whyte, Iain Boyd. *Bruno Taut and the Architecture of Activism*. New York: Cambridge University Press, 1982.

Whyte, Iain Boyd (ed.) *The Crystal Chain Letters: Architectural Fantasies by Bruno Taut and His Circle*. Cambridge, MA: MIT Press, 1985.

Wichmann, Hans. *SepRuf: Bauten und Projekte*. Stuttgart: Deutsche Verlag Anstalt, 1986.

Wighton, Charles. *Adenauer: A Critical Biography*. New York: Coward–McCann, 1963.

Wise, Michael. *Capital Dilemma: Germany's Search for a New Architecture of Democracy*. New York: Princeton Architectural Press, 1996.

Wolf, Werner. *Luftangriffe auf die deutsche Industrie 1942–45*. Munich: Universitas, 1985.

Wright, Janet. *Crown Assets: The Architecture of the Department of Public Works, 1867–1967*. Toronto: University of Toronto Press, 1997.

Index

Index